GALATIANS
BACKSTORY / CHRISTORY

Phillip A. Ross

PILGRIM platform books

Marietta, Ohio

Copyright ©2016 Phillip A. Ross
All rights reserved.

ISBN: 978-0-9820385-6-7
Edition: 2017.06.01

Library of Congress Control Number: 2015958411

Published by

Pilgrim Platform
149 E. Spring St., Marietta
Ohio, 45750
www.pilgrim-platform.org

Biblical quotations are from the English Standard Version, Standard Bible
Society, unless otherwise cited. The Net Bible®, New English Translation
(NET), ©1996 by Biblical Studies Press, L.L.C.

Printed in the United States of America

Dedicated to

Whosoever in the twenty-first century
John 3:16-17

Books by Phillip A. Ross

The Work At Zion—A Reckoning, Two-volume set, 772 pages, 1996.

Practically Christian—Applying James Today, 135 pages, 2006.

The Wisdom of Jesus Christ in the Book of Proverbs, 414 pages, 2006.

Marking God's Word—Understanding Jesus, 324 pages, 2006.

Acts of Faith—Kingdom Advancement, 326 pages, 2007.

Informal Christianity—Refining Christ's Church, 136 pages, 2007.

Engagement—Establishing Relationship in Christ, 104 pages, 1996, 2008.

It's About Time! — The Time Is Now, 40 pages. 2008.

The Big Ten—A Study of the Ten Commandments, 105 pages, 2001, 2008.

Arsy Varsy—Reclaiming The Gospel in First Corinthians, 406 pages, 2008.

Varsy Arsy—Proclaiming The Gospel in Second Corinthians, 356 pages, 2009.

Colossians—Christos Singularis, 278 pages, 2010.

Rock Mountain Creed—The Sermon on the Mount, 310 pages, 2011.

The True Mystery of the Mystical Presence, 355 pages, 2011.

Peter's Vision of Christ's Purpose in First Peter, 340 pages, 2011.

Peter's Vision of The End in Second Peter, 184 pages, 2012.

The Religious History of Nineteenth Century Marietta, Thomas Jefferson Summers, 124 pages, 1903, 2012 (editor).

Conflict of Ages—The Great Debate of the Moral Relations of God and Man, Edward Beecher, 489 pages, 1853, 2012 (editor).

Concord Of Ages—The Individual And Organic Harmony Of God And Man, Edward Beecher, D. D., 524 pages, 1860, 2013 (editor).

Ephesians—Recovering the Vision of a Sustainable Church in Christ, 417 pages, 2013.

Poet Tree—Root, Branch & Sap, 72 pages, 2013.

Inside Out Woman—Collected Poetry, Doris M. Ross, 195 pages, 2014 (editor).

TABLE OF CONTENTS

INTRODUCTION

Galatians–Backstory/Christory articulates a biblically based approach to the metanarrative revealed by the rending of the veil during Jesus' resurrection, a framework that will challenge church and ministry leaders to discern gospel and law in the light of the history of Israel. One of the things discernible is that there is both a social and a personal dimension of salvation for both Israel and the gentiles inclusively. Ross confirms that the relationship between law and freedom of the gospel is at the heart of Paul's letter to the Galatians. The very first chapter of Ross' Galatians provides a brief overview of the history of ancient Israel which sets the context for Christ's mission. In the light of Old Testament history and Christ's redemptive mission, Paul's letter frames the New Testament conflict, which actually continues to manifest even today.

The clearest example of that conflict came in what we call Jesus' cleansing of the Temple, the purpose of which can be seen only in the light of Israel's history and Christ's mission. This act of frustration and justifiable anger preceded His resurrection. Jesus witnessed against the old symbolic, legalistic temple culture and called the whole world to God's future, drawing all of humanity into what might be called our right future possibilities—the coming Kingdom. Jesus' cleansing of the temple upturned the tables of those who were holding human history hostage for their own personal benefit, those who thought that God's blessings were exclusively for themselves, their own group. Thus, Paul's witness to the Galatians reveals the centrality of the relationship between law and gospel, and shows how they both define and clarify one another in both personal and corporate contexts.

The wholeness of the metanarrative relating the messy contextual backstory of God's chosen yet disobedient people, who were veiled to

i

the good news of Christ's story of actually living out the coming Kingdom, provides an important perspective and inspires imagination to creatively confront with renewed insight and vigor the serious error that continues to echo and resonate yet today. We, God's people, are still in the grip of an error of perspective today, as God's people were in Paul's day. Our problem is that if the Bible is understood too literally, or if its literalism is completely rejected or discounted, then the grand biblical metanarrative story that reveals the wholeness of Christ's mission remains unknown. Ross says again and again that Christ does not contradict or deny the value and veracity of the Old Testament, He fulfills it. He completes it. He brings it to fruition. He makes it real, even for us today in the twenty-first century. The holism of the gospel's call to witness combines "knowing" (faith) with "yielding" to His Holy Spirit (grace) in such a way that it finds worldly, cultural expression in "seeing" (hope) and "doing" (love)—the four gospel elements of the pattern and power for imitating Christ, for identity in and union with Christ.

What then must we do? Ross says that the most important story of the Bible is about the relationship of Jesus Christ to the Old Testament, and about God's enduring relationship with His people. Because it is metanarrative, it is not a story that is found in the Bible. Rather, it is a metastory about the Bible. Ross calls it "metabiblical." As such, it's not in the Bible, it's in history. It's in the moment. It's not about telling the story, but is about actually living the story. It is the metastuff of which stories are made. And we must come to understand that the story of the Bible is not about the past, it's about the present, our present right now. Ross works here and now to attune us to God's right future possibilities.

Ross talks about two points that are necessary for humanity to survive. Without clarification of these two points humanity will be lost, or at least confused and conflicted. The two points are necessary in order to plot a path to a sustainable future, and without them we will languish. Jesus was always future oriented, but never lost His historical roots or His foothold in the present. He taught us to pray, "Thy kingdom come," and to live an affective paradigm to love God and neighbor. We are to do justice and love mercy, to live righteously and protect the weak. We must learn how to live wisely, live compassionately, to serve neighbors by responding to our calling. And yet....

The biblical metastory, the Christory, provides the metadata for the foundation of a biblical metaphysics of moral truth that could bridge the gap between a widening moral conflict between science and religion, between church and state, between Christian and Jew—and Muslim! This enduring conflict is about methodological analysis and impacts both our understanding of the world and our action in the world, our moral judgments and actions. It seems to me as an engineer with thirty-seven years of professional work, including work on the establishment of world-wide production standards, an international scientific patent, and experience as a life-long Christian—a Presbyterian elder, that Ross has put his finger on something significant. If we look at the issues of gospel and law in Galatians as setting moral standards, we can examine some significant premise-nested paradigms relating to methodological analysis leading to the process of standards adoption that has very wide application. The role that standards play in the contemporary world cannot be under-emphasized. Standards creation is, in fact, the role of law in society.

The conflict in the contemporary world has come about because the world is in the midst of rapid social, political, and legal change. Old standards of all sorts are being swept away and new standards are being formed. In actuality, the dispensation from the Old Testament to the New Testament is still in process. Thus, the process of standardization, of normalization, is of critical importance. The most important issue regarding the standardization process is the basis from which standards are proposed and established, the foundation upon which they depend. Thus, the conflict manifests as a conflict between science (reason) and the Bible (faith), between the state (secularism) and the church (religion), and between the historic biblical religions—Judaism, Christianity, and Islam.

Ross has provided an analysis of Galatians, of law and gospel, that speaks to both biblical history and our contemporary situation in a way that I have not heard before, and yet appears to be solidly grounded in the best aspects of faithfulness to historic, biblical Christianity. His analysis may provide a foundation for significant conflict resolution in all of these areas—or at least some interesting ideas for disucssion. Yet, there is much work that needs to be done to further evaluate his insights.

My study and analysis of his work suggests that he has shown the biblical roots of a long-standing, religious, philosophical, and historic conflict between human ends and means, between what we ought to do and what we can do, between how we ought to live and how we can live, between the purpose of humanity (being) and the practice of humanity (doing). The beauty of his work in Galatians is that he brings together Paul's treatment of the abstract, intellectual, philosophical, historic, and biblical dimensions of this issue of changing social standards (Old Testament to New Testament) with the practical, moral issues of everyday life in a refreshing, insightful, and helpful way that opens up a potential path for significant conflict resolution in the light of Christ in our contemporary world. Ross's work comports with my own work in the areas of peace-making and the relationship of corporate sin in terms of monetary policy founded on usury—interest. The setting of financial and monetary standards falls into the same pit, the same problems evidenced in Galatians, because the same methodological analysis is applied to these contemporary standards. It should not be surprising that the same methods produce the same results across the board.

Ross teaches that human society cannot thrive without biblical morality, Trinitarian morality, a morality of mutual understanding and cooperation among all sorts of very different kinds of people. If there is no God, not only is there no right or wrong, but there can be nothing but confusion and conflict regarding law and social, corporate standards, as the history of the world clearly reveals.

A new battle for the Bible is afoot because the wholeness of the Bible has been ill perceived apart from what Ross calls the Backstory/Christory, Paul's understanding of Israel's history in the light of Christ. One of the ways that we see this is from the fact that modern Western culture, which is a child of Christianity, is awash in sin—personal sin, corporate sin, sexual sin, financial sin, etc. Poverty and planetary despoliation are primary examples. We are caught in the grip of an ingrained world-spirit of denial, deceit, jealousy, gossip, theft, fraud, and covetousness that manifest as wide scale personal and social brokenness. Contemporary people have no sense of the holism of the biblical story in the light of Christ. We are in the grip of a divisive narrow-mindedness on both the Right and the Left that is inadequately holistic, among both conservatives and liberals. Whatever understanding we have of biblical morality has been compromised through accommodation into an all-pervasive acedia, an epidemic of religious sloth that is the very first trigger in a causal chain of the seven deadly sins.

There is a battle for the Bible that has been raging for a very long time, but it is a battle that most Christians are not prepared to engage. Average pew sitters are lambs to the slaughter because the self-centeredness of the world trumps the self-centeredness of Christians—their timid identity with Christ, their tentative union with Christ, and their tepid commitment to Christ. Christians are rightly conflicted about their self-centeredness, the world is not. The world is much better positioned to win that argument, as we see daily. What must we do? Read the Bible holistically! Ancient Israel was destined to fail in her wider mission to the world because ancient Israel was a culture in transition, it had one foot in the Old and nothing but hope for the New. Very early in Israel's history she began serving two metaphorical "masters."

Cain was jealous of Abel because God preferred Abel's sacrifice. The jealousy arose because of a religious problem. The whole of the history of the Old Testament is the outworking of this religious problem, this transition and establishment from one culture to another. God blessed Israel and set Israel apart to wander in the desert in order that Israel could worship God rightly. Israel was called out of that old pagan, ancient way of worship, which was based on domination, justice, and revenge—a law-based culture—to become a culture based on mercy and forgiveness—a grace-based culture. Ancient Israel was a culture in transition between the Old and the New. And yet when Jesus further illuminated the truth of the New, Israel, because of her exclusive understanding of God, rejected Jesus' Gospel. Jesus inaugurated a change, a change of law and a change of worship, where His resurrected body is now the Temple of God (John 2:19; Matthew 26:59-64). Jesus inaugurated a new way of worship based on cooperation, mercy, and forgiveness—grace.

The entire story of humanity over the past five to eight thousand years is about replacing the ancient retributive religious habits of domination, justice (understood as vindication against wrongdoing), and revenge. Jesus taught the values and habits of cooperation, justice (understood as the righteousness of not doing wrong), and forgiveness. The New Testament teaches mercy, gracefulness, and forgiveness. The general historical outlines of this issue is coming to a head today through the long-standing conflict between Islam and Christianity, which employ competing systems of culture and morality. In our day, Christianity is in the process of abandoning her historic moral understanding, teaching, and commitment, and that abandonment then fuels Islamic hatred of the West. The best thing that Western people can do to extricate themselves from bearing the brunt of Islamic Jihad is to stop being such a prominent target—by repentance. We must repent by claiming biblical moral understanding, teaching, and commitment in the light of Christ, in the light of Ross' Backstory/Christory. Doing that requires both a reaching back to our biblical history and reaching forward with biblical hopefulness to a sustainable future, a future that is only available in the light of Christ.

Ross essentially argues that the holiness of God is the wholeness of God in Christ, that the purpose of God is the establishment of God in Christ in the world, that the end or purpose of history is the reign of Christ, not as some sort of ancient tyrant, but as a loving Father, as a Bridegroom who is madly in love with His bride.

"I declare the end from the beginning, and from long ago what is not yet done, saying: My plan will take place, and I will do all My will" (Isaiah 46:10, Holman Christian Standard Bible).

Ray V. Foss
February 2016
Parkersburg, West Virginia

ACKNOWLEDGMENTS

No one has been a more consistent and faithful reader of my books than my wife, Stephanie, whose love and support make my work possible. It is very helpful to have other people read and respond to your writing because it is also quite easy to read your own words and only see what you *intended* to say, not what you actually said. Thanks also to my many friends who were willing to suffer through the first draft: Eric Brown, Jim Lopreste. Rev. Jim Sallie, Mic Cox, Dr. Paul Krolick, Paul Williams, Dr. David Kimberly, Scott Craig Mooney, and special thanks to Ray V. Foss.

PREFACE

The relationship between law and freedom is at the heart of Paul's letter to the Galatians, at the heart of the original conflict between Catholics and Protestants, and at the heart of the ongoing conflict between conservatives and liberals. For Martin Luther, the essential issue of Christianity was the question of the freedom or bondage of the human will, calling it the "hinge on which all turns." Luther, following Paul, argued that we are all naturally and historically in bondage to sin and Satan until Christ supernaturally frees us.

In a similar way, the relationship between law and freedom is at the heart of the world's most contentious conflict, which has recently blossomed into flower with the proclamation of the Islamic Caliphate known as Islamic State of Iraq and Syria (ISIS), Islamic State of Iraq and the Levant (ISIL), or Da'ish or Daesh, from the Arabic.[1] Islam, which developed out of a faulty understanding of Christianity,[2] is intent upon imposing Sharia Law upon the world; and at the same time the Western world is intent upon imposing International Law (secularism) upon the world. Shariah Law is based upon a literal reading of the Qu'ran, which misunderstands both Christianity and the Old Testament. In contrast, Western International Law[3] is based upon a kind of freedom that issues from the abandonment of religious laws and values, particularly those associated with biblical Christianity. Note that both Islam and Western culture as currently expressed fail to understand God's grace, as did ancient Israel. The insight and foundation of God's grace though Jesus Christ has played a critical role in the foundation of Western society and alone can correct both of these errors. While this book does not deal di-

1   https://en.wikipedia.org/wiki/Islamic_State_of_Iraq_and_the_Levant
2   Dalrymple, William. *The Holy Mountain: A Journey Among the Christians of the Middle East*, Holt Paperbacks, 1999.
3   http://www.un.org/en/globalissues/internationallaw/

rectly with these contemporary issues, it lays important biblical groundwork that can contribute to their resolution. The application of this groundwork is left to others, but demonstrating its importance and foundation as Paul's perspective regarding law and gospel is the purpose of this book.

An important point of this book is that Christ came to free people from bondage to the law of Moses, but not through the absolute abandonment of all law. Paul's training as a Pharisee made him the most biblically competent of the Apostles, which is reflected by his dominance as an author of the New Testament letters. My intention here is not to impose a foreign metanarrative upon the text, but to reveal the actual metanarrative of the Old Testament in the light of Christ as Paul presented it to the Galatians. That metanarrative was not what he had been taught as a Pharisee, nor what they had been taught by the Temple establishment. It was shockingly different, but it made undeniable sense of the Old Testament. The Temple establishment version was full of ancient mystery and symbolism that was difficult to understand, and cast the role of Israel as the hero of the story. Paul's version, on the other hand, was clear, simple, and practical—though it required the abandonment of much well-established Temple superstition. And Paul's version cast the role of Jesus Christ as the hero.

While understanding the story of the Old Testament in the light of Christ is not difficult, abandoning our own false presuppositions about it requires some personal tenacity. Jesus continues to challenge our ideas about who we are and our role in history, in God's story. The story that Paul grew up with was the story about the importance and purity of the Temple. But the story that he learned from Jesus was about the corruption and failure of the Temple. Similarly, Christians today are Sunday-schooled in the importance of the institutional church, but the actual ongoing story in the light of Christ is about the corruption and failure of the church as an institution. In the following pages you will see that this story has played out over and again throughout history because of the pertinacity of sin.

We need to know how this story is revealed because it requires familiarity with the story arc or metanarrative of the Old Testament. It's not so much that the story arc of the Old Testament is *in* this or that verse, or even *in* this or that story. Rather, the metanarrative is in the flow of the stories, in the interrelationships of the stories.

To "get" it we must know, trust, and value the story and the source of the story. Stories, being narrations based on a chain of related events or facts, also provide meta-information about the facts they provide. The biblical story is not merely about this or that event, or this or that fact, but is about how the events and facts are related. All stories issue from reflection about events and facts, but they are not a random stringing together of events and facts. Stories are about cause and effect, about purpose and meaning. Stories convey lessons. Stories endeavor to explain some situation or reality, to explain how or why something is the way it is, based on how it came to be and what happened. By definition, stories are not merely *in* or subjective to the events or facts they reveal, but issue from outside of them. Stories string the facts together. In addition, there are no stories apart from storytellers. Thus, the story of the Bible, the story of humanity, begins with the storyteller—God. If there is no storyteller, there is no story to tell.

What I call *The Backstory,* a brief history of the Old Testament in the light of Christ, provides the context for Paul's understanding of Christ, of his own ministry, and supports his understanding of law and gospel that he shared with the Galatians. Of course, *The Backstory* is not the whole story, but is an integral part of the real story. It is structured to help us understand the major thrust of what Paul understood about the facts of the history of ancient Israel, how they fit together, and the necessity for Christ. It is not an unknown story, but has been little emphasized over the last century or so because of the misunderstanding that it casts ancient Israel and contemporary Jews in a negative light. While the story emphasizes Israel's failure of obedience to God apart from Christ, the great story of the Bible is not intended to cast the people of Israel or the Word of God in any sort of inferior or negative light. No people would have done any better than ancient Israel did. Rather, the story of ancient Israel simply provides a case study and is representative of all humanity. Paul's point was that the Old Testament story is not the whole story, that Christ brings the story to fulfillment.

Nor does *The Backstory* negate or denigrate the value or veracity of God's Word, the Bible. Every word of the Bible is God-breathed, true, trustworthy, and able to teach what God intends it to teach. However, too many theologians of all kinds have traditionally interpreted and understood the Bible in a hyper-literal, wooden way that occludes deeper truths and more subtle lessons. Liberals tend to abandon the truth and teachings of the Bible altogether because they deny the fundamentalist reading, but they fail to provide an alternative reading that maintains biblical truth. The fundamentalists say that the Bible teaches their fundamentalist perspective, and the liberals say that the Bible is wrong because it teaches the fundamentalist perspective. Note that both believe that the Bible actually teaches fundamentalism. Such belief is a serious error at the foundation of both fundamentalism and liberalism, and our contemporary world is locked in conflict over this error. Following Paul, I find that both sides of this argument make the same error, but in different ways.

The purpose of *The Backstory* as I have laid it out is to highlight the essential purpose and correction[4] that Christ brings to the Old Testament, an error that was worming its way into the Galatian church. It is not that Christ contradicts or denies the value and veracity of the Old Testament, but that He fulfills it. He completes it. He brings it to fruition. He makes it real.

In these pages you will find a restatement of *The Backstory* several times in different ways and in different contexts in order to demonstrate how it makes better sense of various Bible stories. While it might appear to be overdone, the intent is to emphasize the explanatory value of *The Backstory* for people who are not familiar with it.

This book is concerned with the big picture of the Bible that is revealed by careful, comprehensive study of Scripture. This view of the history of Israel in the Old Testament will be shown to be the biblical view revealed to Paul in the light of Christ. It is not an argument against traditional theology, though it may at first seem to challenge various aspects of traditional theology. Rather, it is an effort to faith-

---

4   Christ fulfilled the law of Moses, and part of that fulfillment involved the bringing to completion of the purpose of Moses's law by the Advent and establishment of Christ in history. The Biblical metanarrative teaches that the law of Moses, unlike the Ten Commandments, was never intended to be universally applicable throughout all history in all of its details.

fully extend the traditional arc or growth of biblical theology as it unfolds in history. Biblical theology is a conversation about Scripture that
has taken place over many centuries. The position articulated here,
however successfully, issues out of and speaks to that discussion. Unlike those who seem to be trying to make a splash in the theological
pool, this is an effort to gently lead into deep water because that is
where Christ led Paul.

NEW COVENANT

Moses received the Ten Commandments, written by the finger of
God on tablets of stone. But in a fit of anger Moses broke the tablets
when he came down from the mountain and found His people dancing before a Golden Calf that had been made by his own chosen
religious representative, Aaron. Broken! What had been written by
God in stone, His didactic commandments in God's original manu-
script, were literally broken by God's own prophet. Don't miss the
importance of this foundational event in the story of God in human
history. When Moses went back up the mountain to replace the broken tablets, God dictated them to him, and he had to carve them in
stone himself (Exodus 34:27-28). Nonetheless, the Ten Commandments stand as the essential message of God from the Old Testament.

> "The Ten Commandments as the heart of the law express in a most
> fundamental way our obligations first of all to God (commands 1-4)
> and next to our neighbor (commandments 5-10). The rest of the law
> is largely an outworking of the implications of these central obliga-
> tions."[5]

In the Old Testament God used various kinds of symbolism to
help ancient Israel and humanity understand themselves, their proper
place in the world, and their proper relationship with Him. These
symbols are found everywhere in many different forms. For instance,
the design and furniture of the Tabernacle provides a wealth of such
symbolic teaching, as do the sacrificial liturgy, and the gifting and division of the land, etc. There is an abundance of literature about this,
so I don't need to rehearse it here.

---

5   Poythress, Vern S. *The Shadow of Christ in the Law of Moses*, P&R Publishing, New
Jersey, 1991, p.103.

The people were afraid to hear directly from God, so they appointed Moses to hear God for them and then tell them what God said (Exodus 20:19). Here we see the difference between the Ten Commandments, which God initiated and dictated, and the laws and statutes, which Moses requested, received, interpreted, and applied. The Ten Commandments came directly from God—as close as humanly possible, but the law and statutes involved Moses' interpretation and application. I'm not saying that God did not give them to Moses— He did! What I'm saying is that Moses had to write them down, and in that process he could not help but engage his own humanity, his own cultural assumptions, and his own personal limitations. This is not saying anything bad about Moses, only that he was human, not divine.

> "These words the LORD spoke to all your assembly at the mountain out of the midst of the fire, the cloud, and the thick darkness, with a loud voice; and he added no more. And he wrote them on two tablets of stone and gave them to me. And as soon as you heard the voice out of the midst of the darkness, while the mountain was burning with fire, you came near to me, all the heads of your tribes, and your elders. And you said, 'Behold, the LORD our God has shown us his glory and greatness, and we have heard his voice out of the midst of the fire. This day we have seen God speak with man, and man still live. Now therefore why should we die? For this great fire will consume us. If we hear the voice of the LORD our God any more, we shall die. For who is there of all flesh, that has heard the voice of the living God speaking out of the midst of fire as we have, and has still lived? Go near and hear all that the LORD our God will say, and speak to us all that the LORD our God will speak to you, and we will hear and do it.' And the LORD heard your words, when you spoke to me. And the LORD said to me, 'I have heard the words of this people, which they have spoken to you. They are right in all that they have spoken. Oh that they had such a heart as this always, to fear me and to keep all my commandments, that it might go well with them and with their descendants forever!" (Deuteronomy 5:22-29).

The Backstory highlights a theme that runs through the law, the Temple, and the liturgy of worship, which were developed to symbolically teach God's people about their own true identity, function, and purpose in the world. The liturgy of Temple worship and sacrifice served to symbolically teach God's people how to properly value, venerate, and apply God's essential message—the Ten Commandments, which were originally housed in the Ark of the Covenant.

And this is precisely what happened. God's people mastered the symbolism of the law, the Temple, and the liturgy as God continued to unfold the story of the Old Testament. Paul then spoke to the Galatians about how this story had blinded them to the greater truth of the Bible. He taught them that the Bible as a whole, Old and New Testaments as we now understand them, were given to show us how to apply God's Ten Commandments, God's essential teaching, in our own lives.

His Story

The history of ancient Israel, like the history of any people, is messy. While there are clear lessons to be drawn from the Old Testament, they are far from neat and tidy. However, the same lessons are presented over and over again, so there are multiple opportunities to connect the dots. It is easy to accuse the ancient Israelites of being hardheaded and stubborn, as the prophets had done again and again. It is easy to charge them with plain old stupidity, and think that we—you and I—would have done much better. But we would not have.

The situations and lessons are repeated in the biblical stories because each generation must learn their own lessons for themselves. Those stories and their accumulated wisdom compose the meat of Scripture. And to complicate things the lessons that each generation needs to learn are similar, but they are not identical. As the story of history grows, it changes. Our historical context is not the same as that of the Ancient Israelites.

The dynamism of growth can be seen more clearly in the modern era because things change so rapidly that the next generation does not experience the same things as the preceding generation. In previous ages the rate of social change and technology was much slower, and then the succeeding generations did actually experience much the same kinds of things. Children could learn from their parents because they had the same kinds of experiences, they experienced the same kinds of situations. Today, the life experiences of my parents were radically different than my own, and my children will experience things that I cannot imagine. Life unfolds today so quickly that the present threatens to overwhelm the past, and in the future the rate of change will threaten to swallow both the past and the present.

Consequently, in order for humanity to persist, for culture to be sustainable in the ensuing tsunami of change we are now experiencing, two things are needed. Two stable points of reference are necessary to plot a faithful path forward. Those two points are located in time, one in the past and one in the future. We must know where we as a people have been, and we must know where we are going. Without these two points of reference, humanity—the current expression of human culture—will be lost. We will languish without direction. How did we come about? Of what are we made? We are explorers, on a journey of exploration, and for the journey to be sustainable we must maintain our biblical supply chain, the resources we need for the journey. We must know what sustained our great grandparents and project what will sustain our children's children as best we are able.

The clearest and most consistent sustenance of those who have preceded us is God's Word, God's history, His story, the story of His people (Matthew 4:4). God has known this all along and has unfolded His story in such a way as to provide these two points of reference for His people in every generation. The record of that story is the story of the Bible.

It is not a pretty story, not a sweet story of ease and plenty with sappy endings. Rather, it is a real story, cut from the rough and tumble of life in a hostile world among belligerent people. Don't get me wrong, God's story has projected an endpoint of great peace, joy, and satisfaction when He will eliminate evil and "wipe away every tear from their eyes, and death shall be no more, neither shall there be mourning, nor crying, nor pain anymore, for the former things have passed away" (Revelation 21:4).

But the question of *our* day is: how do we get there? Quickly or slowly? Magically or meticulously? All at once or little by little? What is the next step forward? That is the question this book endeavors to address, but because the answer must be real it must also be tough enough to last long enough to actually work. Simple answers cannot address hard questions. The hard questions deserve solid answers.

The most important story of the Bible is about the relationship between God and humanity. That story is reconciled by the story about
its two testaments, about the relationship of Jesus Christ to the Old
Testament, and about His enduring relationship with His people. It is
not a story that is found *in* the Bible, but is a metastory *about* the Bible.
It is metabiblical, like metaphysics, only biblical. The point of the story
is not *in* the Bible, but in human history, not on the page, but in the
moment, not in the telling, but in the living. The point or application
is the stuff for which biblical stories are made.

The Old Testament teaches this story through various symbols
that are full of meaning, connection, and purpose. And the history of
the Old Testament reveals that there are two phases to the process.
First, people must learn about God, and that is what the Old Testament symbolism is about. But learning is not enough, people must also
put that learning into practice—and that is what the New Testament is
about.

SYMBOL & REALITY

Law is about learning how to be a good person, and how not to
be a bad person. In general, good people obey the law. Ancient Israel
failed this lesson. But again, their failure was not about them being inferior, rather it was about the whole of humanity being caught in the
grip of something they could not control—something that we still
cannot control. The biblical name for that something is *sin*, defined as
an *offense* to God. The dictionary defines *offense* as: "1. a lack of politeness; a failure to show regard for others; wounding the feelings of
others...." While the biblical definition of sin is much more serious
than this, we are nonetheless offensive to God. We treat God shal-
lowly, lightly, casually—and worse!

The resolution of the sin problem comes from knowing who we
are and whose we are, knowing our proper place in this world, our
proper relationship with God-in-Christ, and with one another. This is
the grand historical project of the Bible, which endeavors to both
teach this through the stories and symbolism of the Bible, *and* to actually manifest it through Christ's gift of the Holy Spirit. Both the
teaching and the manifesting are necessary.

"The coming of Christ brings a reality and an accomplishment that supersedes Old Testament symbols in depth and finality. Old Testament symbols are fulfilled and replaced by reality."[6]

Can the reality of the manifestation of Christ in His people be as simple as the practice of common concern and manners? Not completely, of course, but it can help a lot. Yet, even that not as simple as one might imagine. For instance, try practicing common concern and politeness in every situation yourself and you will see that it is easier said than done. Now try to not offend God. In order to do this, we need to know what offends Him, which brings us to His law. And even if these things are not the *sin qua non* of Christian mystic fulfillment, they are most certainly a very good place to begin, and to make much significant headway.

The distinction between symbolism and reality is not hard and fast. There are many subtleties, shades, nuances, overlaps, and traditions that make it obscure. Even so, this distinction grows in importance every day as humanity matures. The point of mentioning this dilemma is that we must understand that a map is not a landscape, nor is a sign a thing signified.[7] And while it is relatively easy to distinguish symbol from reality intellectually, it remains difficult to do so in life. For example, highly intelligent scientists and intellectuals commonly mistake computer modeling for reality. Our modeling has gotten so good that we easily mistake our models for the reality. And while the differences are increasingly subtle, they are also increasingly important.

The Old Testament provides many case studies of this general difficulty as the ancient Israelites and their priests and leaders repeatedly mistook the symbolism of worship for the reality of Godly living. They repeatedly mistook the engagement of liturgical symbolism to be a substitute or equivalent for moral living. We do the same thing today when we think that we are good people because we go to church, or because we receive communion or absolution by the priest. I'm not

6   Ibid, p.146.
7   https://en.wikipedia.org/wiki/Map–territory_relation. We can see this issue playing out today in the article by Natalie Wolchover, December 16, 2015 "A Fight for the Soul of Science, Quanta Magazine, https://www.quantamagazine.org/20151216-physicists-and-philosophers-debate-the-boundaries-of-science/

saying that any of these things are bad, only that they are inadequate to the reality of the Bible.

The many stories of the prophets accusing the people, priests, and kings of idolatry provide lessons for us about mistaking symbolism for reality. This error is the very definition of idolatry—thinking that statues have divine power, or that the liturgy of sacrificial substitution provides everything needed for God's forgiveness. The mistaking the map for the geography is also a kind of idolatry.

"What to me is the multitude of your sacrifices? says the Lord?" (Isaiah 1:11), Isaiah proclaimed. The Old Testament is the story of God's people getting stuck in the symbolic teaching that God had given them, of failing to actually engage God in the process. The symbolism was right, and good, and valuable—and God Himself had indeed provided it. But the symbolism is not the reality, and by thinking that the symbolism was sufficient, they kept themselves from the reality of living truly Godly lives, from engaging God fully, wholly.

Jesus came to address this problem, to move people from the symbol to the reality. He came to manifest the character of God that God had called them to imitate. In order to do this, there would need to be a significant change in the culture and the lives of God's people, and such a change would need to be authorized by law.

> "For when there is a change in the priesthood, there is necessarily a change in the law as well" (Hebrews 7:12).

Jesus changed the law in order to change the people. However, the law was not in error. It was not wrong. In fact, God's law continues to provide much incredibly good, valuable, helpful, truthful, beneficial symbolism—and some valuable insights that are waiting to be discovered. How could Jesus change the law without changing the symbolism the law demonstrated? Jesus didn't abandon the law, not a jot or tiddle. So what changed? What changed is the subject of Paul's letter to the Galatians and of this book.

> "Thus the distinction between permanent principle and the temporary symbolical form is not merely some artificial idea from a later age or from later revelation; it was embedded already in the original Mosaic revelation to Israel. Israelites would naturally not have all the answers immediately, but they would have a vague, almost subcon-

scious sense of there being a distinction between what was more
central and what was less, between what was more permanent and
universal and what might possibly be temporary,"[8]

8   Ibid., p. 105.

THE BACKSTORY

Understanding the New Testament apart from an understanding of the general arc of the Old Testament story is a well-worn recipe for misunderstanding the role and purpose of Jesus Christ in the Bible as a whole. Paul's letter to the Galatians is commonly misunderstood because people don't understand the Old Testament as Paul came to understand it in the light of Christ. Paul's understanding of the Old Testament changed radically when he met Christ. Schooled as a Pharisee, he understood it as the Jews had understood it for a thousand years. But after his conversion his views changed and ultimately came into conformity with Jesus' understanding of the Old Testament. To understand Paul's letter to the Galatians we need to understand Paul's new perspective in the light of Christ.

This problem of misunderstanding Scripture is at the heart of the very old argument about Paul's treatment of law and gospel in Galatians. It is also contrasted in his treatment of works and grace (Romans 11:6), letter and spirit (2 Corinthians 3:3-6), and elsewhere in Scripture. Paul was not writing in a vacuum, but was responding to the historical situation of ancient Israel, in which he was well-versed. Paul was a well-educated, high-ranking, well-placed officer of the Temple establishment in his day. So, when he was converted on the road to Damascus he brought all of that training and understanding into his new perspective. This is what made Paul's experience and perspective so important. He was quite different from the other disciples of his time, but not so different than Jesus.

The history of this problem is long and complex. Consequently, my intent here is not to do it academic or historical justice, but to provide a hopefully sufficient but brief overview of the salient events and features of the history of the Temple. Why focus on the Temple? Because it was the heart and focus of Old Testament law and Jewish society. The history of the Temple reveals the arc or general track of Israel's history. The areas that have not received adequate attention by our contemporary churches will be of special interest, and may seem to be new. But there is nothing new about any of this, other than it has not been broadly taught for many years.

My remarks here must be understood in context. They are not stand-alone, out-of-context snippets for use in ever-popular Internet flame wars. Rather, my hope is that this study will undergird a better understanding of the Bible as a whole, of Jesus Christ, of Galatians, of Paul, and of the New Testament context generally. It is my contention, based on my own history and growth, that nearly everyone in the church has misunderstood something important about Paul's argument centered in Galatians. But where to begin!

Because Paul was not introducing anything new, it is important to see that this issue is as old as Scripture itself. The history of the Bible begins with the introduction of a problem, and that old problem has led to our current problem because it continues to dog humanity. The problem began during the second week of creation in the Garden when the Serpent raised a question for clarification, and reached out to Eve with some "good news" of his own. Eve understood the Serpent right away. The tree that God forbade was actually "good for food, and ... a delight to the eyes, and ... was to be desired to make one wise" (Genesis 3:6), she said, following the Serpent's lead. God had been mistaken about it leading to death, probably because He had some unresolved issues about sharing, or so insinuated the Serpent.

The result of that ancient garden conversation was that from that point forward all humanity for all of human history was off on the wrong foot in our dance with destiny, our moral maturity. The Old Testament story of sin or the Fall teaches that all humanity was caught up in the imitation of Adam, who had followed the serpent—Satan. For this reason people are not guilty because of Adam's sin, but because they imitate Adam through the manifestation of their own sin. This is an important point to remember because it is so easy to forget. It is the driving force behind the arc of the central story that unfolds in the Old Testament, but it is not the only force that plays a role in the story. This particular story paints in primary tones of bleak and dreary because of the sin of Eve and Adam, and that makes it hard for us to hear.

Of course there are genuine highlights of hope in the details, so the details tend to dominate our attention. We tend to focus on the trees, the details, and miss the proverbial forest, the larger story. Scholars, who teach the pastors, who teach the people, who teach their children get so caught up in biblical minutia that we all fail to see the central story of the Bible to one degree or another. We human beings love our stories to be bright and rosy, and our selective memories tend to filter out what is painful, disturbing, and uncomfortable. Disobeying God seems much more pleasant than conforming to the harshness of self-denial. We much prefer to remember and serve only the good as we ourselves define *good*. And that is at the heart of the problem.

The hope found in Scripture is very real, but it exists in a vast sea of historical trouble, struggle, and muddle. The hope is the hope of the coming of Christ prefigured in the Old Testament, and *that* hope will come to dominate the story as it flowers into the New Testament. But not yet.[1] In the Old Testament the power of hope is magnified by the dark, dank blackness of hopelessness without Christ that dominated the people of every nation. Against this dark backdrop the Old Testament hope for Messiah shines.

My intention here is to increase our understanding by using the light of Christ in order to highlight the darkness of the human situation in the Old Testament without Christ, in order to demonstrate the usefulness of that light in our contemporary world. I want to share a reading or perspective of the Old Testament that will provide the necessary backdrop for Paul's teaching about law and gospel, apart from which his teaching—which is really Jesus' teaching—will always be misunderstood.

---

1   There are two dangers for Christians: 1) to read the Old Testament without the light of Christ, thinking that the most authentic reading is to read it as Old Testament people would have understood it, and 2) to so overemphasize the light of Christ as we read the Old Testament that we fail to appreciate the historical development that was necessary for the manifestation of Christ. The principle used here comes from 1 Corinthians 10:6, where Paul said that events in the Old Testament occurred for the benefit of people in his own time. God was creating lessons that would be useful later in history. The whole Bible is like that for us, so we must see what God has in it for us, for our time.

THE BEGINNING

Murder haunts the biblical story of human history almost immediately. Cain slew Abel, the first human child, over a worship issue. Cain was jealous, angry, and vengeful—and that is at the heart of the problem! Cain took the law into his own hands, serving as prosecution, defense, jury, judge, and executioner. The whole thing was his idea, his judgment, and his action against his brother.

But God in His astonishing mercy spared Cain in spite of his guilt, and Cain propagated and prospered. One of his more famous sons was Tubal-cain, who "was the forger of all instruments of bronze and iron" (Genesis 4:22)—weapons. Another was Lamech, who said "If Cain's revenge is sevenfold, then Lamech's is seventy-sevenfold" (Genesis 4:24). Lamech multiplied Cain's spirit of murder and revenge, which made him very powerful. Weapons and revenge made for a powerful argument—still do. This basic pattern has been repeated throughout history. Disobedience leads to rebellion, which turns to revenge and violence. Envy grows into jealousy, which grows into pride and greed, which grow into lust, which turns into wrath and violence.

Of course, these were not the only children of Adam and Eve. Seth was born to replace Abel (Genesis 4:25), and so the line of Cain would struggle against the line of Seth evermore. That struggle is the underlying story of the Old Testament. Cain's lineage seems to have dominated until the Flood, when God flushed the whole thing away, except for Noah and his family. Then there was a new beginning full of new hope, sealed with a rainbow.

Noah was a righteous man when compared to Cain's lot, yet Noah had his problems conforming to God's law. His children then inherited his problems. Humanity began again with Noah and his family under an expanded promise/covenant with God. Noah's clan all spoke one language and in time they moved from the mountains to the plain of Shinar, where they built a city called Babel and a tower intended to reach to the heavens. Over the years they lost their concern about pleasing God, or perhaps they thought that God would be pleased by their accomplishments, their works. But God was not pleased with them nor their effort to build their own way to heaven. So He confused their language, which undermined their project and scattered them across the globe, which accounts for the beginning of the various nations. At this point, then, Noah's children had universally displeased the Lord.

ABE

The Shemites were one of those scattered people groups, from which came Abram, and with whom the biblical history of God's people is founded. Abram's father, Terah, had been a priest of some sort. Terah led his family to embark on a long and mysterious journey to Canaan (Genesis 11:31-32). We don't know why Terah began that journey or why the journey ended in Haran rather than Canaan. It has been suggested that Terah was a man in search of greater truth, and perhaps old age curtailed his journey. Nonetheless, Abram picked up his father's torch and continued the journey of God's people to Canaan.

It's important to note that Abram *continued* Terah's mission to Canaan. There is no biblical evidence whether Terah and Abram agreed or disagreed theologically. We might understand them as evangelists on a mission. They were priests who set out with a people on a mission from God. Jewish tradition says that Abram's religion was different than his father's, but there are no such biblical records. All we really know is that Terah was aiming for Canaan, and Abram continued that journey. The biblical treatment of Terah is brief because the focus of the story is on Abram. Abram listened to God and took a troupe into the desert, not knowing how to find Canaan but trusting that God would lead him. And that trust in God became the foundation stone of the nation of Israel, and later of Christianity and Islam.

Abram's mission was to forge a great nation (Genesis 12:2). And as he engaged that mission he had various adventures. In one story his nephew, Lot, was captured and carried off by desert raiders. Abram pursued them, and following the rescue of his nephew he met a priest by the name of Melchizedek, who was the king of Salem, a city that would later be known as Jerusalem. Abram's sortie to rescue Lot had yielded a lot of booty, and Abram tithed—gave a tenth—of it to Melchizedek, apparently as a symbol of a lesser power to a greater power. Melchizedek then blessed Abram in a ceremony of shared bread and wine. That brief meeting in the desert would later prove to be most auspicious (Hebrews 5-7). I'd say more but very little is known about Melchizedek or this event.

Nonetheless, the story goes on. God changed Abram's name to Abraham in honor of God's new covenant with him, which included the promise to make Abraham the father of many, and was sealed with the rite of circumcision, a practice that continues today as a central element of Judaism. The birth of the promised child was delayed, so Sarah, Abraham's impatient and barren wife, eventually decided to provide a child another way. She gave her servant, Hagar, to Abraham as a surrogate mother, who then produced the first born son of the family—Ishmael.

Later Sarah became pregnant at a very old age and had a son of her own—Isaac. Sarah then reneged on her surrogate mother deal with Hagar and dismissed Hagar and Ishmael so that Isaac would become their son of inheritance. That dismissal appears to have been a kind of divorce of Hagar and a disavowal of Ishmael. Scripture then identified and chronicled this event as a source of ongoing regional conflict. It even appears that this dismissal is the origin of the ongoing Israeli/Islamic conflict today.

One day God called Abraham to take Isaac into the wilderness and offer him as a blood sacrifice, to kill him as an act of worship. And Abraham obeyed! It is at this juncture that the issue of whether Abraham's religion was different from his father's comes to a point. We have difficulty thinking of Abraham being actively involved in a child sacrificing blood cult at this point in the story, yet Abraham's obedience appears to confirm the discomforting idea that Abraham would go so far as to prepare his own son for such a sacrifice. Child sacrifice to a god was common among surrounding peoples. Traditionally, it is understood that God was essentially asking Abraham if he loved Him as much as the pagans loved their gods. But we must also note that Abraham fully understood the protocol for sacrifice, and was willing to do it.

This story is central to the mission of Jesus Christ because it prefigures the lengths that God would go with *His* Son in order to save humanity from certain destruction. God appealed to the necessity for blood sacrifice in order to atone for human sin—not because He needed it (God needs nothing!), but apparently because humanity needed it. We laud Abraham for his obedience and careful listening to God, who then stopped him at the last moment. Yet, God did sacrifice His own Son for the redemption of humanity. Perhaps Abraham had some moral qualms about this proposed dastardly deed, but Scripture is silent in this regard. Abraham is portrayed as simply being obedient to God, which according to the story is exactly what God wanted—simple obedience. It was a test to see how far Abraham would go in his obedience. Fortunately, God intervened, stopped the slaughter in the nick of time, and provided a lamb in the stead. Christians breathe a sigh of relief at this point, and relish in the symbolism that points to Christ's sacrifice as the lamb of God.

Nonetheless, our dismay over Abraham's radical obedience in this regard is very real. God's action of providing a substitute sacrifice—a lamb (John 1:29)—prefigured the climax of the larger biblical story of Christ's substitutionary sacrifice on the cross that would come much later. And as inspirational as that story is, serious questions remain: Why would God stoop to engage the horrific methods of a child sacrificing blood cult as the way to reveal His unbounded love and grace through His only begotten Son? If God is all-powerful and can do anything He wants in the twinkling of an eye, surely He could find a better way than working through an ancient blood sacrificing cult!

God's Task

But not if God's intention was to reach those who were actually living in a world ordered by laws and principles that were dominated by such a cult. In a different world God would have done things differently. But in this world dominated by sin and vengeance illustrated by child sacrificing blood cults God worked with the sinful mess created in the wake of Adam and Eve's sin. Actually all worlds (cultures, eras, or dispensations) since the Garden in Eden are manifestations of the Serpent—Satan—because Adam, Eve, and all of humanity followed in the rebellion of Satan. Or at least we could say that those who lived in these cultures, eras, and dispensations since the Garden followed in Adam's stead, who followed the Serpent, who was Satan (Revelation 12:9, 20:2). God had created the world represented by the Garden in Eden, which was corrupted by Satan and destroyed by the Flood. All subsequent worlds followed Noah's sin, which was a reiteration of original sin.

In this world of sin God worked with those existing, blood-guilt laws and principles, and the people who believed them, in order to provide a time-oriented (historical) solution that would speak to such people. The world exists in time, so the solution would also need to manifest in time if it was to be understood by humanity. It isn't that God needed to work in this way, from within the culture of a child sacrificing blood cult, but that humanity required it because that was their world. For whatever reason(s), which can be traced back to Cain's vengeful blood-lust against Abel, all humanity seems to have been caught up in the values, beliefs, and cultures epitomized by child-sacrificing blood cults. And no doubt, such a reality flooded humanity with guilt and shame, and all of the psychological disorders associated therewith. So, to extricate humanity from a culture of blood-lust, guilt, shame, and vengeance—which were the products of the Serpent's deceit, God would need to lead from within, by being with people who were so inflicted. God could not simply decree a fix from above, from outside of time, outside the laws and principles of such a humanity. He would need to change the hearts and minds of those sinners, to free those people from their slavery to sin without violating the motivating force of human freedom or the spirit of creativity with which He had originally endowed people.

The first step toward this solution would involve God's companionship, His presence with people in that world. He needed to be with those He intended to free, to be with them where they were in their captivity and depravity, to be one of their own kind so that they would trust Him, and to speak in terms that they understood, in terms of justice, which they understood at that time as blood for blood—vengeance. Again, it was not that God needed this, but that this was how humanity had understood God from the depths of their enculturated sin and guilt. This is important because it is from this point of Abraham's simple obedience to God that three world-changing religions trace their origin—Judaism, Christianity, and Islam. It is commonly understood that these three are the primary monotheistic religions, and that is what makes them unique, what they have in common, and what makes them clearly distinct from other religions.

But that is *not* what I am arguing here. Here I am arguing that Christianity alone is Trinitarian.[2]

At this point in the story Ishmael had been dismissed from Abraham's house, and plays no further role in the central arc of the story, though his descendents are repeatedly identified as enemies of Israel. So Isaac carried on his father's tradition, even doing many of the same things that Abraham had done, quarreling with the same people, even lying about his wife, Rebekah, being his sister. When Rebekah gave birth to twins a new chapter of the story began.

JACOB & ESAU

The story of human conflict that began with Cain and Abel now emerges within the lineage of Seth through Jacob and Esau, which suggests that familial or cultural separation provides no protection from it. Its origin is not outside humanity, the family, the clan, or the culture. Jacob and Esau, born at the same time from the same mother into the same culture, turn out to be radically different. And those differences appear to be a function of the blessing of God.

At this point in the larger story, the blessing of God is not universal. Rather, it is particular, limited. The story portrays the blessing as going to Abel not Cain, to Isaac not Ishmael, and now to Jacob not Esau. In each case the issue is the father's blessing, which provides an inheritance. The Jews mistakenly thought that the inheritance the Bible was talking about was a function of bloodline, so they kept meticulous track of families and were family centered.[3] And while this

2 The importance and biblical understanding of the Trinity is discussed my books on 1 & 2 Corinthians, Colossians, Ephesians, and 1 & 2 Peter.

3 This is an important issue and beyond the scope of this book. Suffice it to say that careful attention to the New Testament genealogies shows that Jesus' lineage doesn't follow a strict blood lineage, but involves some adoption into Israel—which is the more important point. See: https://carm.org/bible-difficulties/matthew-mark/why-are-there-different-genealogies-jesus-matthew-1-and-luke-3.

"For it must be remembered that, back of the problem of reconciling the virgin birth and the Davidic origin of Jesus, lay the far deeper problem—to harmonize the incarnation and the Davidic origin. This problem had been presented in shadow and intimation by Jesus Himself in the question: 'David himself calleth him Lord; and whence is he his Son?' It is further to be noticed that in the annunciation (Luke 1:32) the promised One is called at once Son of God and Son of David, and that He is the Son of God by virtue of His conception by the Spirit—leaving it evident that He is Son of David by virtue of His birth of Mary. With this should be compared

is not a bad thing, family lineage is not the source of God's blessing. This has proven to be a hard lesson to learn, but is the point of the story of the twins, Jacob and Esau.

In the biblical story the father's blessing conveyed the blessing of God, as well. The characters in the story were in the process of being freed from sin, freed from the false religion(s) that dominated their region and their time. But God was not merely freeing individual people from sin, His intention was—and still is—is to free human culture from sin. So, the understanding of God's blessing portrayed in the Old Testament would fall short of the fullness of God's intention. God's ideal for Abraham was to be a blessing for *all* humanity (Genesis 12:3). Our goal as recipients of the biblical story today is to understand the nature and scope of God's blessing because this appears to be the root of human conflict, in that God's blessing was revoked at the Fall, yet in some sense it continues to be a concern of Scripture.

Jacob and his mother seem to have understood the idea that blood kinship was somehow involved in God's blessing because they worked hard to insure that Jacob would be the one to receive his father's (and God's) blessing as the son of inheritance. They conspired and schemed and lied in order to trick Isaac into pronouncing his blessing on Jacob rather than on Isaac's favorite son, Esau. Esau was an outdoorsman, a hunter—hairy and haughty, a man's man. And Jacob was sensitive, a mama's boy, a nerd, a reader, a thinker—some called him a schemer.

Rebekah and Jacob pulled it off, and got Isaac to bless Jacob rather than Esau through a series of deceitful tricks. It's a wonder that the Lord would go along with such mischievousness. But He did, and He

---

the statement of Paul (Romans 1:3,1): 'He who was God's Son was 'born of the seed of David according to the flesh, and declared to be the Son of God with power, according to the spirit of holiness, by the resurrection from the dead.' This is at least most suggestive (see Orr, *Virgin Birth of Christ*, 119, with note, p. 121), for it indicates that as Paul and Luke were in very close sympathy as to the person of our Lord, so they are in equally close sympathy as to the mystery of His origin. The unanimity of conviction on the part of the early church as to the Davidic origin of Jesus is closely paralleled by its equally firm conviction as to His supernatural derivation. The meeting-point of these two beliefs and the resolution of the mystery of their relationship is in the genealogies in which two widely diverging lines of human ancestry, representing the whole process of history, converge at the point where the new creation from heaven is introduced" (http://www.internationalstandardbible.com/G/genealogy-of-jesus-christ-the.html).

did it for a reason—it fit His long range plan to free this sinful people from the evil of sin. God's plan was to demonstrate the futility of humanity's religious understanding and practices that originated in their fallen, sinful, child-sacrificing, blood-vengeance cult(s). He would adapt and use the organs of that ancient religion to prophesy its own end, its own destruction, and plant the hope of true religion in its rotting carcass. And this is what He did, captured in the story in the Old Testament.

Jacob had twelve sons through four wives: by Leah—Reuben, Simeon, Levi, Judah, Issachar, and Zebulun; by Zilpah—Gad and Asher; by Bilhah—Dan and Naphtali; by Rachael—Joseph and Benjamin. These sons became the twelve tribes of Israel. Why not the twelve tribes of *Jacob?* Because God changed his name.

NAMING

It is important to understand what the biblical practice of naming actually was. Adam's first job in the Garden was to name the animals, so we must understand what Adam was actually doing. Naming is a science called taxonomy. Adam was classifying the animals, which would serve as a model of how to understand the world. Classification by kind, type, or character is the first order of science. Think of botany. Aristotle is historically credited with this, but it actually began with Adam. This kind of naming or classifying requires an understanding of the character and nature of the things to be classified.

This practice of naming was common in the Old Testament, particularly with regard to naming children. A child's name conveyed meaningful information about the person's character, relationships, history, and/or station (employment). This idea was in wide use until the modern era. Thus, we understand that the ancient relatives of the Smith family were iron smiths, and the ancient relatives of the Porter family were porters, etc. A person's name conveyed important information about the person. This understanding of naming is essential to the story of Jacob's name change because it pointed to his change of character. Jacob would become a changed man, which was God's plan for people everywhere. When Jacob's character changed, God changed his name to reflect the change in character. The Holy Spirit is the agent of human change.

One night Jacob wrestled with God, who had appeared in the guise of a man. God did not defeat Jacob, but put his hip out of socket. God seriously wounded Jacob, but still Jacob's pride kept him from conceding defeat. So, God renamed him, *Israel*, which means one who wrestles with God. Jacob then limped through the rest of his life, leaning on God for support. That was the model—wounded pride, leaning on God.

EGYPT

Joseph was Jacob's favorite son, sensitive and intelligent like himself. Joseph's coat of many colors was a robe of authority and honor. But because Joseph was the youngest son, his older brothers were jealous of the authority and honor his father accorded him. So, they made a plan to kill him. Reuben disagreed with the plan and suggested an adaptation. *Don't kill him*, he said, *but throw him in a pit and leave him for dead*. Reuben's secret plan was to rescue Joseph later in order to get into good graces with Jacob. They all agreed, and threw him into a pit. But a caravan of Ishmalites passed near, so they decided to sell Joseph into slavery, pocket the money, and then bloodied Joseph's robe as evidence that he was dead.

The plan worked splendidly, and Joseph was carted off, ending up in Egypt and eventually occupied the highest office in Egypt under Pharaoh. And so it was that Joseph saved Egypt—and Israel—and many of the surrounding nations from starvation through a process of buying and storing grain in anticipation of a famine. Eventually Israel and his children went to Egypt to escape the famine. And that is how the people of Israel came to be in Egypt. At this point the story of God's law gets serious.

MOSES

Eventually Joseph died, and Israel remained in Egypt for four hundred years. During that time Israel devolved from having a special status and protection under Joseph to become abused slaves on the bottom rung of Egyptian society. Moses, through an unlikely turn of events, had been raised in Pharaoh's court. Late in his life he found and reclaimed his Jewish heritage, and God then called him to lead Israel out of Egyptian slavery. The plan was for Israel to go out into the wilderness to worship God. Moses knew himself to be a poor leader so he recruited his brother, Aaron, to be his spokesperson and chief priest, while Moses concentrated on dealing with God.

One day God gave Moses Ten Commandments written in stone, which has become a pivotal event in human history. The idea was that by living in obedience to these Ten Commandments people would avoid entanglement with sin, and these Ten Commandments would then be the basis for a new society, free of Egypt and the old, sinful, religious ways. But when Moses brought them down from the mountain to show Aaron and the people what God had provided, he found them all dancing before a golden calf that had been fashioned by Aaron, and served as a symbol of ancient paganism! God burned with anger for their faithlessness and threatened to destroy them all, but Moses intervened on their behalf, arguing with God that they could be redeemed, that God should not just kill them all. God relented, and He and Moses began a plan for their redemption.

Israel was not ready or able at that time to conform to God's original plan regarding the Ten Commandments as a way to avoid the evil of sin. At that point in their maturity, for Moses to simply give them the Ten Commandments would have been, as Jesus would later say, like giving pearls to swine, which would be a meaningless effort. I'm not suggesting that there is any problem with the Ten Commandments. The Ten Commandments, sometimes called the Law, are perfect and will accomplish their purpose, but at that point in history the people were unable to engage them. They had struggled for many years in the desert trying to make them work, but the people were habituated in their old ways and habits, which created many problems and difficulties. Again, note that the difficulties are not with God or with His law, but with the people.

SANHEDRIN

Eventually, Moses took the advice of his brother-in-law, Jethro, and appointed seventy elders to help administer the Ten Commandments in the midst of their growing population. Jethro was revered as a priest of Midian (Exodus 3:1). The Midianites through their connection with the Moabites are thought to have worshiped a multitude of gods, including Baal-peor and the Queen of Heaven, Ashteroth. The Midianites may also have worshiped Yahweh, but not exclusively.

Nonetheless, we must not lose sight of the fact that the idea of appointing the seventy came from Jethro, nor the fact that God conceded to it. Or we can understand God to have inspired Jethro, a Midianite pagan, to give the idea to Moses.

God's original idea was for His people to simply live by the Ten Commandments, which would provide eternal guidance. They were written in stone to suggest their eternal value. Following the Ten Commandments would keep the people from entanglement with the evil of sin. But people, being people, needed help applying the Commandments to daily life. Life was full of so many extenuating circumstances that it was difficult for them to know how best to apply the Commandments in differing circumstances. Moses' council of seventy were tasked to help the people apply the Ten Commandments.

So they began providing advice, rendering judgments when conflicts arose, and eventually began to codify their extensions and adaptations of the Ten Commandments to meet the needs of the day. Of course, God guided the seventy and provided support and authority for their codification of what became known as the Deuteronomic Law. However, it is important to note that the effort of the seventy was not God's best plan for His people, but was an alternate, temporary measure, introduced by Jethro and aimed to help and to mature His people so that they would eventually be able to live by His Ten Commandments, to apply them themselves, with the direct help of the Holy Spirit. But for now the council of seventy, which eventually became known as the Sanhedrin, would provide help. The Sanhedrin, who were aided by the Holy Spirit, would stand in the gap until the greater dispensation of the Holy Spirit would manifest more fully through the long-expected Messiah. The promise of that manifestation was part of the hope for the coming of the Messiah.

The Sanhedrin, with help from God, created a body of law that would establish and direct the people of Israel to become a nation in the midst of a world captured by sin, epitomized by the religion(s) of blood vengeance. The Sanhedrin worked to forge a righteous people in the midst of overwhelming sin and corruption. Moses had led them out of the dominant Egyptian religion, into the desert where they could carry out this social project apart from false religion and its influence. That effort involved creating various laws and regulations for worship, family life, health, business, government, etc. They were building a new social order. The laws and regulations they created were both detailed and extensive, covering every aspect of life as they knew it. And those laws have proven to be among the best the world has ever seen! God worked with them to make their worship and laws reflect the reality of God and the world, yet they were also crafted for their particular situation in the wilderness.

However, they did not represent God's best plan for His people to avoid the evil of sin, though they continue to provide a useful guide in the light of Christ. They were a stopgap measure aimed at providing immature people with immediate order, health, and genuine well-being while human culture matured to the point that people could live by the original Ten Commandments under the direct aid of the Holy Spirit when He would manifest more fully in history through Christ. But for now, the Sanhedrin provided invaluable guidance for the fledgling nation.

THE TABERNACLE

Part of the law developed by the Sanhedrin provided for worship and the construction of the Tabernacle, a large, portable worship area made of tents. The Tabernacle would provide the central focus for Israelite worship and culture during their nomadic stage. Establishing a nation required significant changes for a people who had originated in nomadic life and who had been steeped in slavery. Significant changes would be necessary, and the Tabernacle played a key role during their transition from nomadism to nationhood. In fact, the building and operation of the Tabernacle would provide important skills and ideas for the development of their future national culture.

Because worship required valuable accoutrements, fine linens, gold, silver, etc., the Tabernacle and the culture that supported it would need protection from desert raiders who had operated in the area from time immemorial. As a result Israel became, among other things, a military force of great reputation. Militarization was necessary for the establishment and survival of the fledgling nation.

And because God was at the heart of the culture providing direction and protection, they became very good at military endeavors. So, we see a lot of wars during this period of nomadic consolidation and national establishment. As they excelled militarily they conquered various armies and nations, taking prisoners (sometimes against God's direction), and learning about the ways of other nations. This exposure to competing religions and cultures brought temptation, corruption, and decay to their own religion and culture. At the height of their nomadic corruption, the people called for a king to lead their fledgling nation because their leaders, Samuel's sons, had themselves become corrupt (1 Samuel 8). They knew that they needed a change.

Samuel, the last righteous judge of Israel, received the request for a king when the people complained about the corruption of his sons, whom he had appointed as judges (leaders).

> "You are old and your sons do not walk in your ways. Now appoint for us a king to judge us like all the nations" (1 Samuel 8:5).

Samuel did not like the idea, and when he took it to the Lord, He said, "they have not rejected you, but they have rejected me from being king over them" (1 Samuel 8:7). The Lord told Samuel to tell them in no uncertain terms that kingship was a bad idea because the king would eventually take their land, their families, and their money through excessive taxation. The king would grow wealthy and wage wars. And the disparity of wealth and the power of war tend to feed corruption. Finally the Lord relented and said to Samuel, "Obey their voice and make them a king" (1 Samuel 8:22). God conceded to their covetous, wayward demand and used it in His plan to demonstrate the errors of their ways.

SHILOH

Again, we must note that this venture into kingship was not only *not* God's idea, but was in blatant opposition to God's best plan for His people. Nonetheless, God again accommodated their foolishness and waywardness in order to allow humanity the experience of learning essential lessons about faithfulness and obedience through the eventual failure of their kingdom. God Himself would help them build the best kingdom possible in order to underscore His previous counsel against building a kingdom at all in the model of the neighboring nations. God's lessons were not simply for them at that time, they were for history, for those who would come later, for us. Those lessons needed to be woven into human history by God Himself becoming an agent in that history.

The first functioning capital of Israel as it transitioned from a band of nomadic tribes into an established nation was the settlement at Shiloh in the northern part of Israel. Shiloh became the home of the Tabernacle and the priesthood during the time of the Judges. And as the story of the period of Judges demonstrates, Israel—exemplified by her rulers, her judges and priests—devolved into sin, idolatry, and corruption while endeavoring to follow the laws of the Moses and the seventy. God's response to this fact ended in the destruction of the Northern Kingdom by Assyria in 721 B.C., with Shiloh functioning as a sort of capital in the north.[4] Let that sink in: the capital of ancient Israelite worship and culture was destroyed in the transition between nomadism and nationhood, and the Ark of the Covenant, the centerpiece of the Tabernacle, was captured and removed from Israel's possession. The Assyrians were simply the means by which God Himself, acting in human history, brought destruction to Israel under the leadership of the Sanhedrin.

Surely the destruction Shiloh and the religion of the Tabernacle that undergirded it provided the central point of that lesson! The best leaders they could muster brought the Tabernacle and its culture to destruction in spite of God's help. But was it enough for Israel to learn that lesson? Far from it. The story continues.

SAUL & DAVID

When Israel set out to find a suitable king, Saul was chosen from the tribe of Benjamin. Again, God relented to the sinful desires of the people in order to teach them about the importance of following God's lead. The Benjaminites were particularly skilled in warfare. They were archers and slingers, and they even trained themselves to be

---

4   "The Bible describes Shiloh as an assembly place for the people of Israel from the time of Joshua. Sacrifices were brought there by the Israelites during the period of judges, and it was also the site of various religious celebrations and festivals. The prophet Samuel was reportedly raised there, and the Ark of the Covenant remained at Shiloh until it was captured by the Philistines in the battle of Aphek during the time of the high priest Eli"
[http://www.newworldencyclopedia.org/entry/Shiloh_(Bible)].

ambidextrous, which provided a great advantage in battle. Saul, because he was tall and handsome, stood out among the Benjamite warriors. God knew that the battles this fledgling nation would still need to wage were important if it was to become a permanent fixture in the region, in the midst of warring nations and desert raiders that was dominated by religious vengeance.

Saul, the people's choice, proved to be a poor king because he would not follow God's lead. So, as he began to establish his faithlessness and corruption, God alerted Samuel that another king would need to be chosen, someone filled with faith and humility, someone teachable, someone willing to be trained for the job. After an extensive search God told Samuel to anoint a young shepherd boy from Judah. David was anointed and assigned to be a musician in Saul's court in order to help subdue the evil spirit that haunted Saul. David then had a ringside seat from which to learn the skills of kingship. David, of course, was not Saul's protege, but God's. Saul provided many useful bad examples that the Lord used to train David for kingship.

The story of Saul and David is filled with adventures, wonder, and intrigue. The lessons learned are valuable for God's people and should be carefully studied. But they are not essential to the arc of the backstory unfolding here. Here we are marking out the development and corruption of the law as Jesus understood it, remembering that Jesus' divinity granted Him an overview of the entire sweep of history. So as we look back from our perspective now, we can be assured that He knew then in some way what we know now—and more![5]

The story of Saul ends with the ascension of David to the throne of Israel, and with David the kingdom of Israel begins in earnest. David was able to establish many significant alliances with various warriors and tribes during the time that Saul considered him to be an enemy. David became a friend of misfits and outcasts as Saul's evil spirit became increasingly clear to the people. David was seen as a man of the people and for the people of Israel, for the common man, and he

5   We can know this because of the reality of the Trinity—Father, Son, and Holy Spirit. Following Christ's resurrection, the fullness of the dispensation of the Holy Spirit, through the reality of regeneration such that He dwells with, in, and among God's people through the light of Christ, provides us with wisdom, direction, and insight previously unavailable. This is a common theme in many of my books, and follows the example of Paul's conversion.

fashioned his band of outcasts into a mercenary force who were loyal to him. The story of David is even more valuable than the story of Saul, but in the same way, most of the details and lessons, essential for the people of God, will draw us away from the story arc that is being described here. So, we will leave readers to explore those stories and lessons in their own time.

RECAP

The Ten Commandments were given to Moses so that God's people could avoid the evil of sin. But the people were not mature enough to make direct use of them themselves at that time. So, Jethro recommended that Moses enlist seventy elders to help administer the Ten Commandments in order to establish God's people, blessed as a nation in the midst of a world of sin and corruption. The seventy elders became the institution of the Sanhedrin, which interpreted and applied the essential law—the Ten Commandments under the guidance of the Holy Spirit—in order to establish the nation of Israel in the sinful, violent, and corrupt center of the world's cultures, to take Israel from its nomadic period into its national period.

The leadership of the nomadic Sanhedrin culminated with the founding and subsequent destruction of Shiloh and the consequent loss of the religious and cultural center, the Tabernacle, the Ark of the Covenant, and the leadership of Israel—all were either destroyed or taken into captivity by the Assyrians. The Tabernacle led to Israel's abject failure, which left Judah remaining in the south. The biblical story is more complex than this, but these important broad-stroke elements of the story provide an overview that is not usually seen.

Saul's experience as the first king provided important training for David, who established Israel as a bonafide kingdom. David's kingship was far more grand, significant, adventurous, and illustrative than Saul's. While David was God's choice for king, the idea of kingship was not God's preference for Israel. Again, God relented to the sinful desires of Israel, but chose David with a plan to redeem His people in spite of themselves. While those stories are not our concern here, this fact is not license to neglect them, for their importance cannot be over estimated.

THE TEMPLE

The story at hand will focus on only one aspect of David's reign—his plan to build the first Temple at Jerusalem. We focus here because the Temple and its religious and social institutions were the first fruits of the law. I'm not disputing the fact that God told David to build the Temple, He conceded to it. But there is much more to the story than that simple fact.

> "For the tabernacle of the LORD, which Moses had made in the wilderness, and the altar of burnt offering were at that time in the high place at Gibeon, but David could not go before it to inquire of God, for he was afraid of the sword of the angel of the LORD" (1 Chronicles 21:29-30).

> "Then David said, 'Here shall be the house of the LORD God and here the altar of burnt offering for Israel.' David commanded to gather together the resident aliens who were in the land of Israel, and he set stonecutters to prepare dressed stones for building the house of God" (1 Chronicles 22:1-2).

David, the king of Israel, was unable to inquire of God through the traditional, nomadic institutions at Shiloh. He would not offer sacrifices at the remnant of the Tabernacle, which at some point had been moved from Shiloh to Gibeon, because the priests who controlled it were idolatrous and the Ark of the Covenant was not with them. This provides an interesting reference for David's faithfulness. The Tabernacle and its institutions brought Israel's nomadic period to complete disarray. It was so mired in sin, idolatry, and corruption that David shunned it.

However, pay close attention to who called for the building of the Temple and who was then called to build it (2 Samuel 7:7-16). David was not a priest, yet he had faithful priests at his side in Jerusalem. Israel was divided as a result of Saul's reign and that division would eventually blossom into of the apostasy of the northern priests and the destruction of the Northern Kingdom by the Assyrians. The Ark of the Covenant had been lost and then recovered by David. But because of the apostasy and corruption at Shiloh David reestablished the capital at Jerusalem. His was the more faithful branch at that time.

But note the absence of the priests and of God in this announcement. *David* said that the Temple would be built in Jerusalem, not a priest, not the Lord, but the king who best represented what God had advised against! The *king*! And whom did David call upon to build it? Resident aliens (גּירר), strangers—not just Israelites (1 Chronicles 22:2)! Of course, David did not build the Temple, he only envisioned it. It would be right next to the king's palace, the home for himself which he had already built. David was a great king, but he was still a king, and represented what God had warned them about. It would be David's son, *King* Solomon, who would actually build the first Temple.

SOLOMON

The transition between David and Solomon was filled with conflict and turmoil. While David had many strengths as a leader, fatherhood was not among them. David's family was a wreck, as the Bible clearly teaches. Rivalry, squabbling, even murder and rape were all part of the story of David's family and his court. Nonetheless, Solomon eventually won the day and became king through scheming and court intrigue. And Solomon is celebrated as the greatest of all of Israel's kings. He was the wisest, the richest, the most successful, and he built the most important Temple ever known to humanity. Solomon became the model and envy of pagan kings everywhere.

David, the king, "ordered all the leaders of Israel to help his son Solomon" (1 Chronicles 22:17) build the Temple and to seek the Lord with heart and soul. That is, David, the *king*, the very embodiment of what the Lord warned against, ordered Israel to worship God in the forthcoming Temple because the Tabernacle had been destroyed. David also called a national convention and reorganized the priesthood from their old nomadic order for their new national order.

> "David assembled all the leaders of Israel and the priests and the Levites. The Levites, thirty years old and upward, were numbered, and the total was 38,000 men. 'Twenty-four thousand of these,' David said, 'shall have charge of the work in the house of the LORD, 6,000 shall be officers and judges, 4,000 gatekeepers, and 4,000 shall offer praises to the LORD with the instruments that I have made for praise.' And David organized them in divisions corresponding to the sons of Levi ...." (1 Chronicles 23:2-6).

Again, it is not that God was opposed to the building of the Temple, or that God did not provide the plans. Rather, the establishment of Israel as a nation among the other nations and the building of the Temple was all part of Israel's disobedience of God's counsel against building a kingdom, which we now know was all part of God's grand plan. The kingdom of Israel was built on the rejection of God (1 Samuel 8:7), even though God continued to pour out His grace and mercy by conceding to their sinful desires. God had a larger plan. While God said, "He shall build a house for my name, and I will establish the throne of his kingdom forever" (2 Samuel 7:13), Israel thought that God would dwell in the Temple at Jerusalem forever. But God did not mean what Israel though He meant. We know that that is not what God meant because history has not established the lineage of David on the throne at Jerusalem. Rather, history teaches that Christ's understanding and teaching about the Temple are the correct way to understand 2 Samuel 7:13. God did not dwell in *that* Temple forever. Yet, it is not that God was mistaken, Israel was. But that's getting ahead of the story.

Solomon built the Temple with the help of Hiram the Phoenician king of Tyre, and with slave labor. Both of these facts should greatly distress us. At the dedication of the Temple, Solomon, the king, took the role of a priest. Solomon, the greatest *king*, had built God a house in which to dwell. Yet Solomon was the very embodiment of what God had counseled against—even more than David! Again, I'm not saying that God was not actively involved in the construction and administration of the Temple. I'm saying that the Temple was the fruit of Israel's kingdom, and that their venture into building a kingdom issued out of disobedience to God's counsel, but to which God had conceded. As great as the Temple was—and it was truly magnificent, it was a tainted project long before the first stone was laid.[6] While Israel

---

6   "The second commandment is closely related to the first. The commandment
     against 'graven images' (idols) is a prohibition against any artistic representation of
     YHWH, for such representation would serve to 'locate' YHWH, to domesticate
     God and so to curb the freedom that belongs to this erupting God (Exod. 20:4-6; see
     2 Sam. 7:6-7). Such images have the effect of drawing God in imagination and in
     practice, away from covenant and relational fidelity and back into a world of objects
     and commodities. The temptation to produce an 'image' of God in artistic form is
     always, everywhere a chance to produce a commodity out of valuable material, at
     best gold if it is available, or lesser valuable material if there is no gold. When a god

believed that it was the very capstone of human history, God knew it to be but a chapter in His unfolding story, a chapter that was destined to end badly.

And yet, there is much value in the study of the Temple, its design, construction, and operation are full of great allusions and lessons regarding the character of God, the reality of humanity, and the nature of reality. Great benefit has accrued to humanity because of the building and operation of the Temple. I'm not suggesting that the Temple was built apart from God's will. Rather, it was God's will to provide a disobedient people (all humanity throughout history) with important, life-changing lessons that would issue from the Temple chapter of God's greater story.

King Solomon, the greatest, richest, wisest, and most successful king in the long history of Israel lived and functioned in essential disobedience to God's best counsel to *not* build a kingdom like those of her neighbors. The wisdom of Solomon, unsurpassed in human history, failed to harken to the voice of the Lord in this regard, and led the people into sin, idolatry, and corruption of huge proportions.

Solomon would be the last king of a united Israel, celebrating the Northern and Southern Kingdoms at Jerusalem as the capital city and the great Temple as the symbol of their unity. Only three kings reigned over a united Israel: Saul, who floundered as he wrestled with an evil spirit; David, who actually brought all the parties together; and

---

is fashioned into a golden commodity (or even lesser material); divine subject becomes divine object, and agent becomes commodity. We may cite two obvious examples of this temptation in the Old Testament. First, in the narrative of the 'Golden Calf' in Exodus 32, it was gold that was fashioned into the image that readily became an alternative god who jeopardized the covenant. The ensuring narrative of Exodus 33-34 tells of the hard and tricky negotiations whereby covenantal possibility is restored to Israel after its foray into distorting images (Exod. 43:9-10). Less dramatically, it is evident that Solomon's temple, designed to 'house' YHWH, became a commodity enterprise preoccupied with gold: (see 1 Kings 6:20-22, 7:48-50).

Even as YHWH was honored by such extravagance, the temple was clearly intended to reflect honor on Solomon and on his regime. The attention to gold objects clearly skewed the simple and direct matter of covenantal possibility. Commodity desire has, for the most part, crowded out the covenantal tradition." — Bruggeman, Walter. *sabbath as resistance—Saying NO to the CULTURE OF NOW*, Westminster John Knox Press, 2014, p. 7-8.

Solomon, who built the great Temple which led to the destruction of the nation.

CIVIL WAR

The end of Solomon's reign was as fractious as the end of David's. Two factions, each headed by one of Solomon's sons, Rehoboam and Jeroboam, vied for the crown. The divided kingdom was represented by Israel in the north, which established a new capital in Samaria, while Judah in the south maintained the capital at Jerusalem. Israel was the more populous and urban of the two kingdoms, and was more closely connected to the ruling houses of Phoenicia. Judah at Jerusalem was more rural and isolated, which helped them maintain the faith. That isolation helped them to be faithful, and yet to maintain a problematic, self-centered focus.

This civil war raged for four hundred years, and involved various other regional powers vying for dominance in the area. Both sides eventually became subject to Assyrian domination by 850 B.C., and were forced to pay tribute. The kingdom of Israel joined in the repeated rebellions of the Phoenicians, whose capital was Tyre, and was punished by Assyria with increasing harshness. In 721 B.C., the Assyrian Kings Sargon II and Esarhaddon conquered Israel and conducted a mass deportation of the ruling aristocracy from Gibeon (Shiloh) to Urartu (ancient Armenia). There the ruling elite of Israel were absorbed into the native population.

Later, in 586 B.C. King Nebuchadnezzar sacked Jerusalem and enslaved the Southern aristocracy, carting them off to Babylon. The Temple was utterly destroyed along with the city, which marked the beginning of the Babylonian Captivity, 586-539 B.C.

This was the result of David's vision and reordering of Israelite culture to serve the Temple establishment. The plan was to create a righteous civilization that gave God praise and glory, all of which is good! However, again it ended with the leadership of Israel doing very well for themselves, and leading the nation into sin, idolatry, and corruption, which ended in destruction. A pattern was emerging.

Jerusalem and the Temple laid in ruins for some seventy years, as Isaiah and Jeremiah had prophesied at the height of Israel's national success at Jerusalem prior to its destruction. Isaiah and Jeremiah were very unpopular writers in their day. Very few people believed them at the time, but history vindicated their prophecies. Once again God laid important lessons about faithfulness and obedience at their feet.

Surely the destruction of Jerusalem and the great Temple that served as the center of their culture provided the central point of that lesson! But was it enough for Israel to learn what God was trying to teach them? Far from it. The story continues.

THE SECOND TEMPLE

The rise of the Persian Empire provided another opportunity for Israel to get it right, or so they thought. Where the Assyrians and Babylonians uprooted those they defeated in order to keep them from having the ability to organize rebellion, the Persians kept those they defeated in place, encouraging their political, social, and religious institutions to flourish so that their vassals could send more tax money to Persia. The Persian model proved to be quite effective.

As the Persians consolidated their empire, Israel came to their attention because the former capital, Jerusalem, lay in ruins, rather than contributing to the tax base of the empire. They knew the stories of Israel's former greatness under Solomon, and moved to reestablish Israel as a source of tax income.[7] Cyrus, king of Persia, issued a decree:

> "Thus says Cyrus king of Persia: The LORD, the God of heaven, has given me all the kingdoms of the earth, and he has charged me to build him a house at Jerusalem, which is in Judah. Whoever is among you of all his people, may his God be with him, and let him go up to Jerusalem, which is in Judah, and rebuild the house of the LORD, the God of Israel—he is the God who is in Jerusalem. And let each survivor, in whatever place he sojourns, be assisted by the men of his place with silver and gold, with goods and with beasts, besides freewill offerings for the house of God that is in Jerusalem" (Ezra 1:2-4).

Nehemiah gave the king the idea to rebuild the Temple, and the king agreed. They would use Persian money because Israel was in poverty as a conquered nation. Again, I'm not saying that God was

---

7   "The Persian leaders required cooperation and imposed a 20 percent tax on all agriculture and manufacturing. They also taxed religious institutions, which despite their wealth had previously not been taxed. The Persians themselves paid no taxes" (http://www.ushistory.org/civ/4e.asp).

not involved. Most assuredly, He was! But Cyrus authorized and paid for it, at least in the beginning, and he returned the various Temple accoutrements that had been taken during the sack of Jerusalem.

Ezra, a priest charged with maintaining Israelite texts and traditions during the Exile, became the leader of the movement and began organizing people to return to Jerusalem and rebuild the Temple, and the city would also come back to life. Once in Jerusalem, they took freewill offerings from those Israelites who had made the journey, who contributed generously as best they could. They rebuilt the altar and reinstituted animal sacrifices before the completion of the Temple. However, as the foundation of the new Temple was laid, many people had mixed responses.

> "And when the builders laid the foundation of the temple of the
> LORD, the priests in their vestments came forward with trumpets, and
> the Levites, the sons of Asaph, with cymbals, to praise the LORD, ac-
> cording to the directions of David king of Israel. And they sang re-
> sponsively, praising and giving thanks to the LORD, 'For he is good,
> for his steadfast love endures forever toward Israel.' And all the peo-
> ple shouted with a great shout when they praised the LORD, because
> the foundation of the house of the LORD was laid. But many of the
> priests and Levites and heads of fathers' houses, old men who had
> seen the first house, wept with a loud voice when they saw the foun-
> dation of this house being laid, though many shouted aloud for joy,
> so that the people could not distinguish the sound of the joyful shout
> *from the sound of the people's weeping*, for the people shouted with a
> great shout, and the sound was heard far away" (Ezra 3:10-13, italics
> added).

The joyful shout was contrasted with the weeping, suggesting that it was *not* tears of joy they shed. It was weeping in sorrow for what was happening. Those who had known the glory of the First Temple were disappointed at the paucity of the foundation of the Second Temple and the way that it was progressing. At this early stage we see divisions in the unity of those who were rebuilding. The builders worked with a trowel in one hand and a spear in the other because of the divisiveness of the local population—their own kin. In addition, those who had been living in the area over the past seventy years—most of whom had been Israelites left in Jerusalem during the Babylonian Captivity—refused to help, and many became violently set against the whole project. The leaders of Israel met the opposition with re-solve:

> "But Zerubbabel, Jeshua, and the rest of the heads of fathers' houses
> in Israel said to them, 'You have nothing to do with us in building a
> house to our God; but we alone will build to the LORD, the God of
> Israel, as King Cyrus the king of Persia has commanded us'" (Ezra
> 4:3).

Note the irony: they didn't want "foreigners" to help build, but acknowledged that Cyrus—a *foreign* king—had commanded it.

DANIEL'S VISION

In the same year that the foundation was laid and restoration be-gan in earnest the Lord gave Daniel a vision. As with Daniel's other vision it was filled with symbolic language, double meanings, and oblique references to the future. But whatever else that vision was, it was not a vision of peace and harmony. It was a vision of future con-flict that would again destroy the Temple by the hand of God who would then send His Messiah.

In the first part of the vision northern and southern kings engaged in battle. They were probably the Persian kings: Cambyses, Smerdis, Darius, and Xerxes. The king of Greece (Daniel 8:1) probably refers to Alexander the Great. And if the king of the south (Daniel 11:5-9) re-ferred to Egypt, those kings would probably be: Ptolemy Soter, Philadelphus and his daughter Bernice, and Ptolemy Philopator. And if the Seleucid kingdom of Syria is the northern reference, then those kings would probably be Antiochus III and Antiochus Epiphanes, who would later desecrate the Temple just prior to its destruction in A.D. 70. Christians understand the second part of Daniel's vision to point to the coming of Christ and His resurrection.

While Daniel's vision thrusts us into the future, we must not get ahead of the story. Nor do we want to get distracted by the details of Daniel's vision. Suffice it to say that the fulfillment of Daniel's vision easily applies to the destruction of Jerusalem and the Second Temple in A.D. 70 by Rome. And the second part of Daniel's vision applies to the manifestation and resurrection of Jesus Christ as the long awaited Mes-siah of biblical prophecy. But all of this gets us ahead of the story.

In 536 B.C. construction of the Second Temple came to a halt. We know this because the Bible has preserved several letters between various parties and the Persian king, Artaxerxes. One such letter reads:

> "To Artaxerxes the king: Your servants, the men of the province Beyond the River, send greeting. And now be it known to the king that the Jews who came up from you to us have gone to Jerusalem. They are rebuilding that rebellious and wicked city. They are finishing the walls and repairing the foundations. Now be it known to the king that if this city is rebuilt and the walls finished, they will not pay tribute, custom, or toll, and the royal revenue will be impaired. Now because we eat the salt of the palace and it is not fitting for us to witness the king's dishonor, therefore we send and inform the king, in order that search may be made in the book of the records of your fathers. You will find in the book of the records and learn that this city is a rebellious city, hurtful to kings and provinces, and that sedition was stirred up in it from of old. That was why this city was laid waste. We make known to the king that if this city is rebuilt and its walls finished, you will then have no possession in the province Beyond the River" (Ezra 4:11-16).

It's not surprising that Israel's enemies were opposed to the rebuilding of the Temple, but many of the locals who opposed it were Jews who had been left behind during the Babylonian Captivity. In addition, we should remember God's promise to Abraham:

> "Now the LORD said to Abram, 'Go from your country and your kindred and your father's house to the land that I will show you. And I will make of you a great nation, and I will bless you and make your name great, so that you will be a blessing. I will bless those who bless you, and him who dishonors you I will curse, and in you all the families of the earth shall be blessed'" (Genesis 12:1-3).

Israel was supposed to be a blessing to *all* humanity, yet many of those closest to Israel were threatened and afraid of Israel. In addition—and more significantly—opposition to the Temple also came from within Israel—those who had wept at the consecration service.

As the construction on the Temple was halted by King Artaxerxes there was a shakeup in the leadership of the Persian Empire as Darius moved against Guamata and gained control of the Empire. Darius was then eager to resume the Temple project in order to increase his tax base. Tattenai, governor of Trans-Euphrates, which included Palestine, balked as construction began and inquired of Darius about the status of the project. Darius replied:

> "In the first year of Cyrus the king, Cyrus the king issued a decree: Concerning the house of God at Jerusalem, let the house be rebuilt, the place where sacrifices were offered, and let its foundations be retained. Its height shall be sixty cubits and its breadth sixty cubits, with three layers of great stones and one layer of timber. Let the cost be paid from the royal treasury. And also let the gold and silver vessels of the house of God, which Nebuchadnezzar took out of the temple that is in Jerusalem and brought to Babylon, be restored and brought back to the temple that is in Jerusalem, each to its place. You shall put them in the house of God. Now therefore, Tattenai, governor of the province Beyond the River, Shethar-bozenai, and your associates the governors who are in the province Beyond the River, keep away. Let the work on this house of God alone. Let the governor of the Jews and the elders of the Jews rebuild this house of God on its site. Moreover, I make a decree regarding what you shall do for these elders of the Jews for the rebuilding of this house of God. *The cost is to be paid to these men in full and without delay from the royal revenue*, the tribute of the province from Beyond the River. And whatever is needed—bulls, rams, or sheep for burnt offerings to the God of heaven, wheat, salt, wine, or oil, as the priests at Jerusalem require—let that be given to them day by day without fail, that they may offer pleasing sacrifices to the God of heaven and pray for the life of the king and his sons" (Ezra 6:3-10, italics added).

The Second Temple would be built by Persian decree, Persian money, and slave labor. What could possibly go wrong! Again, I'm not saying that God didn't order it. He did! But this point remains as a lesson for us to learn.

> "There is a class of temple functionaries called the Netinim (or Nethinim) mentioned once in Chronicles and several times in Ezra-Nehemiah. As mentioned earlier, this group is widely thought to have been comprised of temple slaves whose origins were explained by the story in Joshua 9. Long lists of their family names appear in three related scriptural texts: Ezra 2, Nehemiah 7, and 1 Esdras 5. What is notable about these names is that they are nearly all non-He-

brew names.[8] Their placement in the list of returnee groups (e.g. after the priests, Levites, gatekeepers, and singers in Nehemiah 10:28) also suggests they were more lowly in status. The fact that a class of non-Israelites served in the Temple is further confirmed by this passage in Ezekiel, which sees their presence as an affront to God:

'Say to the rebellious house, to the house of Israel, Thus says the Lord God: O house of Israel, let there be an end to all your abominations in admitting foreigners, uncircumcised in heart and flesh, to be in my sanctuary, profaning my temple when you offer to me my food, the fat and the blood. You have broken my covenant with all your abominations. And you have not kept charge of my sacred offerings; but you have appointed foreigners to act for you in keeping my charge in my sanctuary" (Ezekiel 44:6–8).'"[9]

Construction continued, but not without difficulty. There were droughts and famines that caused the people to put off the work until they could better afford it. It was during this time that Haggai and Zechariah began preaching to encourage the people to return to the Lord. Haggai said that the droughts and difficulties came because of the faithlessness of the people, and that God would remove such difficulties as they got back to faithfulness. And the people responded by getting back to work. But was that what the Lord meant?

Zechariah also preached:

"The Lord was very angry with your fathers. Therefore say to them, Thus declares the Lord of hosts: Return to me, says the Lord of hosts, and I will return to you, says the Lord of hosts. Do not be like your fathers, to whom the former prophets cried out, 'Thus says the Lord of hosts, Return from your evil ways and from your evil deeds.' But they did not hear or pay attention to me, declares the Lord. Your fathers, where are they? And the prophets, do they live forever? But my words and my statutes, which I commanded my servants the prophets, did they not overtake your fathers? So they repented and said, 'As the Lord of hosts purposed to deal with us for our ways and deeds, so has he dealt with us'" (Zechariah 1:2–6).

8　Ran Zadok, "Notes on the Biblical and Extra-Biblical Onomasticon," *The Jewish Quarterly Review* (New Series), 71(2), 1980.

9　https://isthatinthebible.wordpress.com/2014/10/05/did-the-jerusalem-temple-use-slave-labour/

Zechariah acknowledged that the First Temple had been destroyed because of the faithlessness of Israel. Don't let the importance of this insight pass you by. Note that in spite of the law, the traditions, the Temple, and the Sanhedrin, Israel had failed to be faithful to God, and the result was the destruction of the Tabernacle and the Temple. All of those things that were intended to provide help to Israel did not cure Israel of her sin, idolatry, and corruption. They just dressed it up. And yet, in spite of it all, Zechariah said, the faithfulness of the Lord will continue as the Lord continues to call Israel to faithfulness.

The people were cautioned from thinking that rebuilding the Temple would solve their problems or put them in good stead with God. *No! It won't*, said the prophets. Association with the Temple is not a substitute for faithfulness. Why were such messages preached? Because Israel was in the midst of those particular temptations—again (or *still*)! No doubt those engaged in this rebuilding project thought themselves to be doing the right thing for the right reasons. No doubt they considered themselves to be faithful, in part because of the work they were doing. But Haggai and Zechariah told them repeatedly that they were in danger of succumbing to the same sins that had brought the First Temple down, and that involvement in the Temple (construction or worship) was not a substitute for lives of faithfulness.

Zechariah prophesied that sin would be removed by God's "servant, the Branch" (Zechariah 3:8), an allusion to Messiah who would soon come. Zechariah was aware of the futility of building the Second Temple as a renewed means to cleanse God's people of their sin. It didn't work the first time, and wouldn't work this time either. There can be no substitute for genuine faithfulness. This was the problem that the major prophets had railed against before the destruction of the First Temple. Remember that Isaiah and Jeremiah prophesied about and prior to the destruction of the First Temple, and any cursory reading of their work will provide adequate evidence of this problem.

We can easily think that the faithful prophets were officials of the Temple calling backslidden Temple attendees to get back to worship at the Temple, but that would be a mistake. Of course there was some of this going on, but that was not the thrust of their complaints. Jeremiah was calling the Temple priests liars and false prophets:

"The LORD said to me: 'Do not pray for the welfare of this people. Though they fast, I will not hear their cry, and though they offer burnt offering and grain offering, I will not accept them. But I will consume them by the sword, by famine, and by pestilence.' Then I said: 'Ah, Lord GOD, behold, the prophets say to them, "You shall not see the sword, nor shall you have famine, but I will give you assured peace in this place."' And the LORD said to me: 'The prophets are prophesying lies in my name. I did not send them, nor did I command them or speak to them. They are prophesying to you a lying vision, worthless divination, and the deceit of their own minds. Therefore thus says the LORD concerning the prophets who prophesy in my name although I did not send them, and who say, 'Sword and famine shall not come upon this land': By sword and famine those prophets shall be consumed" (Jeremiah 14:11-15).

"Do not listen to the words of the prophets who prophesy to you, filling you with vain hopes. They speak visions of their own minds, not from the mouth of the LORD. They say continually to those who despise the word of the LORD, 'It shall be well with you'; and to everyone who stubbornly follows his own heart, they say, 'No disaster shall come upon you'" (Jeremiah 23:16-17).

Jeremiah had a major confrontation with Hananiah recorded in Jeremiah 28. The Temple priests were preaching lies and falsehood. Jeremiah called them on it, and he was ostracized for it, vilified in public opinion, and shunned. But history has proven him right. Isaiah, a Temple priest himself, preached the same thing.

"Hear the word of the LORD, you rulers of Sodom! Give ear to the teaching of our God, you people of Gomorrah!" (Isaiah 1:10).

We can easily think that Isaiah was talking about people who lived in Sodom and Gomorrah, but he was not. He was calling his fellow Temple priests names, equating them with the idolaters who led Sodom and Gomorrah to destruction.

"What to me is the multitude of your sacrifices? says the LORD; I have had enough of burnt offerings of rams and the fat of well-fed beasts; I do not delight in the blood of bulls, or of lambs, or of goats. When you come to appear before me, who has required of you this trampling of my courts? Bring no more vain offerings; incense is an abomination to me. New moon and Sabbath and the calling of convocations—I cannot endure iniquity and solemn assembly. Your new moons and your appointed feasts my soul hates; they have become a burden to me; I am weary of bearing them. When you spread out your hands, I will hide my eyes from you; even though you make many prayers, I will not listen; your hands are full of blood. Wash yourselves; make yourselves clean; remove the evil of your deeds from before my eyes; cease to do evil, learn to do good; seek justice, correct oppression; bring justice to the fatherless, plead the widow's cause" (Isaiah 1:11-17).

This was not directed at the people, but at the Temple priests and the leaders of society. Prior to the destruction of the First Temple, Jeremiah and Isaiah revealed the futility of Temple worship, long before Jesus said it, as well. Jesus was just being faithful to Scripture.

Construction of the Second Temple was completed in 349 B.C., but because some of the original Temple items were lost it did not contain: the Ark of the Covenant, which held the Tablets of Stone and before which were placed the pot of manna and Aaron's rod; the Urim and Thummim (divination objects contained in the Hoshen); the holy oil; or the sacred fire. Some of the Israelites believed that the Second Temple was flawed because it was missing some of the central items that had been required by God. Others undoubtedly thought it was flawed because it had been built by foreign people or with foreign money, and money always comes with "strings."

However, given the teaching of the prophets, none of that would make any difference because God was not looking for the reconstruction of the Temple as it had been misunderstood and abused by the priests of the First Temple. God had something completely different in mind. The Temple descriptions were always intended to be understood as analogies that would help us understand our relationship with God, as Jesus understood it.

The Second Temple was doomed for many reasons long before it was built. The rebuilding of the Temple would stand as a confession of the failure to understand the Temple as an analogy, and would contribute to the same sin, idolatry, and corruption that destroyed the First Temple. The language of the prophets needs to be carefully read to distinguish between building the Temple as Christ would come to understand it—as flesh and blood, and building the Temple as King David had understood it—as bricks and mortar.

OVERVIEW

Very early in her history Israel lost sight of Leviticus 19:18 and began an overemphasis, not on moral purity, but on ceremonial purity
rites as a substitute for personal moral purity. Had ancient Israel
heeded her own prophets, the Second Temple would not have been
built, at least its sacrificial practices would not have been modeled on
the first. God repeatedly told Israel that He was no longer interested in
feasts, ceremonies, rites, etc., which *modeled* moral purity. Rather, He
was interested in the actual *practice* of morality in the lives of His people, which was to be practiced and modeled by Israel's leaders. But
Israel, long known as a stubborn, hard-headed people, rebuilt the
Temple anyway, and doubled-down on ceremonial purity rites during
the centuries that followed. Jeremiah was well aware of this problem:

> "I did not speak to your fathers or command them concerning burnt
> offerings and sacrifices. But this command I gave them: 'Obey my
> voice, and I will be your God, and you shall be my people. And walk
> in all the way that I command you, that it may be well with you'"
> (Jeremiah 7:22-23).

To hear these words aright can generate some confusion regarding
God's commands pertaining to burnt offerings and sacrifices. Did God
not command such things? Indeed, He did! They served a purpose at
the time. So, was Jeremiah wrong? No! How then are we to reconcile
these two ideas? Calvin said that

> "the Jews were sedulously attentive to sacrifices, and yet neglected
> the main things—faith and repentance. Hence the Prophet here re-
> pudiates sacrifices, because these false worshipers of God had adulter-
> ated them; for they were only intent on external rites, and over-
> looked their design, and even despised it."[10]

Calvin and Jeremiah differentiated between following the letter of
God's commands—doing the rites—and the spirit or intent of God's
commands—actually engaging faith and repentance personally. And
this was Jesus' concern as well. But again, note that this message did
not originate with the New Testament, but was in full expression at all
times (Leviticus 19:18), and especially through the prophets during the
exile and the Second Temple period.

10 Calvin, John. *Calvin's Commentaries*, Jeremiah 7:22, public domain.

But again, this does not mean that building the Second Temple was not part of God's plan. Rather, it means that the world was not yet ready for the manifestation of Christ until He came to inaugurate God's Kingdom for the whole world by closing the chapter on the misunderstood Temple sacrifices and ceremonies in A.D. 70.

Israel faced a theological crisis during the Second Temple period involving their understanding of the nature, power, and goodness of God; and they were also threatened culturally, racially, and ceremonially as they were thrown into proximity with other peoples and religious groups while in exile in Babylon. The absence of recognized prophets later during the intertestamental period[11] left them without divine guidance at a time when they felt most in need of God's support and direction. A second crisis was the growing influence of Hellenism in Judaism, evidenced by the completion of the Septuagint,[12] which culminated in the Maccabean Revolt of 167 B.C. And a third crisis was the Roman occupation of the region, beginning with General Pompey and his conquest of Jerusalem in 63 B.C.

The Second Temple was consecrated in the spring of 516 B.C., more than twenty years after the return from captivity in the sixth year of the reign of King Darius, amid great rejoicing and weeping on the part of the people. It was, however, evident that the Jews were no longer an independent people, but were still subject to a foreign power. This fact led to a different milieu, a different mindset from the Jews of the First Temple, and colored their religious and social practice of their religion. It drove them inward. They became self-focused—even more than the First Temple Jews had been and forgot that God had counseled them before the First Temple was destroyed:

11 The intertestamental period was the period of time between the writings of the Hebrews Old Testament and the Christian New Testament texts. Traditionally, it is considered to be a roughly four hundred year period, spanning the ministry of Malachi (c. 420 B.C.), the last of the Old Testament prophets, and the appearance of John the Baptist in the early first century A.D., almost the same period as the Second Temple period (530 B.C. to 70 A.D.). It is referred to as the "four hundred silent years" because it is believed to have been a span where God revealed nothing new to his people.

12 The Septuagint is the most ancient translation of the Old Testament into Greek, and consequently is invaluable to critics for understanding and correcting the Hebrew text.

"Thus says the LORD of hosts, the God of Israel, to all the exiles whom
I have sent into exile from Jerusalem to Babylon: Build houses and
live in them; plant gardens and eat their produce. Take wives and
have sons and daughters; take wives for your sons, and give your
daughters in marriage, that they may bear sons and daughters; multiply there, and do not decrease. But seek the welfare of the city where
I have sent you into exile, and pray to the LORD on its behalf, for in
its welfare you will find your welfare" (Jeremiah 29:4-7).

But once back in Jerusalem after the exile, rather than being free
they were *still* captive. Jerusalem was occupied and taxed. Once back
in Jerusalem they did not work to blend in with their captors, as they
had in Babylon. They did not seek the welfare of all. The Second
Temple period was a time of inwardness, separation, and self-absorb-
tion led by their own religious leaders in denial of the very Scriptures
and prophets they "honored." One of their first concerns was to restore
their ancient house of worship by rebuilding their destroyed Temple
and reinstituting the sacrificial rituals known as the *korbanot* or *korban*,
offerings and animal sacrifices. And yet, their own prophets told them
repeatedly *at that time* that God was not interested in sacrifices and ceremonies, that the value of sacrifices and ceremonies was allegorical.
But they persisted, in spite of the fact that they were neither politically
free nor independent—or perhaps because of it.

The Second Temple had come under the influence of Alexander
the Great when the Persians were defeated in 332 B.C. The Seleucid
kingdom then dominated the region. During this time Judaism was
significantly influenced by Hellenistic philosophy, developed from the
third century B.C., notably by the Jewish diaspora in Alexandria, which
culminated in the compilation of the Septuagint, the only extant version of the entire Old Testament, written in Greek.

The relations between Hellenized Jews and traditional Jews dete-
riorated and led the Seleucid king Antiochus IV Epiphanes to impose
decrees banning certain Jewish religious rites and traditions. As a result, the orthodox Jews revolted under the leadership of the
Hasmonean family, also known as the Maccabees. This revolt led to
the formation of an independent Judean kingdom, under the Hasmon-
aean Dynasty, which lasted from 165 to 37 B.C. The Hasmonean
Dynasty eventually disintegrated as a result of civil war. The people,

who did not want to be governed by a foreign king but by the San-hedrin, then appealed to Rome, who deferred to the local control of the Sanhedrin as long as Rome could appoint the High Priest. Rome sent General Pompey, who brought peace by the sword, quelling the revolt. Not long after, Herod the Great established himself as a new pro-Roman king of Judea.

CONTEXT

This was the ambiance of the Second Temple period into which Jesus came and in which Paul grew up. The Second Temple period was a time of religious self-centeredness, corruption, and impurity, so it is no surprise that Israel's leaders emphasized purity from others and separation, and did so in opposition to their own prophets and God's initial vision for them. Paul had been schooled in this perspective, so he knew it well. He was very familiar with the culture of his day, Sec-ond Temple culture, and most of his life he shared the values and assumptions of that culture.

But Christ gave him a vision of a different culture with different values and assumptions—not different from Scripture, but different from the Temple establishment. The important thing about Paul was not his shared Second Temple ideas, but his Christ-is-the-Temple ideas. Sure, his language and thought patterns had been saturated in Second Temple language, ideas, and assumptions, but what makes Paul important is that he broke out of those ideas and assumptions. Paul was instrumental in the laying of the foundation for a different culture. Paul's importance as a theologian has little to do with the Sec-ond Temple culture in which he had lived, other than the fact that he rejected it in favor of a different understanding of the Temple and the Law that supported it.

JESUS & THE TEMPLE

With this background in mind, we turn to Jesus' cleansing of the Temple because both the context and the lesson of the that event were focused on the history herein discussed. John wrote in response to Je-sus' cleansing of the Temple

> "The Passover of the Jews was at hand, and Jesus went up to
> Jerusalem. In the temple he found those who were selling oxen and

sheep and pigeons, and the money-changers sitting there. And making a whip of cords, he drove them all out of the temple, with the sheep and oxen. And he poured out the coins of the money-changers and overturned their tables. And he told those who sold the pigeons, 'Take these things away; do not make my Father's house a house of trade.' His disciples remembered that it was written, 'Zeal for your house will consume me'" (John 2:13-17).

This story is in all four gospels. In Matthew, Mark, and Luke it appears at the end of their books, while it appears early in John's. Some scholars conclude that there must have been two cleansings, one early in Jesus' ministry and one later. Perhaps. But in all of the gospels this story is short, awkward, and a bit stark. For many people it seems to be out of character for Jesus. But it's not. Rather, it is central to the message of the prophets of old and to the message of Jesus. It is the failure to understand the importance of Jesus' cleansing of the Temple that is at the heart of the misunderstanding about law and gospel, works and grace, letter and spirit.

To understand the story rightly we need to see it in its larger context, which I have labored to provide in the preceding pages. To emphasize this fact John's version places this story directly following the miracle at Cana, changing water to wine, and follows it with the Jews requesting a sign or miracle from Jesus. Jesus enacted his first miracle at his mother's bidding by changing the water into wine at the Cana wedding. He immediately went from there to the Temple where He went ballistic, wreaking havoc and throwing people out in a fit of apparent anger, frustration, and rage. The Jews then asked Him to produce a miracle as a sign of his authority, which means that they either weren't aware of the Cana miracle or they denied it.

> "So the Jews said to him, 'What sign do you show us for doing these things?' Jesus answered them, 'Destroy this temple, and in three days I will raise it up.' The Jews then said, 'It has taken forty-six years to build this temple, and will you raise it up in three days?' But he was speaking about the temple of his body" (John 2:18-21).

Whatever the case, the Jews are portrayed as not seeing the significance of the cleansing of the Temple, not understanding Jesus' rage, which is not surprising because the story of the Old Testament is the story of this particular blindness on the part of the Jews. On another occasion the Pharisees asked a similar question of Jesus:

> "Then some of the scribes and Pharisees answered him, saying, 'Teacher, we wish to see a sign from you.' But he answered them, 'An evil and adulterous generation seeks for a sign, but no sign will be given to it except the sign of the prophet Jonah. For just as Jonah was three days and three nights in the belly of the great fish, so will the Son of Man be three days and three nights in the heart of the earth. The men of Nineveh will rise up at the judgment with this generation and condemn it, for they repented at the preaching of Jonah, and behold, something greater than Jonah is here. The queen of the South will rise up at the judgment with this generation and condemn it, for she came from the ends of the earth to hear the wisdom of Solomon, and behold, something greater than Solomon is here'" (Matthew 12:38-42).

The "three days" Jesus referred to pertained to His death and resurrection, which are related to his understanding of the Temple. We know from our side of His resurrection that these verses were about the impending (at that time) destruction of the Second Temple and His resurrection, which He alluded to as the raising up of God's Temple, referred to as His body, the church, "built on the foundation of the apostles and prophets, Christ Jesus himself being the cornerstone" (Ephesians 2:20, see also Ephesians 2:22 and 1 Peter 2:5).

And the sign of Jonah would be the astonishing outpouring of un-merited grace upon the gentiles that they experienced following Jonah's preaching at Nineveh. Remember Jonah's story: God called Jonah to preach repentance to the Ninevites. Nineveh may have been the largest city in the world at that time, which made it a thriving metropolis of gentiles. But Jonah could not bring himself to offer God's forgiveness to *those people*. He refused God's calling and tried to run away. So God sent a great fish to deliver him to the shores of Nineveh against his will. Jonah finally relented and preached to the Nivevites. And to his consternation they responded to his preaching and repented —and God saved them. That was the sign that Jesus would provide to the Jews—a great outpouring of God's grace to the gentiles that would bring them to repentance and faithfulness.

The cleansing of the Temple event was not about money, nor about selling stuff in the Temple, nor about changing money for a profit—none of that. The moneychangers were doing nothing wrong, according to Old Testament law. They had the blessing of the High Priest and the Temple establishment. Rather, Jesus attacked these things because they were simply manifestations (fruit) of Temple corruption, manifestations of the ongoing Jewish blindness. Jesus' whole ministry was focused on the origin or source of the corruption, not the particular ways that the corruption manifested. Jesus was after the root of the problem, not the fruit. The Temple cleansing provided a witness against 1) accommodation to Roman authority, 2) corruption of Temple worship as legalism focused on sacrifices rather than on God's calling, and 3) the injustice and idolatry of the Temple sanctioned system of mammon, a term that was used to describe gluttony, excessive materialism, greed, and unjust worldly gain.

TORAH

Jesus understood the history of the Temple much as I have laid it out. This is what motivated His desire for reform. He understood that the Temple itself was the fruit of what the Jews called the *Torah* or law of God. They clung to the law, and the Temple was the centerpiece of their law-based culture. The first five books of the Old Testament are often referred to as the *Torah*, so today Christians usually equate Torah with biblical law, as part of the sixty-six books that comprise our Bible. But that is *not* how Jesus or Paul understood the term.

In rabbinical literature *Torah* denotes more than the first five books of the Bible. The Rabbis include *Torah Shebichtav* (Torah that is written), and *Torah Shebe'al Peh* (Torah that is spoken). The Oral Torah consists of interpretations and amplifications which according to rabbinic tradition have been handed down from generation to generation, following the tradition of Moses' seventy elders, and are now embodied in the *Talmud* and *Midrash*. A version of these sources of oral Torah were in use at the time of Jesus. And the reason I mention them is that they take us beyond the Bible.[13]

13   Heschel, Abraham Joshua. *God In Search Of Man: A Philosophy Of Judaism*, Farrar, Straus and Giroux, New York, 1955, renewed 1983, p. 274.

In contrast to this, Christians—and mostly Protestants—use the word *Torah* in a way that excludes all extra biblical references. And that is an error because neither Jesus nor Paul understood Torah that way. Paul, trained as a Pharisee, would have used it as the Pharisees used it at that time, in this expanded way to include the Old Testament, the Talmud, and the Midrash. While the Talmud and Midrash were oral traditions in the first century and were committed to writing later, the point remains. Jesus would have understood it in this way, too. But He would also have been aware of the truth of Israel's history as sketched out here. Jesus understood the many ways that the Jews had misunderstood and abused God's teaching on the Temple, and that is precisely what He came to correct by providing a new adaptation and application of God's law, and by appealing to a culture of blood-vengeance through His atonement for sin. But He couldn't just correct them about the Temple because the Temple was the fruit, not the root of the misunderstanding. The law or Torah, as Israel had understood and abused it over the centuries, was the root. Jesus needed to treat the problem at the root, at the level of law, of Torah.

Jesus taught a lot about the law and many of the things that He said about the law began with, "You have heard that it was said," followed by, "But I say to you," mostly in Matthew 5-7, in His sermon on the mount. Among scholars the sermon on the mount is understood to be Jesus' giving of the new law for a new people in a new era. Jesus was the new Moses, the new law-giver, giving—not a new law, but the old law, the original law, the original intention of the Ten Commandments. Jesus returned to the Ten Commandments, not the Torah. He would reform the Ten Commandments—reiterate them—for a new people in a new era, in a similar way that Moses and the seventy had done for ancient Israel.

THE LAW OF CHRIST

Among all of the things that Jesus taught about the law, the most important are found in three contrasting teachings:

> "Do not think that I have come to abolish the Law or the Prophets; I have not come to abolish them but to fulfill them. For truly, I say to you, until heaven and earth pass away, not an iota, not a dot, will pass from the Law until all is accomplished" (Matthew 5:17-18).

"And one of them, a lawyer, asked him a question to test him.
'Teacher, which is the great commandment in the Law?' And he said
to him, 'You shall love the Lord your God with all your heart and
with all your soul and with all your mind. This is the great and first
commandment. And a second is like it: You shall love your neighbor
as yourself. On these two commandments depend all the Law and
the Prophets'" (Matthew 22:35-40).

"A new commandment I give to you, that you love one another: just
as I have loved you, you also are to love one another. By this all people will know that you are my disciples, if you have love for one another" (John 13:34-35).

First, Jesus said that He had not come to change the law; then He
summed up the Ten Commandments in two commandments: love
God and neighbor; then He said that He was delivering a new commandment: to love one another. It's not surprising that people get
confused. Which is it? Did He change the law or not? The answer is
both no and yes. Some things changed and some things didn't.[14]

The clearest example of the changing of the law can be seen in the
Sabbath Commandment, one of the Ten Commandments. The Jews
were commanded to worship on the Sabbath, which they understood
as Saturday. Christians worship on Sunday, so something changed.
There are, of course, many Old Testament laws that changed from the
Old to the New Testaments, i.e., blood sacrifices, food and clothing
laws, stonings, etc. Yet, at the same time Christians argue that the Ten
Commandments are still in force, that they are eternal. But if the Ten
Commandments are still in force, why do obedient Christians worship
on Sundays? These are some of the concerns that drive this issue about
whether Jesus changed God's law. And they are fraught with various
difficulties, yet the truth of the matter is quite simple. This was the issue that Paul addressed in his letter to the Galatians.

Finally we have before us a brief overview of the backstory or
context regarding Paul's letter to the Galatians in its essential points.
These were the issues that confused the Galatians. Paul was writing to
the Galatians to bring clarity to these issues. So with all this in mind,
we turn our attention to that letter. It is important to see how this per-

---

14 This is not a new insight. See Westminster Confession, Chapter 19, Of The Law Of
God, and the Westminster Larger Catechism, Questions 91-150.

spective helps us understand what Paul was saying to the Galatians, and to the world. So, we will examine Galatians carefully so we can see how Scripture alone through *The Backstory* brings clarity to Paul's words, exposes sin, and shows the way forward.

1. Not From Nor Through

Paul, an apostle—not from men nor through man, but through Jesus Christ and God the Father, who raised him from the dead—and all the brothers who are with me, To the churches of Galatia: Grace to you and peace from God our Father and the Lord Jesus Christ, who gave himself for our sins to deliver us from the present evil age, according to the will of our God and Father, to whom be the glory forever and ever. Amen. —Galatians 1:1-5

As usual, Paul began by identifying himself, by clarifying his identity in Christ. He was writing as a man with a message, not from men or though men, but from and through Jesus Christ. It is important not to miss the importance of what he was saying here. Paul's message did not originate with nor was it authorized by human authority. He did not learn it from any academy or from any group of human beings. Thus, his message was not to be associated with any religious or political party at the time, or since. He was not associated with any of the various Gnostic or Jewish cults of the day. The effort to link his message with any such group, or to impose the context of any such group on his message would be an error. Rather, he said, his message was coming directly "through Jesus Christ and God the Father" (v. 1). It is a message from the Holy Spirit.

Paul was establishing the source and credibility of his message. And the first thing to notice is that he was not concerned about appealing to the authority or credibility of the Jewish establishment of his day, neither to the power of their priests or the intelligence of their scholars. He was not writing as an associate of the Pharisees or Saducees, nor the Scribes or Essenes, nor the Maccabees or the Zealots, etc. Quite the opposite! He was saying that the authority and credibility of his message was *not* associated with the Jewish establishment, the Roman establishment, the Greek establishment, nor any of the many pagan establishments.

To put this idea in our contemporary context, Paul would say that his authority and message did not come from any religious, denominational, or academic institution, nor from any political party, nor was it associated with any historic group, nor was he funded by any such group. Rather, Paul's authority and message originated from outside all existing cultural and historical groups, and must not be associated or tainted with ideas related to any such groups.

Of course, since Paul penned these words every Christian group imaginable, and then some, have claimed to rightly understand his message and have incorporated their understanding of his understanding into their theology. Over the centuries there have been a gazillion such groups and even more interpretations of Paul's meaning in Galatians. Some of the larger such groups include Catholic, Orthodox, Protestant, Mainline, Liberal, Conservative, Calvinist, Arminian, Evangelical, Lutheran, Baptist, etc., etc. Today we find so much ink spilled on Paul's treatment of law and gospel in Galatians that it would take more than a lifetime to just read all of the various interpretations. So, how are people to know which is true or false, better or worse? All of that spilled ink has provided a plethora of confusion among believers, which has produced a harvest of disdain and disbelief among too many people, in the church and out.

So, what has possessed me to think that I could add anything to this long and complex historical discussion about biblical law and the gospel of Jesus Christ? Like Paul, I come without academic credentials, denominational backing, seminary support, foundation authorization, or think tank camaraderie. I'm not trying to grow a church, raise support, or empower some historic theological position. Rather, I'm simply interested in clarifying the truth as best I can in the time in which I live, trusting Jesus' promise that the truth will make us free (John 8:32). Like Paul, I have been thinking about this issue for a long time, and an idea has occurred to me that seems to comport with the Bible generally. So, I'm simply trying to clarify it for myself. If it has any merit beyond that, God only knows.

Few people that I have met are prepared or able to engage the depth or breadth of the related literature or a sustained meditation on the biblical text that are necessary to seriously consider Paul's message. So I write in the hope that my meager effort might be useful to people that I don't know. I'm certainly not the sharpest crayon in the box, nor the most disciplined student on the block. But for whatever reason the Lord has kept me interested in this issue for quite a long time. So, my intent is to simply share my thoughts for others to engage as the Lord leads. My intent is to maintain the character of Paul's message, which was "not from men nor through man, but through Jesus Christ and God the Father" (v. 1), from one follower of Jesus Christ (Matthew 4:19) and of Paul (1 Corinthians 4:6, 11:1) to another.

May the words of my mouth and the meditations of our hearts be acceptable in thy sight, O Lord, our Rock and Redeemer.

RAISED

Paul's message, which is much more important than his authority or identity as an individual, was *from* and *through*—and I will add, *about* —Jesus Christ. Paul used both words (ἀπό and διά) to indicate some- thing important. *From* suggests a source in the past, while *through* suggests an ongoing effort in the immediate present. Together they suggest the transcendence of time, and only God the Father transcends time. But to enforce the reality of the immediate presence of the Spirit in the process, Paul added that God had raised Jesus from death. And the fact of Jesus' resurrection and the reality of the Holy Spirit places Him in the immediate present as a contemporary actor in the drama of life, for Paul and for us still today. Jesus was not dead, but was very much alive and present with Paul as he penned these words.

And more than this, Paul himself had been raised from death on the Damascus Road (Acts 9). Paul, like Jesus, was a resurrected man. Paul had been regenerated. He had a new beginning, which created a new life in Christ. His former self as a Pharisee and an officer of the Temple establishment had died as the scales fell from his eyes and he rose up and was baptized (Acts 9:18).

Regeneration and resurrection are loosely related. They point to the same reality—new life in Christ. To say that they are identical ar- gues too much, but to say that they are completely different ignores their commonality. Suffice it to say that our resurrection is the completion of what begins with our regeneration. Thus, Jesus' resurrection is a kind of foreshadowing of the believer's regeneration, and the believer's regeneration is a kind of foretaste of future resurrection.

Here Paul established that personal regeneration was a mark of Christian identity. So, when he mentioned all the brethren who were with him, he didn't simply mean those who were in the room when he wrote the letter. Rather, he meant to suggest the unity of the brethren with regard to his forthcoming message to the Galatians. All of the regenerate Christians, those who were living new lives in Christ, were *with* Paul regarding what he was about to say. That is, all of the regenerate Christians were in agreement about his forthcoming argument.

Paul was writing to the "churches of Galatia" (v. 2). But when he said *churches* (ἐκκλησία), he didn't mean what we mean when we say *churches* today. Today churches in contemporary culture are understood to be membership clubs, places or institutions that exist for the benefit of their members, places where members gather. While I understand that the translation of ἐκκλησία as *church(es)* is correct, today it does not reflect what Paul was saying. The word actually means an assembly of people in an area convened at the public place of the council for the purpose of deliberating community concerns. We would call them town meetings today, and they would be open to all who resided in the town or area, led by local officials. Paul did not mean membership clubs. That idea developed long after Paul, during the time that Christians were persecuted and hid from public attention. Unfortunately, that persecuted, place-to-hide understanding of the word has continued through history. It's long past time to return to Paul's intention and abandon that historical error. That alone would bring tremendous reform to Christianity because it would end denominationalism. Paul was writing to all of the Christians in Galatia, not just some.

GRACE & PEACE

When I graduated from high school (1965) the hippie peace movement was in full flower. Peace was the great cry of people everywhere. The Viet Nam war was raging and people wanted peace. That movement has not abated, yet America is still engaged in war—now the longest war in American history, and it is still raging. Why is there no peace?

We have approached the problem as if peace is something that we must accomplish. We think that we have to build a sustainable peace, yet all of our efforts to do that have not brought it about. So, let me suggest that our assumptions about peace must be wrong. It seems that we are approaching it in the wrong way.

Paul called for grace and peace to be with the recipients of his letter. He was not calling them to accomplish or make peace, but to receive it. Peace is a gift of God, a gift that issues from God, from God's Word, from God's order, from the order of the world that God created. And while the gift and the experience of peace are very real, very visceral, peace itself is a byproduct. This means that it cannot be had directly, but is the natural consequence or result of something else.

Paul put grace and peace together, in that order. First comes grace, then comes peace. Clearly, grace is not something that we do, either. Grace is a gift, a consequence of God's character. God is graceful, full of grace and mercy. Grace is a character quality, modeled by God, by Jesus Christ, and is to be imitated by God's people. Thus, we receive grace in order to imitate God's character, His gracefulness. God's mercy toward us allows us to be merciful toward others. God's grace to us inspires us to be graceful to others. Thus, peace is achieved, not by striving for peace, but by reflecting God's grace and mercy to others.

It is not accidental that this is the first thing that Paul said to the Galatians because it is where Christianity begins. We must not only receive God's grace, we must reflect it. It must be reflected in and though us. Reflecting it demonstrates that we have received it. In contrast, the failure to reflect God's gracefulness, God's mercy, to others, indicates the failure to accept it. These two aspects of grace always come together. There can be no reflection without reception. So, how do we make reflection happen?

First, it's not a matter of *doing*, it's a matter of *being*. Yet, it's wrong to say that we don't have to do anything because being graceful means doing everything gracefully. Yet, our every effort to master gracefulness will end in failure because such efforts are a matter of doing rather than being. Trying to be graceful is like trying to dance. We either dance or we don't. Sure, we may dance well or poorly, but we either dance or we don't. As Yoda said, "There is no try." You cannot try to take a nickel out of my hand. You either take it or you don't. You do it or you fail to do it.

But, while grace is a free gift, it is possible to receive it and ignore it. Receiving the gift is not sufficient. Just because God is graceful and merciful to me doesn't mean that I am automatically graceful and merciful to others. In fact, this is the situation of everyone in the world. Jesus' accomplishment on the cross has already provided sufficient grace for all humanity (2 Corinthians 12:9). The gift has already been extended to everyone! It's a done deal. Yet, hoards of people simply ignore it. Most people (because most people are not Christian) live in ignorance or denial of the most precious and beneficial gift that has ever been given. Ignorance can be fixed, but denial constitutes the unforgivable sin. It is unforgivable, not because God cannot or will not forgive it, but because those who are already in possession of God's forgiveness deny their own possession of it, or they deny that God is the giver, or deny that it makes any difference. And denying it, they do not engage it, so it does nothing for them—not because it is impotent to work for them, but because they themselves turn away from it. They cannot escape from Satan's grip that was instituted at the Fall.

The prerequisite for world peace is for the people of the world to reflect God's grace and mercy to one another. It's not rocket science, but it is necessary for the production of the byproduct—peace.

FROM GOD

Paul told the Galatians that grace and peace come from God and Jesus Christ. He was acknowledging that his apostleship, his message, was an instance of God's grace. It came to him unbidden, unexpected, and unwanted on the Damascus Road as a gift from God. He had done nothing to earn it, nor was he the slightest bit interested in receiving it. Christ had pursued him, he had not pursued Christ (though he was literally pursuing Christians). Of course, he thought that he had been pursuing God as a Pharisee, but he quickly learned that all of his efforts actually led him further away from the only real God, the Lord and Father of Jesus Christ. Imagine the shock and depth of his surprise.

We can, therefore, look for Paul's reflection of God's character in this letter to the Galatians because Paul was modeling how to be graceful. And as we model God's grace, we must be careful not to confuse gracefulness with nicety. Paul will say some shocking things to the Galatians in order to shake them out of their habitual responses to what they perceived to be religious ideas, as Christ had done to him. Those habitual responses are not merely individual, they're also cultural. Most of our religious and spiritual ideas are far more habitual than people realize. These habits are ingrained early and cling to our deepest structures of identity throughout our lives. It is rare for anyone to think about or react to religious or spiritual ideas apart from these habits, partly because enforcement of them is social and cultural as much as it is personal. Deviation from accepted social norms tends to offend others, especially when those deviations affect religious and social ideas of personal and group identity.

This is true even in the midst of our contemporary culture of diversity and acceptance, in the sense that anything other than wide open diversity of values and acceptance of social behaviors is vilified in the public media by those who claim to value diversity and acceptance. Such people have mastered the art of social control by affecting the mechanisms of public discourse, by setting the terms of debate. In former times such activity would have been called gossip and discouraged from the pulpit and dinner table. Unfortunately, today too many churches and Christians are working hard to establish themselves as players and authorities in this arena in order to reestablish some idea or other of past Christian social glory. It is unfortunate because the arena in which they seek leadership is built on gossip, innuendo, covetousness, and pride. These are the things that influence the world, or so they think. Therefore, they are working to master them—for Christ, of course! Yes, I'm being facetious to suggest that they are actually working against traditional Christian values.

God's plan is to "deliver us from the present evil age" (v. 4), not to advance the very things that make it evil. What Paul called the "present evil age" was the age of the Second Temple. Paul lived during the height of that age, amidst its rampant corruption and confusion. Paul lived on the cusp of the fading Second Temple age and the beginning of the Christian age. And while his letters anticipated the coming Christian age, he lived on the other side of the culminating event that marked the transition from the old to the new age—the destruction of the Temple and Jerusalem in A.D. 70.

WILL

First Paul said that his apostleship was not through or by man, but through God. And in verse 4 he repeated the same idea, that deliverance from evil times would happen "according to the will of our God and Father." Indeed, the idea of God's will or free will continues to be a problem in that free will is both widely discussed and broadly misunderstood under the heading of *predestination*. The concept of will is also central to the discussion about law and the gospel of grace in Galatians. I will assume familiarity with the classic literature on this subject and not rehash it here.

However, I do want to introduce an idea that I have not seen in the literature. While there is nothing new that can be wrung from the biblical presentation of will, greater understanding may come from keeping the idea in its proper context. At issue is the degree and extent of individual free will. Nearly all of the time that the word (*will*) is used in Scripture it refers to God's will. Yet, no one seriously doubts that human beings have free will. What is debated is the extent of that will.

> "The decisive point is whether freedom in the Christian sense is identical with the freedom of Hercules: choice between two ways at a crossroad. This is a heathen notion of freedom. Is it freedom to decide for the devil? The only freedom that means something is the freedom to be myself as I am created by God. God did not create a neutral creature, but his creature. He placed him in a garden that he might build it up; his freedom is to do that. When man began to discern good and evil, this knowledge was the beginning of sin. Man should not have asked this question about good and evil, but should have remained in true created freedom. We are confused by the political idea of freedom. What is the light in the Statue of Liberty? Freedom to choose good and evil? What light that would be! Light is light and not darkness. If it shines, darkness is done away with, not proposed for choice! Being a slave of Christ means being free."[1]

---

1   Barth, Karl. *Table Talk*, 1963, p. 37.

To frame the issue as *free will* is quite different than framing it as *will power*. All of the classic discussions frame it as *free will*, but if we frame the issue as God having given human beings the power to accomplish His will, rather than the freedom to accomplish our own, the whole conversation veers in a different direction. God gives His people sufficient will power to live *in* Christ and *for* Christ—to be what God created us to be in Christ. Being a Christian is not a matter of being able to do what *we* want, it's a matter of wanting what God wants us to be and do in Christ. *Ya gotta wanna*, in slang. We are not given the will power to break the bonds of freedom—Christ alone has done that. Rather, we are given the will power to follow Christ, who alone has set the model and pattern of our freedom.

The issue is to discern the origin of the desire. Is it available to all who seek it? Or does it manifest only in those to whom God gives it? This is the root issue of the classic discussions, and it is not easily resolved because Scripture itself can be legitimately lobbied to support both views. Therefore, both views must be true or valid. However, for both views to be valid, both realities must be manifest in the lives of people in order to qualify them as believers. Christ came to Paul on the road to Damascus unbidden, unexpected, and unwanted. Only later did Paul's subjective desires come into conformity with God's will. But Peter wanted to be a follower of Jesus long before his will was sufficiently conformed to God's will. Peter, ever the eager beaver, wanted to be faithful his own way, which put him at odds with Jesus on more than one occasion. Only later, when Peter received the Holy Spirit through regeneration (John 20:22) did he have both elements in his life. So, both views are true because people are different.

The lesson here is that it is not enough to want to follow Christ, nor is it enough to have the call of Christ on your life. We cannot follow God by exercising our own free will. I cannot be a Christian "*my way*," as the old Frank Sinatra song would have it. God's way is the only way and conformity to His way is the only path. And yet, the effort toward conformity will fail apart from the genuine, personal desire to conform. While discipline is necessary, discipline alone is not sufficient. Jesus said,

"You shall love the Lord your God with all your heart and with all your soul and with all your strength and with all your mind, and your neighbor as yourself" (Luke 10:27).

This is the definition of worship. Worship includes gathering, praying, singing, serving, and all the things Christians do on Sunday mornings. Yet, Sunday morning worship alone does not qualify as genuine worship. Genuine worship is better defined as what people do with their time, twenty-four-seven. True worship is an attitude, a posture, a preference, a way of being in the world.

2. Ouch!

I am astonished that you are so quickly deserting him who called you in the grace of Christ and are turning to a different gospel—not that there is another one, but there are some who trouble you and want to distort the gospel of Christ. But even if we or an angel from heaven should preach to you a gospel contrary to the one we preached to you, let him be accursed. As we have said before, so now I say again: If anyone is preaching to you a gospel contrary to the one you received, let him be accursed. —Galatians 1:6-9

Having identified himself and his authority as an apostle of Jesus Christ, Paul greeted the Galatians with a slap in the face. Can you imagine any denominational leader greeting any congregation in this manner today! In addition, these verses alone should put an end to the falsely conceived idea of "once saved, always saved" that has infected too many churches. One cannot desert principles or beliefs that one never held. Yet, Paul did not give up on these deserters. Rather, he poured himself out to them in complete honesty, which made him vulnerable.

Paul spoke a word of encouragement to these backsliding Christians. He was trying to bolster their courage (the root of *encouragement*) to help them maintain the faith by identifying their root problem. First, this letter was an encouragement in that he hadn't given up on them, and he could have. Many of us have given up on people who have done far less. And second, he was like a physician probing a sore spot in order to properly diagnose an injury. His intention was to help them, to heal them. Paul thought that he knew what their problem was, so he probed them right where he thought it would hurt in order to confirm his suspicion. And he was right!

Had their affliction been limited to their own church, had it been a small problem in one errant congregation, Paul's letter would not have been preserved as it has been. The fact that this letter made it into the canon tells us that this was then, and has always been, a major problem in the church(es). Paul's letter intended to correct this problem. His hope for this wayward people provided help, not just for them, but for countless people over many generations.

The disputed misunderstanding that has haunted Paul's letter to the Galatians over the centuries has to do with Paul's contention with them. What was Paul's beef with them? What had they done that set Paul off? The Galatians had allowed other leaders—people teaching the old history of Israel—to contradict what Paul had taught them, what Jesus had taught Paul. What was it that the Jews so disliked?

That is the rub, and it is my contention that it was about what I have called *The Backstory*, previously described. Paul had made Jesus' understanding of Old Testament history, and the faithlessness of the Temple establishment understanding of that history, the foundation of the gospel of Jesus Christ. Paul was setting Jesus Christ as the end (*telos* —solution and purpose) of that misunderstanding, and the Temple establishment were threatened by it because it undermined their authority and their understanding of who *they* thought they were in God's plan.

Paul's letter does not use the word *Temple*, nor does it focus on the idea of the Temple, rather it contrasts the ideas of law and gospel. This reading of Paul's letter will use the idea of the Temple establishment, meaning the existence of the Temple itself and all that it entailed as the religious and social center of Jewish society, as the referent of Paul's term *law*. The culture of the Temple was the primary fruit of the law. This understanding does not come from the etymology of the Greek word νόμος (law), but from history and the context of the Old Testament and Jesus' ministry.

The issue was not simply about getting church liturgy correct, nor about personal morality or purity, nor about church membership requirements, nor about getting the particulars of Old Testament law right. Rather, it was about the character of God's law, the integrity of God's promises, and the inability of humanity to meet the demands of God's law apart from the presence of the Holy Spirit through regeneration. The fruit of God's law is not bricks and mortar, not rules and laws. Rather, the fruit of God's law is hearts and minds in Christ, living stones built into a spiritual economy, the replication of Christ's character in human lives. My abbreviated history of the Temple provides a brief overview of the historical context of Paul's letter. It demonstrates the purpose of Christ's ministry and the historical background against which the gospel of Jesus Christ shines.

The issue was that the gospel that Paul had taught the Galatians—and everyone else—explained the history of Israel differently than the Temple establishment understood it. The Temple establishment believed and taught that *they*, the Rabbis, were the authoritative mouthpiece of God on earth. But with the Advent of Christ, *Jesus* was the authoritative mouthpiece of God. In Christ, the Holy Spirit through regeneration is the authority, not the past, not the Temple hierarchy.

In contrast, these other leaders were reasserting that old perspective in Galatia by trying to bring Jesus' gospel under the Second Temple administration by bringing Christian converts under the authority of Temple law and practice. But Paul had taught them that the purpose of the manifestation of Jesus Christ on earth was to put an end to the charade of the Second Temple. Christ exposed the faithless corruption of the Temple establishment, just as the prophets had been doing for centuries. And while the ancient prophets had been honored by collecting and preserving their writings, the Temple establishment either failed to understand them or was able to nuance an interpretation of them that declawed them. The Temple establishment was able to deflect the accusations the prophets had hurled at them.

What was new in the New Testament was Jesus' restatement of the original intent of God's law, God's purpose—to be a blessing to all humanity. Jesus did not bring a new message for the world. He brought the old message that had been lost under thousands of years of accumulated half-truths, political wrangling, magnified self-importance, lust for empire, and accommodation with mammon. It was never a *new* testament, but has always been a *renewed* testament. It is not that Jesus' gospel was novel, but that it was reinvigorated, rekindled, reconfigured, reborn. The difficulty in trying to communicate this idea is that the old adage, "it takes one to know one," applies.

In verse 8 Paul said that "even if we or an angel from heaven should preach to you a gospel contrary to the one we preached to you, let him be accursed." It is astonishing that he included himself. He meant that even if he somehow changed his mind about what he had taught them previously, that change would be cursed by God. Even if the wisdom of angels could prove some other view with superior, angelic logic, the logic of that proof would be flawed. This means that opposing views of the history of the Temple establishment could be based on apparently solid reasoning and sound logic, and still be wrong! Logic, human or angelic, is not sufficient for biblical interpretation. The significance of this verse is devastating to the endeavor of secular academics apart from faithfulness as a tool of biblical analysis.[1] Any other analysis or interpretation of the history of the Temple and its establishment would throw the world into hopelessness. Christ is the Messianic hope of the Old Testament, and because the Messiah did manifest in the historic person of Jesus Christ, the denial or ignoring of Christ's presence in history is far worse than the hopelessness of the Old Testament apart from God's Messianic promise. The blatant denial of Christ is far worse than ignorance of His actual presence.

---

1   I have written about this issue which I call "presuppositional trinitarianism" in many of my books, and won't go into further detail here other than to say that all analysis requires making assumptions, presuppositions. And the assumptions required for the correct analysis and interpretation of the Bible are the assumptions of faithfulness. Apart from faithfulness the Bible cannot be correctly understood as God intended.

3. No Human Source

For am I now seeking the approval of man, or of God? Or am I try-
ing to please man? If I were still trying to please man, I would not be
a servant of Christ. For I would have you know, brothers, that the
gospel that was preached by me is not man's gospel. For I did not re-
ceive it from any man, nor was I taught it, but I received it through a
revelation of Jesus Christ.   —Galatians 1:10-12

Paul literally opposed the whole world. His understanding of the purpose and value of Jesus Christ opposed all of the views held by gentiles, even though Paul's view opened God's Kingdom to the gentiles. And his understanding of the purpose and value of Jesus Christ also opposed all of the views held by the Jewish Temple establish-ment, even though his view also opened God's Kingdom to the Jews. The Temple establishment thought that they were God's chosen people, that they already had a kingdom reservation that could not be revoked. They didn't realize that they had gone off the proverbial rails centuries earlier. They believed their own press, and couldn't smell the rancid stench of their own breath.

The truth of the identity of God's chosen people was never intended to be based on human bloodlines, but was always based on God's grace. It was never a matter of race, and always a matter of grace. God has al-ways seen humanity as one family, that is the biblical testimony from Genesis to Revelation. When we see Israel hyper-focused on family or blood kin we are seeing Israel's misunderstanding and the self-justifica-tion of that misunderstanding. God's story was never supposed to be centered on the building of the Temple in Jerusalem, but had always been centered on building the temple (understood as an allusion or illus-tration, as Jesus understood it) of humanity in Christ. The Jerusalem

Temple was but a scaffold, a temporary support that allowed the real building (humanity in Christ) to be constructed by the Lord.

The idea that Paul did not seek human approval of his authority and doctrine shocked those who first heard it, whether they were Jews or gentiles. It was, and still is, a revolutionary idea, and it will always be rejected by established authorities. Establishment authorities are established precisely because the society in which they are established views them as having authority, power, and gravitas. All established authorities hold their social positions as authorities because the majority of people in any society confer authority upon them by believing them, by trusting their opinions, by yielding to their ideas. And such social belief and trust exists on the basis of the approval of man, on social approval, social validation.

GOD'S OTHERNESS

However, the gospel of Jesus Christ necessarily stands outside and apart from all established authority, all social approval or validation. And this fact will always be true because the witness of history is that human authority overflows with pride, sin, and error. In order for God's truth to be eternally true it cannot be dependent on the foibles and failures of human opinion or history. Yet, God has entered history to provide His eternal truth to time-bound creatures. God's truth must be eternally renewable, every generation and every Christian must make God's truth their own, or must be made God's own by His truth. It must be renewed in them, and they must be renewed by It. And that renewability is rooted in heaven, not in the earth or the things of the earth.

As such, there was no earthly school, nor any group of people that Paul could go to in order to learn about the true gospel of Jesus Christ, not in the sense or in the context of the history of the Temple as I have sketched it out above. Nor did I find this understanding in any established schools or traditions. The true story of Israel's history devastates —utterly destroys—the false, prideful, racist, and narrowly conceived story of Israel as a group of faithful, godly people struggling against an unfaithful world. Israel's true history was a history that includes faithless abandonment of both her leaders and her people, yet seasoned with a genuine desire for God's truth. But the abandonment began with and was institutionalized by her leaders, her kings and priests, and always issued out of her kingdom success. The record of Israel's prophets testifies to the reality of this truth, of Israel's consistent misunderstanding of themselves and their divine calling apart from Jesus Christ.

It's not that God didn't choose Israel to be His people, nor is it that God has not protected Israel throughout her history. Rather, God chose Israel to be an example, to conclusively demonstrate beyond all doubt that humanity apart from God in Christ is doomed to damnation and extinction. This is what lies under the veil that blinded Israel. God veiled this from Israel in order to fan her fickle flame of Messianic hope.

THE VEIL

Moses was instructed to make a tabernacle for a meeting place where God might dwell with Israel (Exodus 25:8), which consisted of two areas divided by a curtain or veil. The inner area behind the veil was called the Most Holy and figuratively represented the dwelling place of God. The Ark of the Covenant was in that area, and the Ark held the two tables of the Law, the Ten Commandments, which were at the symbolic center, source, or origin point. On top of the Ark was a Mercy-seat of gold with decorative cherubim (angels) fashioned on each end. God then caused His presence to dwell between or in the midst of the cherubim (Exodus 25:22, 26:33). All of this created a picture or symbolic representation of the presence of God dwelling in their midst, with the Ten Commandments at the center. This is a critical element that plays a key position in the Bible and in this analysis.

In the Old Testament the High Priest alone was allowed behind the veil, and only once every year on the Day of Atonement (Leviticus 16:2, 12:17) at a culminating high, holy worship service. According to Jewish tradition, God inscribes each person's fate for the coming year into the Book of Life on Rosh Hashanah, and waits until Yom Kippur to seal or finalize their verdict. During the Days of Awe, Jews try to amend their behavior and seek forgiveness for wrongs done against God and against others. The evening and day of Yom Kippur are set aside for public and private petitions and confessions of guilt. At the end of Yom Kippur, the Jews hoped that they were forgiven by God.

David followed the same pattern when he replaced the Tabernacle with the Temple. The Ark of the Covenant was placed in the Most Holy which was separated by a veil from the rest of the Temple. When Herod restored the Second Temple the same pattern was maintained. The book of Hebrews explains that the place behind the veil represented the presence of God into which Jesus ascended after his resurrection (Hebrews 6:19).

"Behind the second curtain was a second section called the Most Holy Place, having the golden altar of incense and the ark of the covenant covered on all sides with gold, in which was a golden urn holding the manna, and Aaron's staff that budded, and the tablets of the covenant. Above it were the cherubim of glory overshadowing the mercy seat. Of these things we cannot now speak in detail. These preparations having thus been made, the priests go regularly into the first section, performing their ritual duties, but into the second only the high priest goes, and he but once a year, and not without taking blood, which he offers for himself and for the unintentional sins of the people. By this the Holy Spirit indicates that the way into the holy places is not yet opened as long as the first section is still standing (which is symbolic for the present age). According to this arrangement, gifts and sacrifices are offered that cannot perfect the conscience of the worshiper, but deal only with food and drink and various washings, regulations for the body imposed until the time of reformation. But when Christ appeared as a high priest of the good things that have come, then through the greater and more perfect tent (not made with hands, that is, not of this creation) he entered once for all into the holy places, not by means of the blood of goats and calves but by means of his own blood, thus securing an eternal redemption" (Hebrews 6:3-12).

"Thus it was necessary for the copies of the heavenly things to be purified with these rites, but the heavenly things themselves with better sacrifices than these. For Christ has entered, not into holy places made with hands, which are copies of the true things, but into heaven itself, now to appear in the presence of God on our behalf. Nor was it to offer himself repeatedly, as the high priest enters the holy places every year with blood not his own, for then he would have had to suffer repeatedly since the foundation of the world. But as it is, he has appeared once for all at the end of the ages to put away sin by the sacrifice of himself. And just as it is appointed for man to

die once, and after that comes judgment, so Christ, having been offered once to bear the sins of many, will appear a second time, not to
deal with sin but to save those who are eagerly waiting for him"
(Hebrews 9:23-28)

Thus it is that the veil represents direct access to God (Hebrews
10:20), which was forbidden until Christ removed it. This is reinforced
by God in the miraculous rending of the Temple veil from top to bottom at the same instant that Christ died because His death provides
direct access to God through Christ (Matthew 27:50). Jesus is now the
only High Priest and through Him alone can we come into God's
presence. Note the connection between access to God and the Ark of
the Covenant, which held the Ten Commandments, and the central
place of the Ten Commandments with regard to access to God
through Jesus Christ.

This picture is not that Christians go to heaven, but rather that the
kingdom of God has come to earth with Christ. Christ's death opened
this access to all who believe in Christ, through whom Christ lives
(Galatians 2:20). Yet, we also live in Christ (Romans 6:11). Thus,
Christ's death provided for a means of His return from death through
the lives of believers. Calvin said of the veil:

> "But by the veil the obscurity of the shadows of the Law was princi-
> pally denoted, that the Israelites might know that the time of full rev-
> elation had not yet come, but that the spiritual worship of God was
> as yet enshrouded in a veil; and thus might extend their faith to their
> promised Messiah, at whose coming the truth would be discovered
> and laid bare. Wherefore, when Christ rose again from the dead, "the
> veil of the temple was rent in twain from the top to the bottom"
> (Matthew 27:51); and an end was put to the ceremonies of the Law,
> because God then presented Himself in His living and express image,
> and the perfect reality of all the ceremonies was manifested. Now,
> therefore, in the light of the gospel, we behold 'face to face' what was
> then shown afar off to the ancient people under coverings (2
> Corinthians 3:14). Yet, although there is now no veil to prevent us
> from openly and familiarly looking upon Christ, let us learn from
> this figure that the manifestation of God in the flesh is a hidden and
> incomprehensible mystery (1 Titus 3:16). It is not without reason
> that Christ Himself compares His body to the temple, because the
> fullness of the Godhead dwells in it (John 2:19). Let us then know as-

suredly that the Father is in the Son, and the Son in the Father (John 17:21); but if it be asked in what manner, this is ineffable, except that the eternal Son of God, who, before the creation of the world, possessed the same glory with the Father (John 17:5), that even He is now man, that 'He might be the firstborn among many brethren'" (Romans 8:29).[1]

Paul wrote to the Corinthians saying that God had blinded the Jews, blinded the Temple establishment. God allowed them to obscure their own vision and understanding, which kept the whole truth from them. This was the function of the Temple veil. They were not able at that time to realize the fullness of God, nor had human history been properly prepared yet, so He allowed them to hide full access to God by the Temple veil. At that time their access to God was through the priesthood and Temple worship. Their establishment in history through Temple worship provided various analogies and social patterns that would become clear when the Messiah was revealed. In the meantime, God simply allowed the seeds of the gospel to grow below the level of social consciousness. The role of the veil in Temple culture created a kind of spiritual dam wherein the Spirit could unconsciously or semiconsciously ripen until the fullness of time when Messiah would appear and release the dammed up waters of the Spirit.

However, the establishment of the priesthood and later the kingdom of Israel brought tremendous wealth and splendor to Israel, which in turn flowered into corruption as the higher class worked to preserve its position and power. God knew that the wealth and splendor would bring corruption because the kingdom had been established on the model of Israel's pagan national neighbors. They wanted a kingdom like the other nations, and that's exactly what they got. Samuel told them that it would not work out well, but they thought that they could manage it. The history of the Old Testament is the story of how they were then mangled by their own success.

Had they correctly understood that the Temple they built and rebuilt would become like the Tower of Babel, a way to breach heaven and usurp the authority of God, the faithful would have long ago abandoned that effort. But the veil kept them from seeing it. God was simply allowing a case history of Israel to develop that would demon-

---

1   Calvin, John. *Calvin's Commentaries*, Exodus 26:31, public domain.

strate the futility of such denial once and for all. Israel, in spite of God's direction, in spite of the law, the traditions, and God's explicit instructions, failed to become what God intended for His people to become—a blessing to all humanity.

They mistakenly thought that God's blessing was intended for *them*, for their clan, their bloodline, their group, their nation, which caused them to become self-focused and narrow-minded as they protected themselves and their cultural experiment in the desert from the vicissitudes of the world and the godlessness of their neighbors. Self-centeredness can produce worldly success, but worldly success undermines God's mission. This doesn't mean that they didn't need protection from the vicissitudes of the world. They did, and God acted in their history on their behalf. And it doesn't mean that their neighbors were not godless, they were. Nonetheless, they became self-centered, as were their neighbors. And as they established a kingdom of their own, they followed the model of their deluded neighbors rather than conforming to the wisdom of God (1 Samuel 8:7). God's people were blind to their own failure, and Paul related that blindness to the Temple *veil*. Using Jesus' understanding of the Temple as an allusion to human development, Paul applied the idea of the Temple veil to the Jewish understanding of their own history. Paul could see all of this because God had removed the veil from Paul.

> "Since we have such a hope, we are very bold, not like Moses, who would put a veil over his face so that the Israelites might not gaze at the outcome of what was being brought to an end. But their minds were hardened. For to this day, when they read the old covenant, that same veil remains unlifted, because only through Christ is it taken away. Yes, to this day whenever Moses is read a veil lies over their hearts. But when one turns to the Lord, the veil is removed. Now the Lord is the Spirit, and where the Spirit of the Lord is, there is freedom. And we all, with unveiled face, beholding the glory of the Lord, are being transformed into the same image from one degree of glory to another. For this comes from the Lord who is the Spirit" (2 Corinthians 3:12-18).

The function of a veil is to hide or obscure and to separate or divide. Israel was blind to the futility of trying to please God apart from the dispensation of the Holy Spirit through regeneration in Christ. And

God allowed that to unfold as it did in order to conclusively and historically demonstrate the futility of such an effort.

This is why Paul could say that "even if we or an angel from heaven should preach to you a gospel contrary to the one we preached to you, let him be accursed" (v. 8). He was aware that God Himself had provided explicit directions to the ancient Israelites—and apart from Christ they still got it wrong! Instructions alone could not undo the sin of the Fall. Man required a divine savior who would model the death of the old self and the birth of the new.

Paul was a servant of Christ, an ambassador of the Lord, and was bound to represent the will and desire of Jesus Christ for the people of God. God's Messiah had come and was manifest in Jesus Christ. This fact was destined to change the world. It would change the destiny of the gentiles, but it would also change the destiny of the Jews, as well. The Jews were not who they thought they were, nor could they continue on the path that they were on. They could not journey to the promised land forever (Abraham). They could not remain desert nomads forever (Moses). They could not establish a godly kingdom using significant elements of the model of a pagan, worldly kingdom. That's what David did. Nor could they rebuild what they never had in the first place. That's what the Second Temple attempted to do. So, just as Jesus Christ had revealed Himself to Paul, Paul was charged to reveal Jesus Christ as Lord and Savior to both the Jews and the gentiles.

We often hide much of this understanding from ourselves by calling Paul the missionary to the gentiles, and think that what he said had no application to the Jews. It is a serious error to do so. No one understood the Jews better than Paul. The very people God needed to reach to correct the error—the Temple establishment—were the people who could best be reached by Paul because he had been one of them. He knew how they thought. Paul was in their orbit and could speak their language as an educated elite. They easily ignored the uneducated fishermen and gentile heathens who had followed Jesus, but they could not so easily avoid the full-throated attack on the Temple establishment that Jesus—Himself a Jew!—had launched, nor could they ignore Paul the Pharisee when he picked up and further clarified Jesus' argument. The gospel of Christ meant the demise of the Temple establishment, which seemed to them to threaten their work, their social position, their families, and the existence of the Temple itself. Nor were they wrong about this!

It is not easy to admit to an error of this magnitude.

REVELATION

Paul learned all of this "through a revelation (ἀποκάλυψις) of Jesus Christ" (v. 12), through an *apokalupsis*. History has so abused this ancient Greek word that it now functions as a veil, it obscures the real meaning of the biblical message. The word *revelation*, which is the English translation, literally means to reveal. But in the spirit of Matthew 13:13, Jesus' words reveal truth to those who have ears to hear, but obscure it for those who do not. The revelation or apocalypse[2] of Jesus Christ is not a prediction about the destruction of the world by the wrath of God. Jesus did not come to destroy the law or the real temple of God, though the Jews charged Him with having made just such a threat. At the conclusion of John's version of the cleansing of the Temple,

> "the Jews said to him, 'What sign do you show us for doing these things?' Jesus answered them, 'Destroy this temple, and in three days I will raise it up.' The Jews then said, 'It has taken forty-six years to build this temple, and will you raise it up in three days?' But he was speaking about the temple of his body." (John 2:18-21).

John was showing us that Jesus had a different understanding of Temple than the Jews did. John's book, originally called The Revelation Of Jesus Christ, is full of Temple imagery, which is why some people have thought that Jesus had come to restore the Temple to it's original glory, and which led to a reinstituted priesthood that reincarnated most of the same errors that had infected the Temple priesthood and produced the building of great cathedrals—all in the name of Christianity. However, the reestablishment of priestly worship and the building of great cathedrals for ceremonial worship is but a slight deviation from the blindness of the Second Temple establishment. It is another effort to rebuild the Temple as the Jews had historically mis-

2   Apocalypse: 1. A cosmic cataclysm in which God destroys the ruling powers of evil. 2. A disaster or cataclysmic event. The contemporary dictionary definition of this word, reflecting its historic usage rather than its root meaning, belies the deeply engrained misunderstanding of the word and the gospel.

understood God's original intention, only in the name of Jesus Christ. But it fails to yield to the understanding of the Temple of God as Jesus taught it. These errant Galatian Judaizers sought to build the church of Jesus Christ on the model of the Second Temple, to incorporate the blindness of the Second Temple establishment into the foundation of the Christian church. And that effort was completely opposed to Christ's mission. This is what tripped Paul's trigger.

4. Counsel Of The Spirit

For you have heard of my former life in Judaism, how I persecuted the church of God violently and tried to destroy it. And I was advancing in Judaism beyond many of my own age among my people, so extremely zealous was I for the traditions of my fathers. But when he who had set me apart before I was born, and who called me by his grace, was pleased to reveal his Son to me, in order that I might preach him among the Gentiles, I did not immediately consult with anyone; nor did I go up to Jerusalem to those who were apostles before me, but I went away into Arabia, and returned again to Damascus. —Galatians 1:13-17

Because this was such a critical issue Paul expounded on the source of his Christian training. The Jews understood the importance of training because it is rare that a student surpasses his teachers, particularly the master teachers. As such the Jews were well acquainted with the phenomenon of various schools of thought that developed well-articulated positions and ardent followers. Among those teachers in Paul's day were Rabbis Hillel, Gamaliel, Shammai, and others. There were also the Essenes, mystics, gnostics, etc. In essence, all of the various schools were grounded in the thought of a particular person, whose scholars then developed and augmented that perspective. All were historical, and the fact of their history contributed to their significance.

Paul briefly mentioned that he had been an exceptional student among the Jewish scholars in terms of both academics and passion. His expertise and commitment had been to the traditions of his fathers, the fathers of Judaism. He had been completely committed to the Second Temple establishment. He understood its history and believed it to be completely true. We would say that he was a Jewish patriot of the highest order. This was Paul's pre-Christian mindset, and this was the mindset that the New Testament referred to as *old* in its various allusions to *old vs. new* in various verses (Mark 2:22; Luke 5:36-39; 1 Corinthians 5:7; 2 Corinthians 5:17; Hebrews 8:13; 1 John2:7, etc.). The old was passing away, behold the new had come! A new chapter of world history had come, and it was not based on past history. It transcended all past history—except perhaps that of Melchizedek, and could not, must not, be attributed to any previous historical movement. So Paul sought to ground it in Scripture alone. Thus, Paul eschewed all historical schools of thought by retreating to the desert to be alone with Christ, in order to be led by faith alone in Christ alone according to Scripture alone to the glory of God alone.

Verses 15 & 16 tell us four things about Paul. He was 1) separated and 2) called by grace to 3) reveal and 4) preach. The idea of his being separated, literally from his mother's womb, refers to his birth. He was saying that this was his destiny from birth, that he believed that he had been born for this purpose. The idea of being called means that the purpose he was to serve was not of his own making. He was called to serve the purpose of another, not his own. Grace was the channel or means through which he was called, which means that his calling was God's idea not his. Strong's first definition of *grace* is "that which affords joy, pleasure, delight, sweetness, charm, loveliness."

Paul was not fulfilling a personal ambition, but had been swept up in a tsunami of God's kindness and blessing that had caused Him to send Jesus Christ to undeserving people of every race and nation. That tsunami was an historical event that occurred during Paul's day, and he had been caught up in it because of his commission to persecute Christians. His new commission in Christ was to *reveal* to others what had been revealed to him (ἀποκαλύπτω, a conjugation of *apocalypse*, literally to remove the cover or veil) and to share the good news of Jesus Christ. The centerpiece of Paul's calling was this process of revelation or revealing, of removing people's illusions, their misconceptions and wrong assumptions about God, about life, about history, about all sorts of things.

When all of this first came to Paul he "did not immediately consult with anyone" (v. 16). Literally, he did not confer with flesh and blood.

He did not consult with human or historical authorities, but retreated to be alone, to be with God, to sort things out. This sounds like such a simple thing that we are tempted to overlook its importance. Paul turned to get advice from his mentor, to the voice that he had heard on the road to Damascus that fateful day. And while Scripture does not say so, I'm sure that that voice never left him. From that day forward it would be his constant personal companion, his muse. This is the heart of evangelical Christianity.

More importantly, Paul also said that he had not gone "up to Jerusalem to those who were apostles before" him (v. 17). It was important that he did not confer at that point with the apostles because the lack of apostolic contact would help him gauge the correctness of his own thinking. Had he simply gone to them he would have fallen into their patterns of thought, their understanding of Jesus Christ. But the Holy Spirit needed to show Paul and establish for the rest of us the fact of His (the Spirit's) leadership and integrity. The whole point of Christianity is for the Holy Spirit to take a leadership role in history, in the lives of men and women—individually, personally, intimately. So, the Spirit sent Paul into the desert, just as He had sent Jesus into the desert, in order to model the process for the rest of us. They did not stay in the desert, and neither are we to remain in retreat mode.

When Paul returned from his journey to Arabia and Damascus the change that Christ had begun earlier was in full flower. Paul came back from that conference with the Holy Spirit full to the brim and overflowing with the gospel of Jesus Christ, the good news of new life in Christ, which he modeled. He hadn't gone to Arabia to consult with the Arabs, he went into the desert, the wilderness, to be alone with God, to dedicate himself to his new understanding of God in Christ. Three years later Paul went to Jerusalem.

CONFIRMATION

> *Then after three years I went up to Jerusalem to visit Cephas and remained with him fifteen days. But I saw none of the other apostles except James the Lord's brother. (In what I am writing to you, before God, I do not lie!)*   —*Galatians 1:18-20*

All of the apostles had received the Holy Spirit directly from Jesus, and Paul was going to Jerusalem to confirm that what he had received from the Spirit was in harmony with what they had received. Doing so would confirm the reality and integrity of the Holy Spirit and the gospel of Jesus Christ. He went to confirm what we call evangelical Christianity, the value and veracity of personal regeneration in Christ. Paul was aware that Christ had breathed the Holy Spirit into the apostles (John 20:21-23), and believed that the same thing had happened to him.

In particular Paul went to Jerusalem to meet Peter. Paul mentioned this detail because he was still laying out his credentials to the Galatians, and he had gone to Peter to lay out his credentials to him, that credential being personal regeneration. He was careful to note that he hadn't had any contact with any other of the apostles, which meant that he hadn't learned what he knew from them. James was the exception, perhaps James had told him how to contact Peter.

Previously we noted that Paul was coming to them with the authority of the Holy Spirit, not the authority of flesh and blood. Peter, like Paul, had also received special treatment from the Lord. Peter had received a special commission from the Holy Spirit.

> "When they had finished breakfast, Jesus said to Simon Peter, 'Simon, son of John, do you love me more than these?' He said to him, 'Yes, Lord; you know that I love you.' He said to him, 'Feed my lambs." He said to him a second time, 'Simon, son of John, do you love me?' He said to him, 'Yes, Lord; you know that I love you.' He said to him, "Tend my sheep.' He said to him the third time, 'Simon, son of John, do you love me?' Peter was grieved because he said to him the third time, 'Do you love me?' and he said to him, 'Lord, you know everything; you know that I love you.' Jesus said to him, 'Feed my sheep'" (John 21:15-17).

Paul also had a special commission and was probably hoping to confirm it with Peter. I suspect that Paul was not looking for apostolic permission, but for camaraderie.

The proof of the reality of the Holy Spirit that Paul was looking for was a commonality of belief, knowledge, and calling that he and Peter would have in common. That commonality pointed to the reality of their common teacher (John 14:16, 26). And because this commonality was such a fundamental thing, it was important that Paul's witness be genuine, not a lie of any sort. This is why Paul said that he was not lying, that his testimony before Peter was true, and that it was inspired by grace alone through faith alone in Christ alone through Scripture alone to the glory of God alone—not by flesh and blood. He wanted to see if Peter was the real deal and to show Peter that he was the real deal, according to what the Spirit had taught him.

Change Of Heart

> *Then I went into the regions of Syria and Cilicia. And I was still*
> *unknown in person to the churches of Judea that are in Christ.*
> *They only were hearing it said, "He who used to persecute us is*
> *now preaching the faith he once tried to destroy." And they glorified*
> *God because of me.*   —*Galatians 1:21-24*

Having made that confirmation Paul went to Syria and Cilicia. It is of interest that Antioch, the capital of Cilicia was where disciples were first called Christians. Something of significance happened there that was fundamental to Christian identity that will be addressed in Galatians 2. This was Paul's lead into that discussion. It is important to note that at this time Paul had no authority or standing with the apostles, but was unknown as a Christian to them. In fact, worse than no authority or standing at all, Paul was known up to this time as the chief enemy of Christianity. He went to Antioch with the proverbial deck stacked against him. So, if Paul could be regenerated, anyone could. And of course, that is the significance of Paul's conversion and the reason that they glorified God.

5. Discussion

Then after fourteen years I went up again to Jerusalem with Barn-
abas, taking Titus along with me. I went up because of a revelation
and set before them (though privately before those who seemed influ-
ential) the gospel that I proclaim among the Gentiles, in order to
make sure I was not running or had not run in vain. But even Titus,
who was with me, was not forced to be circumcised, though he was a
Greek.   —Galatians 2:1-3

Fourteen years later Paul led a troupe to Jerusalem to defend a revelation (ἀποκάλυψις, *apokalupsis,* another conjugation of *apocalypse*), to test it in counsel with the apostles. It appears that Paul had been preaching his doctrine of the veil at Antioch because he spoke of a revelation, which by definition is the revealing of something previously hidden. The Second Temple had established a veiled understanding of the Old Testament law that obscured the good news of God's salvation, and Jesus had removed that veil.

Barnabas was the pastor of the church at Antioch, and Paul had much in common with him. They also took Titus, a pastoral student, which made three preaching elders from the church at Antioch who went to settle an argument that occurred, not just at Galatia, but was rampant everywhere. Peter and James had also gotten caught up in its deceit.

Paul had gone to talk privately with Peter because he was influential, because Peter represented what the apostles believed. Paul was not interested in the position or office that Peter may have held among the apostles, but was interested in the fact that Peter's understanding and beliefs represented the apostles' understanding and beliefs. Peter was "first" among the apostles, not because he was smarter, holier, kinder, etc., but

because he was always the first to shoot off his mouth and the first on
the scene, the first to make a mistake and often the first to learn from
it. The biblical testimony about Peter shows him to have been brash,
eager, and careless. He tried to walk on water with Jesus (Matthew
14:28-31). He openly rebuked Jesus when he thought Jesus was
wrong. (Matthew 16:22-23). Peter denied that he would ever fall away
or deny Jesus—he would rather die! He couldn't even stay awake one
hour with Jesus in the garden (Matthew 26: 40). Then he fell away and
denied Jesus three times. Peter was not a paragon of faithfulness, intelligence, or courage. His only redeeming quality was eager willingness,
which was sufficient. Paul went to see Peter to share his vision of the
Second Temple establishment and the corrective purpose for which Jesus had come. Peter was not a scholar, he was a fisherman, so he would
not have understood Jesus' mission as Paul did. Nonetheless, Paul was
convinced that he was on to something important, and wanted to run
it by Peter.

The fact that the Christian church was birthed in a such a fundamental argument is no minor detail, nor should it be overlooked.
Argument is an essential response to the removal of the veil. We can
assess the scope of the argument by the fact that Peter represented the
Jewish view, which was the Second Temple establishment view
slightly modified to better comport with his, at the time, immature
understanding of Christianity. Paul opposed the effort by some Jewish
Christians to bring the Second Temple establishment view of biblical
history into Christianity. Paul knew that view and increasingly rejected it as he received the waxing light of Christ, because Christ
rejected it. Paul represented Christ's view, the historic, prophetic view
of Israel's history described above in *The Backstory*. This is the essential
argument that was prosecuted in Paul's letter to the Galatians.

Paul was being criticized because his gospel, his perspective regarding biblical history and Jesus' place and role in that history, was
radically different from the generally accepted Second Temple establishment view. The overwhelming majority of Jews held to the
Second Temple view because that was all that had been preached and
taught for centuries. The intertestamental period, those four hundred
silent years, were truly the dark ages of Judaism. It was not simply that
God did not reveal anything new to His people during this time, but

that His people were in active denial of what God had revealed through the very prophets they claimed to cherish—and they had been in that denial since before the prophets put quill to parchment.

Jesus Christ brought light into *that* darkness. *That* was Paul's darkness that the blinding light of Christ had pierced on the road to Damascus. It took a while for Paul's eyes (his insight) to become accustomed to *that* light, *that* version of Jewish history. He then spent the next fourteen years preaching and refining that view, working out the details, coming to terms with the implications, and honing his argument to razor sharpness. And only Paul could do this, only Paul among the apostles had the necessary academic abilities and credentials within the Second Temple establishment to understand the fullness of the gospel of Jesus Christ as the long awaited Messiah who was the Savior of the world. Of course, in one sense Paul's credentials did not equip him to understand the gospel in any more fullness than any of the other apostles. He declared himself to be the least of the apostles and that all of his academic credentials were dung. Nonetheless, because Paul was a Pharisee, he simply had a superior understanding of Israel's history and Second Temple Judaism.

WORLD

Exactly what or whom had Christ come to save? The cosmos (κόσμος), the age (αἰών)—what? We are so thoroughly modern in our outlook that we cannot envision anything other than the material sense of these words. But that is *not* what the Bible means by these words. The Bible is not a modern book, and the ancient understanding of those words was not weighed down with the accumulated barnacles of material scientism, like we are. We are so accustomed to viewing the Bible though the magnification glass of modern academic studies that we are blinded to its stories, to their greater context, their point and purpose.

We can better assess the biblical meaning of these words by looking at their etymological history. The English word *world* comes from the Old English *weorold* (-uld), *weorld*, *worold* (-uld, -eld), a compound of *wer* "man" and *eld* "age," which thus means roughly the "Age of Man." The corresponding word in Latin is *mundus*, which literally means clean, elegant. The Latin was a translation of Greek *cosmos*, which means an *orderly arrangement*. And the Germanic word suggests a mythological idea of a human domain, an environment in which human beings can live.

While it is important to understand what Scripture may have meant at the time that it was written, a faithful reading will always strive to understand what it means to us, to its contemporary readers because its deepest and most essential meaning, its purpose, will be the same in every generation. That's why the Bible is alive—it speaks today. And to miss what it says to us today in whatever age we live, is to miss its deepest and most essential meaning—its purpose, its life.

Jesus did not come to preserve us in some kind of perpetual, Platonic, ideal, abstract existence. He came to save us from extinction as a race, a biblical kind—to keep us from destroying ourselves.[1] Heaven is not simply a place to go when we die, it's a way that humanity can flourish, a way to dissipate the accumulated momentum of denial, alienation, fear, self-concern, and revenge that threatens the well-being of humanity, of the whole world. History is the story of that accumulated momentum, and as it accumulates it becomes easier to see. Today it is the proverbial elephant in the room of history. And one day soon that historical momentum will be undeniable and the whole world will be astonished at its revelation, at the apocalypse (uncovering) that will mark its climax.

However, that apocalypse is not about the destruction of the world, but is about the remodeling of human society on the model provided by Jesus Christ in the New Testament.[2] To be remolded in the likeness of Jesus Christ is to be remade in the image of God. Of course, that remodeling, remolding, and remaking requires the end of the old, the end of life in the image of Adam. But that rekindling does not result in physical or ultimate death, anymore than the emergence of a butterfly results in the death of the caterpillar. The caterpillar does not die, it is transformed—but not into something else. It remains the creature it always was, but in its maturity it comes to the fullness of its unique character as a creature. The butterfly is not the end or death of the caterpillar, but provides for the enduring life-cycle of the species.

1   Ross, Phillip A. *Varsy Arsy—Reclaiming The Gospel in Second Corinthians*, Pilgrim Platform, 2009, Marietta, Ohio, "Extinction."

2   Ross, Phillip A. *Peter's Vision of Christ's Purpose in First Peter*, 2011, *Peter's Vision of The End in Second Peter*, 2012, Pilgrim Platform, Marietta, Ohio.

The impending apocalypse of Jesus Christ has similarities, though the impetus for this transformation is not endemic to our humanity. Rather, it comes from God who is both immanent and transcendent in this world.

CONFLICT

The traditional understanding of Galatians is that as gentiles converted to Christianity, a dispute arose among Christian leaders as to whether or not the gentiles needed to observe all the tenets of the law of Moses. In particular, the issue was whether gentile converts needed to be circumcised or observe the dietary laws. However, it was not just these things, but rather the whole of Torah obligation that was in view.

In addition and around the same time period, the subject of gentiles and the Torah was also debated among the rabbis and recorded in the Talmud. This resulted in the doctrine of the Seven Laws of Noah,[3] which were to be followed by gentiles, as well as the determination that gentiles did not need to be taught the Torah. One eighteenth century teacher, Jacob Emden,[4] taught that Jesus' original objective, which he thought Paul continued, was to convert gentiles to the Seven Laws of Noah, while allowing Jews to continue following the Mosaic Law. This view then developed into dual covenant theology.[5] It

---

3   The seven Noahite laws are: 1) do not deny god, 2) do not blaspheme god, 3) do not murder, 4) do not engage in incestuous, adulterous or homosexual relationships, 5) do not steal, 6) do not eat of a live animal, 7) establish functioning courts of law. According to Rabbinic tradition, the Noahite laws were derived exegetically from the few commandments which were given to Adam in the Garden of Eden (Genesis 2:16), and a seventh precept regarding animals, which was added after the Flood of Noah.

4   Jacob Emden. also known as Ya'avetz (1697-1776), was a leading German rabbi and Talmud scholar who championed Orthodox Judaism against the Sabbatean movement. Moses Mendelssohn, founder of the Jewish Enlightenment movement, wrote to him as "your disciple, who thirsts for your words." Emden did not approve of the Hasidic movement which came about during his lifetime, his books are well-respected among the Hasidim.

5   Dual-covenant theology is a Christian view of the Old Covenant which holds that Jews may simply keep the Law of Moses, because of the everlasting covenant (Genesis 17:13) between Abraham and God, whereas gentiles must convert to Christianity or alternatively accept the Seven Laws of Noah to be assured of a place in the world to come. I argue against this theology throughout this book.

should be noted that dual covenant theology amounts to the refutation of the essential teaching of Jesus and the Old Testament prophets as described in *The Backstory* (above), which Paul argued in Galatia.

Emden made the case for continuing the blindness of the Second Temple establishment by clinging to the idea that God's eternal covenant honored everything in the Torah. Nonetheless, this is the position that Jesus came to correct and which Paul argued against at Galatia. Yet Emden refused that correction by denying the Lordship of Jesus Christ. And today some misguided Christians agree with Emden in the name of Jesus Christ! Of course, Emden lived much later than the first century, but the spirit of his argument was alive and well in Galatia in the first century.

It seems that Peter had traveled to Antioch where he and Paul got into a dispute. It isn't clear whether it happened before or after the Council of Jerusalem (Acts 15), but it was the same argument. To Paul's dismay, the Jewish Christians in Antioch sided with Peter, including Barnabas (Galatians 2:13). Paul called the error *hypocrisy*, which was the same accusation made by the Old Testament prophets against the Second Temple establishment, whom Jesus quoted (Matthew 13:14, 15:7) and called them a "den of thieves" (Matthew 21:13)—all of which suggests the same error. This was the argument that Paul prosecuted among the apostles, to ensure that he had understood Jesus correctly and was not arguing in vain. This very argument has not been fully resolved to universal agreement to this day, and is a concern of this book.

Paul mentioned that Titus had not been circumcised, and yet Titus was widely accepted as a viable Christian brother. Indeed circumcision was the issue of presentation, but was not the issue of substance. While they argued about circumcision, the actual argument was about the covenant, of which circumcision had been given to the Jews as a sign. The issue was about God's eternal covenant (Genesis 17:7). If there was a change regarding the sign of the covenant, was there a corresponding change in the content of the covenant? Christianity answered this question by calling the new covenant the *New Testament*, which completes and fulfills the Old. Christianity has argued ever since that there is something new and something enduring in God's covenant, that there is both continuity and discontinuity from the Old to the New Testament. The nature and extent of that continuity and discontinuity is the issue.

6. THE GAUNTLET

Yet because of false brothers secretly brought in—who slipped in to spy out our freedom that we have in Christ Jesus, so that they might bring us into slavery—to them we did not yield in submission even for a moment, so that the truth of the gospel might be preserved for you. And from those who seemed to be influential (what they were makes no difference to me; God shows no partiality)—those, I say, who seemed influential added nothing to me. On the contrary, when they saw that I had been entrusted with the gospel to the uncircumcised, just as Peter had been entrusted with the gospel to the circumcised (for he who worked through Peter for his apostolic ministry to the circumcised worked also through me for mine to the Gentiles), and when James and Cephas and John, who seemed to be pillars, perceived the grace that was given to me, they gave the right hand of fellowship to Barnabas and me, that we should go to the Gentiles and they to the circumcised. Only, they asked us to remember the poor, the very thing I was eager to do. —Galatians 2:6-10

Immediately Paul labeled those who opposed him as *false brothers* who had been smuggled into the Galatian fellowship to spy on Paul and the *freedom* (ἐλευθερία) of his preaching message. There were two aspects to Paul's message. The first was that the gospel of Jesus Christ came to people freely, without effort, cost, or expectation. It could not be earned or achieved. And second, it produced freedom in the believer, freedom from what Paul called the *law* (νόμος). What Paul meant by this word is a major subject of this book.

Paul argued that the view of these false brothers led to slavery and bondage (καταδουλόω), the slavery and bondage that the Jews had been caught up in for centuries. The false brothers continued in the blindness of the Second Temple establishment in that they failed to heed the preaching of the prophets, Jeremiah, Isaiah, etc., whose ancient message Jesus had rekindled. Of course, there was more to Jesus' message than this, but this is where it began, especially for the Jews because of their long history of blindness and denial. Jesus aimed his most critical harangues at the Pharisees of the Second Temple establishment, calling them "whitewashed tombs, which outwardly appear beautiful, but within are full of dead people's bones and all uncleanness," saying that they "outwardly appear righteous to others, but within you are full of hypocrisy and lawlessness" (Matthew 23:27-28).

Paul said two important things in verse 6 about those apostles who were influential—Peter, James, and John. First, he said that it didn't matter what sort of people they were, by which he meant that God was not concerned with their special skills or abilities, or about any human offices they may hold as a result of their skills or abilities. Paul did not seek Peter out because Peter was the head apostle. Rather, Paul's interest in Peter was that Peter's views represented (provided a representative example of) the apostles' views. Second, Paul reiterated God's policy of showing no partiality to individuals. Paul captured this idea later in this letter when he said, "There is neither Jew nor Greek, there is neither slave nor free, there is no male and female, for you are all one in Christ Jesus" (Galatians 3:28). While God loves us as individuals, and people are actually more individual in Christ than not, God's love does not increase or decrease because of our individuality.

In that same sentence (v. 6) Paul also said that those influential apostles (Peter, James, and John) added nothing to him. Their views on the conflicted issue were worthless to him because they didn't understand *The Backstory* at that point. They did not help resolve the conflict. He had gone to the apostles for counsel, and their counsel was worthless, of no help, it added nothing to him.

Verse 7 is the source of dual covenant theology in that the English translation makes it look as if this verse teaches that Paul's theology best fit uncircumcised gentiles, while Peter's best fit circumcised Jews. However, that is not what Paul meant to say. Again, the issue of presentation was circumcision, but the actual issue was the law, how the law related to each group. Note also that this duality came from the apostles, not from Paul. The deeper conflict was whether dual

covenant theology was biblically valid. One side thought that everyone ought to be circumcised (follow the Old Testament law) and the
other thought that Christ had abrogated the law. However, those who
thought that Paul was teaching that Christ had abrogated the law misunderstood Paul. That was not what he taught, and clarifying this
confusion is the subject of this book.

Verse 7 begins by noting that what follows in the verse is contrary
to Paul, that it belonged to those who added nothing to Paul's thinking. Paul argued and was entrusted with his view issuing out of *The
Backstory,* and Peter represented a view of the gospel that was unin-
formed or unconvinced by *The Backstory*. Yet, verse 7 tells us that in
spite of the opposition Paul believed that there was truth in both per-
spectives. Paul was clear at this point that he did not agree with the
apostles, but also sensed a common thread between them. And when
James, Peter, and John saw the grace that had been given to Paul,
when they felt his love, his passion, and his willingness to engage with
them they welcomed Paul and Barnabas, and we assume Titus as well.
However, the apostles suggested that Paul's group would be best suited
as evangelists to the gentiles and they, Peter's group, would be best
suited as evangelists to the Jews.

This is very curious division because as it happened Paul was con-
tinuously hounded by the Jews throughout his ministry. The Jews
seemed to follow him everywhere he went in order to stir up trouble.
Peter, then, became the leader of the gentile church at Jerusalem, and
later at Rome, a gentile capital. It was never intended that Paul evangelize gentiles and Peter evangelize Jews. Rather, Scripture simply
acknowledged that Paul's theology was more in line with gentile theology in that it did not depend on strict obedience to the law, and
Peter's theology was more in line with Jewish (Second Temple) theology in that it depended on strict obedience to the law. Neither Peter
nor Paul made an effort to limit their outreach in any way. So, the idea
that Peter was the missionary to the Jews and Paul to the gentiles is
simply false.

Verse 9 then tells us that the two groups were willing to meet and
discuss the issue as brothers in Christ, with the stipulation added by the
apostles that they remember the poor. While persecution of Christians
may not have been in full flower yet, both the Pharisees and the Ro-

mans were quite displeased with the Christians. Persecution always begins socially and economically as the disfavored group becomes increasingly alienated from the sources of social influence—money and power. The apostles in Jerusalem were particularly aware of this and called it to Paul's attention because Paul had been a high ranking Pharisee and businessman. Like his father, Paul ran a tent-making business on the side.

CONFLICT

> But when Cephas came to Antioch, I opposed him to his face, because he stood condemned. For before certain men came from James, he was eating with the Gentiles; but when they came he drew back and separated himself, fearing the circumcision party. And the rest of the Jews acted hypocritically along with him, so that even Barnabas was led astray by their hypocrisy. But when I saw that their conduct was not in step with the truth of the gospel, I said to Cephas before them all, "If you, though a Jew, live like a Gentile and not like a Jew, how can you force the Gentiles to live like Jews?" We ourselves are Jews by birth and not Gentile sinners; yet we know that a person is not justified by works of the law but through faith in Jesus Christ, so we also have believed in Christ Jesus, in order to be justified by faith in Christ and not by works of the law, because by works of the law no one will be justified.
>
> —Galatians 2:11-16

Calvin uses these verses to prosecute his argument against the Papacy by translating the phrase as "because he was worthy of blame" (v. 11b).

"Peter was chastised and struck dumb. The observation of Chrysostom, that, for the sake of avoiding scandal, they would have talked in private if they had any difference, is frivolous. The less important must be disregarded in comparison of the most dangerous of all scandals, that the Church would be rent, that Christian liberty was in danger, that the doctrine of the grace of Christ was overthrown; and therefore this public offense must be publicly corrected.

The chief argument on which Jerome rests is excessively trifling. 'Why should Paul,' says he, 'condemn in another what he takes praise for in himself? for he boasts that 'to the Jews he became as a Jew' (1 Corinthians 9:20). I reply, that what Peter did is totally different. Paul accommodated himself to the Jews no farther than was consistent with the doctrine of liberty; and therefore he refused to circumcise Titus, that the truth of the gospel might remain unimpaired. But Peter Judaized in such a manner as to 'compel the gentiles' to suffer bondage, and at the same time to create a prejudice against Paul's doctrine. He did not, therefore, observe the proper limit; for he was more desirous to please than to edify, and more solicitous to inquire what would gratify the Jews than what would be expedient for the whole body. Augustine is therefore right in asserting, that this was no previously arranged plan, but that Paul, out of Christian zeal, opposed the sinful and unseasonable dissimulation of Peter, because he saw that it would be injurious to the Church."[1]

As much as I value Christian unity and have argued for the same in all of my books, I think Calvin was right about what was going on in these verses. This conflict, which preceded the birth of Christ, who was simply arguing as the prophets before him had argued during the Second Temple administration, has never been satisfactorily resolved to this day! And it cannot be ignored or swept aside in the name of Christian unity because it lies at the very heart of human health and well-being. This issue is about much more than the Pope, and to focus it on the Pope is wrong-headed because it makes the issue about a person rather than principalities and powers (Galatians 1:16, 2:25). Nonetheless, it remains an issue today, and is in need of proper focus.

In verse 11 Paul simply said that Peter was wrong. Apparently, Peter had understood grace correctly before James brought some of his people, Judaizers, to convince Peter otherwise. And they succeeded. Peter had been fellowshiping and eating with all comers until James came to "correct" him. No doubt James appealed to history, to the centuries of the Second Temple administration and its "well documented" teachings. Paul observed that Peter feared the circumcision party. Only a fool would not have feared them! They were the Jewish establishment and they controlled everything Jewish. To cross them would lead to tremendous social difficulties that would result in being shunned and ruined, financially, socially, politically, religiously, etc. Paul knew well their power, their reach, and their vindictiveness.

1   Calvin, John. *Calvin's Commentaries*, Galatians 2:11, public domain.

Paul then accused the other Christian Jews of hypocrisy (συν-υποκρίνομαι), not treason or heresy. This particular accusation suggests that they were guilty of the same thing that the prophets had accused people of centuries earlier, and the same thing that Jesus accused the Pharisees of. It was the same accusation because it was the same issue, described by what I have called *The Backstory*.

The fact that Christians fellowshiped with all believers was a very early doctrine that all Christians agreed with. Its source was the dispensation of the Holy Spirit in Acts 2. That was the Spirit of Christianity that had gone out to all the world. But from the perspective of the Second Temple establishment, such a thing was viewed as heresy of the highest order because they thought that it threatened the integrity of the Torah. And it did!

Hypocrisy means saying one thing and doing another, which is exactly what Paul had observed about Peter. So he called him out on it. Peter's new "conduct was not in step with the truth of the gospel" (v. 14). He was a Jew who had been living like a gentile, but after James' visit, Peter asked gentiles to live like Jews. He couldn't have it both ways. Neither would Paul accept the Noahite covenant, which would make the gentiles Jewish-lite. It was simply a different version of the same thing. For God's grace to truly be a product of God's graciousness, grace had to be completely divorced from human expectations and behavioral demands.

Paul acknowledge that he, like Peter, was Jewish by birth. They were not gentiles,

> "…yet we know that a person is not justified by doing what the Law requires, but rather by the faithfulness of Jesus the Messiah. We, too, have believed in the Messiah Jesus so that we might be justified by the faithfulness of the Messiah and not by doing what the Law requires, for no human being will be justified by doing what the Law requires" (v. 16, *International Standard Version*).

The ISV provides a clear expression of Paul's meaning. Note that justification is not produced by what we do, not even by our own believing. Rather, justification is produced by what Jesus did, by His faithfulness unto death. This means that not even Christ in the flesh was justified because of His obedience to the law. Rather, He was justified by His faith, just as we are justified by His faith, not His

obedience to the law. Christ is the model for our justification, so He
needed to model it for us. Of course, Christ did not *need* to be justified
at all, so we can understand it as an additional grace given to Him, not
for His sake, but for ours, for our understanding. Christians emulate
Christ's faith; we reproduce it. Obedience is a fruit, belief is the root.
Obedience issues out of belief, belief does not issue out of obedience.
The cart is incapable of pushing the horse.

7. Not Through Obedience

But if, in our endeavor to be justified in Christ, we too were found to be sinners, is Christ then a servant of sin? Certainly not! For if I rebuild what I tore down, I prove myself to be a transgressor. For through the law I died to the law, so that I might live to God. I have been crucified with Christ. It is no longer I who live, but Christ who lives in me. And the life I now live in the flesh I live by faith in the Son of God, who loved me and gave himself for me. I do not nullify the grace of God, for if righteousness were through the law, then Christ died for no purpose.   —Galatians 2:17-21

When Paul mentions "our endeavor to be justified" (v. 17) he includes himself and Peter and those whom Peter was defending, the Judaizers. We must be clear about whether this verse is about them as Jews or about them as Christians. They understood themselves to be Jewish Christians or Christian Jews. Clearly, he was talking about the Christian endeavor to be justified by Christ because Jews loyal to the Second Temple establishment would not have so endeavored.

The point he was making was that Jews who followed Christ could only do so by confessing their sin apart from Christ. Their confession of sin was an admission that participation in Temple sacrifices had not cleansed them of sin. Jewish Christians confessed that following the Torah had not kept them from sin and that they too needed Christ. And it was the teaching of Christ that pointed this out, which led to Paul's question about Christ being a servant of sin, since Christ's ministry made it clear that all were sinners. It seems that Christ's ministry increased the awareness of sin. Did that mean that Christ increased sin? No, not at all!

A second argument against Peter and the Judaizers was that as Jews they believed that obedience to the Torah would save them. Then as Christians they found freedom from the Torah and fellow-shiped with gentile Christians without concern for the law. But with James and the Judaizers, they changed their minds again and refuted their previous freedom from the Torah. Such back and forth beliefs insured that whatever position was ultimately true, they would have transgressed it at some point because they had changed their minds more than once. "Whoever commits sin transgresses also the law: for sin is the transgression of the law" (1 John 3:4). Thus, the law revealed their sin because of the law's inefficacy, and the revelation that the law could not save them, leaving them in death. They were then open to salvation through God in Christ.

At that point Paul broke out into a doxology about being crucified with Christ. It appears that this idea originated with Paul, and is likely related to the idea of being *in Christ*. Here's the logic: Because Christ is eternal and the saved are with Christ in heaven, and heaven is not merely a location but is primarily a way of being in the world (as it is in heaven), Christ's goal is to bring heaven to this world. The faith of believers is Christ's faith which resides in them through union with Christ (Colossians 2:10), and not their own.[1] Therefore, because the faith of the One who was crucified for the salvation of the world is the same as the faith of the believers in the world, the crucifixion of Christ was tantamount to the crucifixion of those who believe and reside in Him. Paul's logic is flawless, yet still requires faith in Christ, union with Christ, as an axiom upon which the logic stands.

Logic does not establish the truthfulness of facts. Rather, logic only establishes the validity of a conclusion. Logic shows that if the initial proposition is true, the conclusion will be valid. Thus, if it is true that the believer has faith in Christ, then the conclusion that the believer has been crucified with Christ is valid. And if it is true that Christ has been crucified, then it is true that belief in Christ logically implies the believer's crucifixion with Christ.

Paul then drew a valid implication: "It is no longer I who live, but Christ who lives in me" (v. 20). Because Christ's crucifixion led to His

---

1   Ross, Phillip A. *Ephesians—Recovering The Vision Of A Sustainable Church In Christ*, Pilgrim Platform, Marietta, Ohio, 2014.

death, His crucifixion was also the believer's death. And because Christ was raised from death, His resurrected life resides in believers through their faith. It naturally follows, then, that the life the believer now lives in the flesh is lived by faith in the Son of God. Consequently, Paul can say that "the Son of God ... loved me and gave himself for me" (v. 20).

> "I do not nullify the grace of God, for if righteousness were through the law, then Christ died for no purpose" (Galatians 2:21).

Verse 21 presents a huge problem that cannot be resolved without first defining and understanding the two central terms: *righteousness* and *law*. The idea of verse 21 is that righteousness is *not* produced by the law or by obedience to the law, and this idea flies in the face of our natural understanding.

RIGHTEOUSNESS

Righteousness (δικαιοσύνη) is defined as the state of being as one ought to be, the condition that makes people acceptable to God, integrity, virtue, purity of life, rightness, correctness of thinking, feeling, and acting; and in a narrower sense, justice or the virtue which gives each his due. Compare this definition of the Greek word with the contemporary definition of the English word, which is: adhering to moral principles. Adhering is a function of obedience. If righteousness is about adhering it is about behavior, but if it is a state of being it precedes behavior. We tend to think of righteousness as a behavioral issue, but Paul defines it as a matter of being. It's the difference between behavior and character. While these two things are related, they are not the same. Behavior manifests outwardly, socially, and character manifests inwardly, personally. Of course, our behavior demonstrates our character, and our character demonstrates our morality, our commitment to righteousness. However, demonstration is not causality.

We tend to think of righteousness as being about morality and behavior, but Paul defines it here as being about character and being. And this is the problem of Galatians in a nutshell because character produces moral behavior, defined as conformity to God's rule. But obedience to rules does not produce godly character. Love will cause us to behave in certain ways, but behaving in certain ways will not cause us to love.

This righteousness does not natively belong to us, but is the result of regeneration in Christ. Righteousness is not a function of behavior, and if it was we could simply conform our behavior to the standards of righteousness and achieve salvation ourselves, without Christ. If this were possible, then righteousness would be something that we do ourselves, which would make it a matter of works. It would be works-righteousness, which is what the effort to live in obedience to law amounts to.

The Bible is very clear to those who have eyes to see and ears to hear that the gospel is grace driven, not works driven. It is a matter of being, not mere behavior, of character, not mere conformity. However, just saying this is an insufficient description of gospel grace because the grace that actually connects to people always elicits a response of love, obligation, and obedience. It doesn't take perfect love and obedience on our part, but it does produce real love and increasing obedience, even if it is as small as a mustard seed. And the actual connection comes through eyes and ears that are both willing and able to connect, and to repent of our failures. Willingness alone is necessary but not sufficient. And the same thing is true of ability alone: ability is necessary but not sufficient. The connection between willingness and ability is the Holy Spirit through regeneration. The Holy Spirit makes the able willing, and the willing able.

When Paul said that this argument does not do away with the grace of God (v. 21), he was saying that this argument rests fully on God's grace. He said it negatively as a response to the accusation that his argument made a mockery of God's grace because it did not require anything from the recipients of grace. Paul argued that it was the false teachers who were making a mockery of grace by suggesting that grace comes with requirements.

Paul was not arguing that there are no consequences that come from reception of God's grace. The desire to please God is the consequence. Obedience, however imperfect, is the consequence. Paul's point was that obedience is the consequence, not the requirement. Obedience, however imperfect, is always involved. Paul never said that it wasn't involved, only that it was not required on the front end. Rather, it is the product, the consequence, on the back end. A gift that entails a requirement prior to reception of the gift is a bribe not a gift.

8. FOOLED

O foolish Galatians! Who has bewitched you? It was before your eyes that Jesus Christ was publicly portrayed as crucified. Let me ask you only this: Did you receive the Spirit by works of the law or by hearing with faith? Are you so foolish? Having begun by the Spirit, are you now being perfected by the flesh? Did you suffer so many things in vain—if indeed it was in vain? Does he who supplies the Spirit to you and works miracles among you do so by works of the law, or by hearing with faith—just as Abraham "believed God, and it was counted to him as righteousness"? —Galatians 3:1-6

Modern people frown on name calling. Yet here is Paul calling the Galatians names in the most unflattering way. Absolutely no one would say such a thing to a live audience today. Sure, preachers call other people names. We all think that people who don't agree with us are stupid, and it is easier and more common than ever to call people names. But the pastor who calls his own flock *stupid* is bucking for a demotion. Yet, here is Paul doing exactly this!

Paul used the word ἀνόητος (*anoetos*), *a,* meaning *not* and *noetos* or *noetic* in English—an adjective meaning *of, or associated with, or requiring the use of the mind.* There are at least two ways to understand what Paul meant. He could have meant it in the crude way, meaning *you idiots!* Or he could have had something more refined in mind, meaning that they were not proficient in the higher arts of philosophy, logic, analysis, etc. Or he could have meant that they were motivated by fear rather than reason. Or he could have meant all of these things. Whatever Paul originally meant, at this point in history we must conclude that Paul called attention to a human malady that education alone cannot fix. We know this because many very smart and highly educated people continue to argue about what Paul meant.

And yet this is about more than a simple misunderstanding. Paul said that they had been duped, fooled, tricked, deceived. It was as if a veil hid the truth from them because, in fact, a veil *had* hidden truth from them for a very long time. It wasn't that the false teachers in Galatia were some sort of new religious sect. Rather, the false teachers were peddling the same old lies that had hidden the truth from Israelites for centuries. It was the same old ideas that had been dressed up in new semi-Christian garb. The Galatian false teachers were not Gnostics, they were Judaizers who were trying to justify their delusion.

If these Judaizers were correct, then Christ had been needlessly crucified. If they were correct, Christians just needed to follow a few Old Testament laws and they'd be good to go. If they were correct, Jesus would be a great teacher and prophet in that he would have shown the world how everyone can be Jewish and reap the benefits of being Jewish, just like the Jews throughout the ages. If they were right, being Jewish-lite would be sufficient. If they were right, the issue was behavior, not character; rules, not grace.

DECEIVED

Paul asked for clarification, "Did you receive the Spirit by works of the law or by hearing with faith" (v. 2)? I would punctuate it differently and make it into two questions: *Did you receive the Spirit? By works of the law or by hearing with faith?* The first concern involves the reception of the Spirit, and the Judaizers would *not* have denied their reception of the Spirit. But they would have understood the Spirit differently than Paul understood it.

They could easily have understood that the Spirit had come to them, not when they first heard Paul, but later when they began to conform to Old Testament law. At that point, they could argue that the Spirit had directed them to correct Paul's earlier view. So, yes, they had received the Spirit and believed themselves to be operating in the Spirit (Matthew 7:21).

This view of things also answers the question about when they received the Spirit, but not in the way that Paul wanted them to answer it. In order for them to believe their view, it was necessary to believe that Paul had been wrong in his initial gospel message. This is probably pretty much what the Judaizers had been thinking, and shows that their message to the Galatians had not issued out of ignorance. This is actually a pretty sophisticated message. It is most certainly not a grossly stupid view of things because it has centuries of Jewish tradition and history to support it.

This argument would run something like this: God had given the Jews the law, and the law was for the whole world—the gentiles, too. But the law was too much for the ignorant gentiles, so Jesus had come to dumb it down a bit so the ignorant gentiles could find a place in the Jewish kingdom until they matured enough to convert to full-fledged Judaism. It is not an unreasonable argument. It is logically and philosophically valid.

However, it completely misses the larger argument about *The Backstory*, the failure of the Jews to manifest the character of God as evidenced by their own prophets, and Jesus' mission to correct this problem. In fact, the Judaizers completely ignored *The Backstory* by believing that the Old Testament was sufficient for the manifestation of the character of God. They assumed that they were just fine, it was the world that was the problem. They believed that the Jews had God, it was the gentiles who needed Him. And in this, they were half-right.

Hearing with faith (v. 2) means believing what you hear. It means bringing faith to the content of what has been heard. Faith is not a substance that gets transferred from mouth to ear. Rather, hearing the gospel is more like having the pillars of falsehood knocked out from beneath you and falling into the arms of the Holy Spirit. The gospel is not a really good argument that inspires our trust, the gospel is so completely unexpected and so *not* like what we expect it to be that it shatters our previous assumptions about God and the world and how we thought things work. The gospel is not a superior argument that sweeps us off our feet and envelopes us in the love of God. At least, that's not our first response to the gospel.

Rather, the gospel takes us by surprise, challenges our core beliefs and assumptions, and upends everything we thought we understood. The gospel is pure grace, pure gift, because it is so other, so different, than what we naturally want, believe, expect, understand, and prefer.

The gospel is not about us, not about how much God loves us—though He does! It's not about how worthy or unworthy we are. It's about the unfathomable wideness of God's mercy and Christ's love. The good news of the gospel is not about the eternal damnation and torture in eternity of the faithless, though this is true. It's about our own ignorance, foolishness, hardheadedness, narrowmindedness, self-centeredness, density, imbecility, and inability. The gospel comes as a gift to produce our humility. It exposes our own hypocrisy and hard-headedness, and humiliates us. The gospel of Jesus Christ is a gift of shame for the pride of humanity.

REPENTING REPENTANCE

Paul originally brought the gospel message to Galatia during his second missionary journey. So, the gospel that converted the Galatians was the gospel that Paul first preached to them, which issued out of his new understanding of *The Backstory*. *The Backstory* was the context of the gospel that Jesus had preached, and which He taught Paul through the power of the Holy Spirit. Understanding Jesus' mission requires understanding the historic context into which He had come and to which He spoke. The problem Jesus came to address was Israel's historic problem—the failure of legalism to deal with sin. Jesus spoke into that historic situation, which involved both the Jews and the gentiles. The gentiles—Assyrians, Syrians, Persians, Romans, Germans, Italians, Americans, Russians, Chinese, etc.—were as guilty of legalism as the Jews. Jesus had come to reconcile the Jews to the God they proclaimed, and to reignite their original mission to be a blessing to all humanity—to the gentiles, to the world.

Paul accused them in verse 3 of having begun their walk in Christ by the Spirit, under the guidance of the Spirit, but trying to complete that walk in the flesh, under various rules of behavior. He used the word *flesh* (σάρξ) because their focus was on diet (Acts 15:29, and other behavioral things in the Noahite covenant). Paul was not saying that there are no behavioral consequences that issue from faith in Christ, only that behavior is the fruit of the faith, not the root.

The Galatians like other Christians had suffered for the gospel because both the Jews and the Romans believed themselves to be threatened by Jesus and began alienating Christians from society. The

Jews did not want them in the Synagogues and the Romans thought they were rebels against the Roman state. So, as family and friends began to shun them socially, the Christians began losing social and financial capital. Soon, outright persecution would break out.

And yet the Spirit had continued to be with them, providing comfort and gifts—miracles. The Greek word δύναμις, although usually translated as *miracles*, doesn't suggest anything contrary to nature. Rather, δύναμις refers to strength, power, and/or ability, a kind of inherent power that resides in a thing by virtue of its nature, or which a person or thing exerts and puts forth. The word is related to our English word *dynamic* and *dynamo*. It's not that such power is not miraculous, but that the miracle is the Spirit who inspires and directs energies and abilities that were not previously manifest.

So, Paul asked them if they thought that the Spirit had come to them because of their obedience to the law, or because they had believed the gospel Paul had initially preached to them. Clearly, the Spirit had not been with them prior to Paul's preaching. The Spirit had come with Paul's preaching, and Paul had not preached salvation by works or obedience to the Torah. Paul had preached a new found freedom in Christ that had come to them apart from the law, apart from or prior to their obedience.

RENEWED

Paul was not teaching some new doctrine. Rather, he was teaching a very old doctrine, "just as Abraham 'believed God, and it was counted to him as righteousness'" (v. 6), quoting Genesis 15:6.

> "...we do not say that Abram was justified because he laid hold on a single word, respecting the offspring to be brought forth, but because he embraced God as his Father. And truly faith does not justify us for any other reason, than that it reconciles us unto God; and that it does so, not by its own merit; but because we receive the grace offered to us in the promises, and have no doubt of eternal life, being fully persuaded that we are loved by God as sons. Therefore, Paul reasons from contraries, that he to whom faith is imputed for righteousness, has not been justified by works. (Romans 4:4.) For whosoever obtains righteousness by works, his merits come into the account before God. But we apprehend righteousness by faith, when God freely reconciles us to himself. Whence it follows, that the merit

of works ceases when righteousness is sought by faith; for it is necessary that this righteousness should be freely given by God, and offered in his word, in order that anyone may possess it by faith. To render this more intelligible, when Moses says that faith was imputed to Abram for righteousness, he does not mean that faith was that first cause of righteousness which is called the efficient, but only the formal cause; as if he had said, that Abram was therefore justified, because, relying on the paternal loving-kindness of God, he trusted to His mere goodness, and not to himself, nor to his own merits. For it is especially to be observed, that faith borrows a righteousness elsewhere, of which we, in ourselves, are destitute; otherwise it would be in vain for Paul to set faith in opposition to works, when speaking of the mode of obtaining righteousness. Besides, the mutual relation between the free promise and faith, leaves no doubt upon the subject."[1]

The reason that belief is counted as righteousness is that righteousness refers to being not behavior, to character not performance, to person not action. The righteousness of Christians is not the result of what they do, their behavior. It is the result of who Christ is, because our righteousness is actually His, in that His Holy Spirit inhabits Christians. Christians are not self-made people, but are remade in the image of Jesus Christ through regeneration—not perfectly in terms of our behavior, but sufficiently in terms of our identity in Christ, our union with Christ.

---

1   Calvin, John. *Calvin's Commentaries*, Genesis 15:6.

9. GOD'S KIDS

*Know then that it is those of faith who are the sons of Abraham.
And the Scripture, foreseeing that God would justify the Gentiles by
faith, preached the gospel beforehand to Abraham, saying, "In you
shall all the nations be blessed." So then, those who are of faith are
blessed along with Abraham, the man of faith. For all who rely on
works of the law are under a curse; for it is written, "Cursed be everyone who does not abide by all things written in the Book of the
Law, and do them." Now it is evident that no one is justified before
God by the law ...."* —Galatians 3:7-11

Paul's observation in verse 7 reveals Israel's folly. However, we must also acknowledge that the mere observation of Israel's legalistic folly does not mean that we are not similarly guilty of the same folly. While identifying a problem is the first step toward a solution, identification alone does not constitute a solution. Israel's folly is humanity's folly, no one is exempt (Romans 3:23). So, we begin with Paul's observation: it's always been about grace, not race; bread (communion), not blood; faith, not family.

This simple observation completely undermined the Second Temple establishment and their cultural focus on exclusiveness—race, blood, and family. The whole purpose of the Second Temple establishment was to return to the glory of the Davidic/Solomonic empire, to the golden splendor of Israel's kingdom dominance as a way to overcome the brutality of Persia, Greece (Alexander), then Rome. The Second Temple establishment wanted God to give these heathen occupiers their come-uppance. They wanted revenge, but called it justice.

They wanted to bask in the light of God's glory once again, but understood that glory in terms of human desire, power, wealth, and success

—just as the heathens did. So, when the light of Christ came with the message of humility, sacrifice, and suffering as the way of God's love, they rejected it. The thing that ancient Israel had feared the most while wandering in the desert was contamination by foreign passions and gods. So, they set up elaborate schemes for maintaining their purity in a contaminated world.

And those practices, those efforts of cultic purity were woven into the fabric of Tabernacle and then into Solomon's Temple establishment. That effort, however, resulted in complete failure as the Tabernacle and then the Temple were destroyed and Israel was taken into captivity by foreign powers. From their Babylonian Exile, a few "faithful" Jews rekindled *that* spirit and convinced Cyrus to permit and fund the rebuilding of the Temple and Israel's fallen grandeur. Again, I'm not saying that this effort was not God-driven. It was! But it was not an example of faithfulness, but of unfaithfulness, of hard-headedness—but not because of what God did, rather because of what Israel did. Cyrus saw the project as a means of tax revenue expansion and stepped up to lend a hand. Decades later *that* spirit was reestablished in the Second Temple culture.

The Jews understood Cyrus' help as a stepping stone to the greater glory of God, which would manifest through the Second Temple. But to their surprise, the Messiah they had waited so long for did not share their enthusiasm for power, wealth, and success as they defined these things. Jesus rejected their exclusivity, but not their zeal for and veneration of moral purity. Genuine purity could not be achieved or maintained by barriers of race, blood, or family. Satan had dominated these concerns from very early antiquity. God's purity can only be received as a gift, and maintained through the disciplines of humility, sacrifice, and suffering.

ABE'S FLOCK

Those who had followed Abram into the wilderness were not Abram's biological children. Most of them were not likely even his extended family. Remember that Abram, like his father was a priest, and he was a priest long before God had called him to go to Canaan. Abram had set out with his father, Terah, who had been a priest of antiquity. Abram then continued Terah's mission into the wilderness, to settle the world.

Abraham and Sarah finally had a biological child of their own quite late in life. The point is that one child does not make a tribe—at least not for quite a while. The initial conflict in Abraham's household was a dispute about inheritance rights between Ishmael and Isaac. Ishmael was the legitimate, elder son who by tradition should have had the right of inheritance. But Isaac was the unexpected son of grace, the long expected son of Abraham's faith in the God who had promised him a son. The point here is that Abraham's tribe was itself not a family clan as Israel (the nation) later came to understand itself.

Abraham's child of inheritance, Isaac, was a child of Abraham's faith in the promise of God. Whereas Ishmael was a child of Sarah's scheming and dependence on the ancient religious laws of inheritance. The difference between Ishmael and Isaac was not a function of blood, it was a function of grace, of Abraham's faith. This was Paul's observation.

> I will bless those who bless you, and him who dishonors you I will curse, and in you all the families of the earth shall be blessed" (Genesis 12:3).

The above verse is intimately associated with Abram's call to "Go from your country and your kindred and your father's house to the land that I will show you" (Genesis 12:1). How could Jews have missed the fact that Abram had been called *away* from his kindred, *away* from his family, his blood ties, and then establish Israel on kindred, family, and blood ties?

No doubt it was in part because the earlier Noahite covenant had been established "with you and your offspring after you" (Genesis 9:9). The KJV reads "seed" and the meaning of the Hebrew word points to offspring, descendants, posterity, children. So, their interpretation is understandable. What they failed to consider was Noah's circumstance, the context of God's covenant with Noah. The world had just been destroyed by the Flood, all except Noah and his immediate family and their wives. In addition, that covenant was not made between God and the individual, Noah, but between God and those who had survived the Flood, Noah being the elder. So, Noah, like Adam before him, was to repopulate the earth. In the context of the biblical story there was no other seed available. So, it wasn't that God was covenanting with Noah and his clan, but that God was re-covenanting with *humanity* through Noah, with the enduring seed of humanity.

We can only understand this if we accept the veracity of the biblical story. If we get all caught up in the extra-biblical ideas that there must have been other people on the earth, or a limited Flood, etc., then we will see the covenant being exclusive with Noah. But if we simply take the biblical story at its face value, its plain reading, then we must understand that the covenant is not with the person or clan of Noah, but with humanity, the remnant people of the earth. Those who fail to trust the biblical story in its simplicity confuse themselves about God's message with all sorts of things that are not part of the story. We can't bring extraneous elements into a story and expect to understand it.

COVENANT

Paul's observation strikes at the heart of ancient Israel's understanding of themselves as a covenant people. There are a variety of ways to understand biblical covenants. One of the more common ways is to enumerate seven covenants: Adamic (original, with humanity), Noahic (postdiluvian), Abrahamic (grace through faith), Palestinian (land based, may be considered part of Abrahamic covenant), Mosaic (Moses and the Ten Commandments), Davidic (Temple based), and New Covenant (Jeremiah anticipates it, Jesus fulfills it).

Scholars then divide the covenants into two groups: unconditional and conditional. The unconditional are understood to be covenants with humanity, and the conditional to be covenants with the nation or people of Israel. Paul's message of radical grace challenges this understanding by suggesting that he, following Jesus, understood them all to be unconditional. And *The Backstory* account of Israel's history suggests that those covenants thought to be limited to Israel were errantly understood as such by Israel, in the same way by various Christians who had been affected by the Judaizers.

The word ('Ιουδαϊκώς) appears in Galatians 2:14 and means *Jewishly* or like the Jews. The Judiazers taught that, in order for Christians to truly get right with God, they must conform to the Mosaic Law. Circumcision was strongly promoted as being a necessary sign of the people of God. They taught that gentiles had to become Jewish proselytes first, and only then could they come to Christ. This teaching was a combination of grace (through Christ) and works (through the keeping of the law). The Jerusalem council determined it to be a false doctrine in Acts 15, and Paul's letter to the Galatians deals with the same subject.

This teaching was the traditional, though errant, understanding of the Jews from antiquity. It was birthed during the time of Abraham, and has proven to be quite tenacious in various forms, even within Christianity. The Christian versions of this works or works related teaching are Pelagianism and Arminianism, both of which modified the details of the doctrine but not its general thrust. Both believe that some form of works or obedience are required *prior* to God's dispensation of grace. In other words, God responds to something that a person does—and belief is understood as something people do (or don't do), rather than the free gift of grace through Christ—by providing them with salvation. The Judaizers thought that those things that people must do had been laid out in the Mosaic Law—circumcision and various purity laws. Pelagius argued that God responded to the believer's belief, and Arminius argued that God and the individual shared the responsibility for salvation, that both had to do something.

BACKWARDS

The true gospel does involve obedience, but obedience is a fruit of the gospel, not a root. This means that obedience is the consequence of belief, not the cause. Obedience is involved in the maintenance of one's salvation or membership in the people of God, but it is not, nor can it be, a condition for salvation or for membership.

God provides grace in various ways. Actually all of life is a function of grace. All of life is pure gift. We don't cause our own birth, nor do we cause the birth of others. Of course, sex is involved, but sex is the means not the cause. God gives, and we respond. God does not initially respond to us, He precedes us. He was here before we were.

This does not mean that God does not respond to people, of course He does! God responds as a function of His relationship with people. But the issue here is the initial action that establishes a faithful relationship. God is the initiator, He begins it, and we respond to Him. Once we are in right relationship with God, He then responds to us, to our actions, thoughts, prayers, activities, etc. And yet, of course, if we are not in right relationship He also responds, but negatively. His absence in our lives speaks volumes.

There are three pieces of this issue: 1) initiation, 2) response, and 3) maintenance. The ancient Jews, the Judaizers, most religions, and various forms of Christianity have all reversed the order of these elements of salvation, or establishing a relationship with God. God initiates the relationship out of His pure grace, that initiation elicits a response, and maintenance then is the product of will. Because those who are already involved in relationship with God are also already involved in maintenance of that relationship, they mistakenly think that people who don't know God can become a part of the people of God by engaging in maintenance activities. So, they require the signs of maintenance of people prior to their knowing God, prior to God's initiation. And this means that many people are required to maintain what they do not yet have, what they do not yet acknowledge—a viable relationship with God—as a means of establishing a relationship with God. While many people do not acknowledge God's call and have not responded to that call, they are expected to perform the signs of relationship maintenance as a prerequisite in order to demonstrate that they have such a relationship.

Furthermore, those who are already in right relationship with God read about and enjoy God's amazing grace, which has been given to them without requirements. They then apply the idea of God's grace to the obligations of relationship maintenance by thinking that God will always maintain the relationship as a function of His radical grace. Thus, they ask people to engage the signs of relationship maintenance before people are in relationship, before people have heard and responded to God's call, God's grace.

But that's not all. Once people are in relationship with God they are too often taught that the maintenance of the relationship is also pure grace, pure gift, which means that they do not need to actively engage in maintenance of the relationship. So, non-believers are expected to show the signs of belief as a way to become believers, and believers are expected not to show the signs of belief, not to engage in the maintenance of the relationship, as a way to maintain their belief. But this is all completely backwards!

This is particularly true among Evangelical Christians since the Second Great Awakening and tends to dominate contemporary Christianity in way too many churches and denominations. This problem (the reversal of the order of the elements of salvation and the maintenance of a personal relationship with God), which originated in antiquity, was a major problem in Solomon's Temple, evidenced by the prophets. The problem was resurrected in the Second Temple establishment, and in spite of Paul's teaching and the destruction of the Second Temple, it continues to be a problem today.

Actually, God initiates a personal relationship by sending His Holy Spirit to inhabit the life of the believer. And once the Holy Spirit so inhabits a person, the Spirit Himself guides and directs the person to respond to God, and to maintain the relationship. So, there is a sense in which God has a relationship with Himself through the Person of the Holy Spirit who inhabits believers. And this special relationship constitutes the believer's union with Christ. Such are the sons of Abraham.

JUSTIFY THE GENTILES

Do what to who? Justify (δικαιόω) means to make a thing what it ought to be, what it was designed to be, to bring a thing to the completion of its created purpose. And because it applies to people in this world, in which time is a central reality, such justification takes time in this time-bound world. It is a process, and like all time-dependent processes it has a beginning, a middle, and an end (*telos* or completion). So, the analysis and understanding of justification must take time into consideration, which means that justification is dynamic, it develops over time.[1]

Paul taught that this justification by God began in earnest through the birth, life, death, resurrection, and ascension of Jesus Christ in history. Of course, God had been planning for this from before the

---

1 This analysis may seem more Catholic than Protestant because this distinction was argued about during the Reformation, and since. The resolution that I offer but not defend here is that the biblical uses of the ideas of justification and sanctification are not as clean and neat as we Protestants tend to make them. And the reality of salvation is that justification and sanctification never appear alone, but always together.

beginning, before time itself, or time as we know and experience it, began. Because justification is like a seed, it required some preparation of the soil. And because this seed was planted in time, in history, the preparation was also historic, progressive. The Old Testament provides the telling of that preparation in history. It foreshadows the coming of Messiah, whom Christians know as Jesus Christ.

God's justification, then, involves all three of the time-related pieces of justification—beginning, middle, and end or completion. Paul argued that the advent of Jesus Christ, His birth, life, and death, qualified as the *earnest* beginning, manifested in history. The Holy Spirit is referred to as the deposit, seal, and earnest in the hearts of Christians (2 Corinthians 1:22; 5:5; Ephesians 1:13-14; 4:30). The Holy Spirit is God's seal on His people, His claim on His property—us. The Greek word translated *seal* (ἀρραβών) in these passages indicates a pledge, that is, part of the purchase price or property given in advance as a security deposit. God does not renege on His promises. He completes His plans, not in the ways that we expect Him to, or in the time frame that we expect, but in His own way and time.

The Holy Spirit has come as a first installment or *earnest* to assure us that our full inheritance as children of God will be delivered. We don't use *earnest* this way much any more, but it means something of value given by one person to another to bind or seal a contract, or in this case a covenant. The Holy Spirit has been given to confirm to us that we belong to God who has granted His Spirit as a gift (Ephesians 2:8-9). God renews and sanctifies us through the bestowal of His Holy Spirit, who produces the desire to love and serve God in His people. God accepts those who love and want to serve Him. Such people are regarded as His adopted children. Christ has given His Holy Spirit as a kind of down payment, a sign of His intention to complete His mission, both individually and in history. The proof of the Spirit's presence in the lives of believers begins with repentance, and flowers into increasing conformity to God's will, a personal passion for prayer and praise, and genuine love for His people, which manifests as the fruit of the Spirit (Galatians 5:22-23). These things provide evidence that the Holy Spirit has begun the renewal process and that the Christian has been sealed or marked for the final day of redemption.

THE GENTILES

Paul said that the message about Jesus Christ that he was teaching was the gospel in seed form that had been given "to Abraham beforehand when it (Scripture) said, 'Through you all nations will be blessed'" (v. 8, Genesis 12:3). Therefore, those who believe this message that Paul was teaching about Jesus Christ "are blessed along with Abraham" (v. 9). Paul's message was what Abraham believed, though Abraham did not know the details of how history would play out. If Abraham was able to believe without knowing the details, then we who have witnessed the details being played out in history and in our own lives should believe all the more. This common belief provides unity with Abraham. It makes believers into Abraham's children. This is the faith that justifies.

God planned on justifying the gentiles (ἔθνος), ethnicities or nations. How many gentiles? All (πᾶς) of them, which brings up an old theological problem that has divided Christians for millennia. The Greek word simply means *all*, but when we look around our world we see that all gentiles are not justified, not all are believers. The traditional attempts to understand this dilemma have lead to the doctrines of universal atonement on the one hand and limited or particular atonement on the other. Believers have been arguing about this issue since Abraham.

Both views lead to theological problems unless time is factored into the equation. Clearly, not everyone in the world believes, yet God's words are clear. And because this justifying of the gentiles is at the heart of God's mission in this world of time and history, time and history are necessary for a correct understanding of God's intention. This means that this issue of who will be saved (all in every nation or some from every nation) is not static but dynamic. It involves time, a process that matures over time, like a seed.

The Old Testament is the story of the preparation of the soil, of history. The birth, death, and resurrection of Jesus Christ culminated in the bestowal of the Holy Spirit (Acts 2), who planted the seed in history. That seed produced the church, which has been growing ever since in every nation on earth. The church in every nation has been producing gospel fruit. And the purpose of fruit is to feed the new seeds that are produced over time. Thus, seeds and fruit are being scattered all over the world, and in time God's crop will dominate the world.

Does this mean that every person who has ever lived in history will be saved? Of course not! But it does mean that all of the ethnicities of the world will be included in the final harvest. It simply means that the church started small and will continue to grow to numerically dominate humanity over time. We get into unnecessary difficulty when we try to apply mathematical specificity to a concept in a narrative form.

UNDER CURSE

In order to understand how and why those who depend on the law are under a curse we need to first understand what Paul means by *curse* (κατάρα) and what he means by *law* (νόμος). The curse is not part of the Ten Commandments, but it is part of the law in a general way because, for instance, Deuteronomy 28:16-35 says that

> "if you will not obey the voice of the LORD your God or be careful to
> do all his commandments and his statutes that I command you today,
> then all these curses shall come upon you and overtake you ...."

Deuteronomy is referred to as the book of the law, yet the first five books of the Bible are also referred to as the law or Torah.[2] Paul was simply pointing to, and the Greek word (κατάρα) literally means through or because of an imprecation, an act of calling down a curse that invokes evil or harm, which is exactly what we find in Deuteronomy 28:15-ff and elsewhere in Scripture.

This raises the issue of whether God is the cause or source of evil, and it poses a significant problem because of the history that testifies to the fact that the whole Bible is the Word of God, that the first five books of the Old Testament are called the Torah, usually interpreted as law, and that the book of Deuteronomy itself is called the book of law. Yet, Paul clearly said here and elsewhere (Romans 3:20) that God's law is the source of our awareness of sin.

The solution to this problem is to understand the difference between *sin and the awareness of sin*, or *evil and the awareness of evil*. The traditional answer to the problem of evil is to note that it originated in

---

2   Yet, *Torah* also refers to much more than this. See *Torah*, p. 40.

this world from the serpent in Genesis 3, and when Adam and Eve disobeyed God by eating of the forbidden fruit. It is no small thing that this act of disobedience is called *fruit*, particularly in light of all that Christ said about fruit, and Paul's injunction to produce the fruit of the spirit (Galatians 5:22-23). In contrast stand the works of the flesh (Galatians 5:19-21), though these could also be called *fruit* of the flesh. Comparing these two kinds of fruit provides a useful picture of two divergent ways of living in the world.

Only when people see that God opposes the works or fruit of the flesh, as Paul has delineated them throughout his various writings, can we come to understand that God's law makes us aware of our sin by forbidding it. Apart from God's proscriptions people would simply assume that such works of the flesh are the ordinary way that the world works, and adapt to them, accept them as being normal. So, God's proscription against them causes us to notice them, to question their normalcy because God has issued an imprecation against them. God's imprecation can almost be understood as common sense, in that if you engage in these behaviors, things will not go well for you.

THE LAW

Also at the heart of this issue is Paul's use of the term *law* (νόμος). What exactly does Paul mean by the *law*? As I argued earlier, Paul's understanding of the term issued from his training as a Pharisee and would have included *Torah Shebichtav* (Torah that is written) and *Torah Shebe'al Peh* (Torah that is spoken). Torah for Paul at that time would have included the Old Testament, the Talmud, the Midrash, and the decisions of the Sanhedrin, the ongoing spoken or living Torah. As a Pharisee, Saul would have been devoted to these teachings, but the converted Paul, who wrote to the Galatians, made a firm and faithful distinction between the intention of the Ten Commandments (spirit vs. letter, 2 Corinthians 3:6), the laws of Moses, and the traditions of the Pharisees.

The essential meaning of νόμος (law) suggests a norm, anything established, anything received by usage, like a custom, law, or official command. We might think of it as meaning the *usual practice*, and in this case, the usual practice of the Jews. But with Paul's new belief in Jesus Christ as the fulfillment of Messiah, Jesus Christ was understood as the new Moses, as a lawgiver whose position in Torah (dynamically as Paul understood it) superseded all of the previous elements of Torah. Jesus Christ, then, superseded or trumped the Old Testament, the Talmud, the Midrash, and the decisions of the Sanhedrin.

Jewish law, the Torah, was also theocratic. It included what we call religious and civil law, and it was dynamic not static. The best of the Jewish commentators had been collected and included in Torah over the centuries and had provided contemporary interpretation and understanding of God's word in the same way that the Old Testament prophets had provided contemporary interpretation and understanding of God's word during the various times in which they wrote. Thus, Torah was understood to be a growing, living, dynamic accumulation of God's word, God's law.

Paul's argument with the errant Judiazing Galatian leaders was that by turning back to what they had known as Torah amounted to ignoring or discounting the contribution of Jesus Christ to Torah, to the law of God. Of course, Jesus Christ needed to be understood in the light of the tradition in which He had come—as did all the prophets, but to return to that tradition apart from applying His corrections was worse than knowing nothing of God's mission through the Jews. It would be worse than being a gentile, an unbeliever.

Paul's position was that God's original and most important communication to His people came from Mount Sinai, the Ten Commandments written in stone that Moses had brought down from the mountain. These original Ten Commandments constituted the heart of Jewish culture and society, and were intended for all humanity. However, Paul had come to learn that Jewish culture and society had turned in upon itself by interpreting and understanding the Ten Commandments to be exclusively for them, for Jews—even though Scripture explicitly said and implied that God's blessings, specifically the giving of the Ten Commandments, were to provide a blessing for the whole world—though the Jews had the particular responsibility of preserving the history of the development of God's blessings to the world. Only the Jews could do this because God's original message, the Ten Commandments, which needed to come to some particular people in written form, had come to *them*.

Paul's position, then, was neither that of the Judaizers nor of the antinomians, errant Christians who denied moral law by invoking grace. Christians were neither bound by Old Testament law, nor completely free to ignore it. Rather, Christians needed to understand Jesus Christ, which meant both understanding the tradition from which He came—the Old Testament law, and to both see the Old Testament in the light of Christ and apply the light of Christ to that tradition. Jesus had come, not with a new teaching, but with a renewed expression of God's original teaching of the Ten Commandments. And this was nothing more than what Jewish Rabbis had been doing themselves for centuries, except that Jesus was now applying correction by providing a new adaptation and application of Moses' law, not simply, woodenly interpreting and applying Moses' words as the Pharisees had been doing.

How do we know that Jesus Christ was authorized to interpret and apply Moses' law differently, to correct the Second Temple understanding of Moses that had been codified and justified by the Pharisees? This is an important concern that has been poorly understood and not universally accepted throughout history. Just as the Second Temple establishment understanding of Israel and her history continued to deny the teaching and corrections provided by her own prophets as the Jewish authorities ignored those teachings because of the veil that blinded them, so that same mindset infected many early Christians, especially these Galatian Judaizers. Unfortunately, many of the Judaizers did not heed Paul's teaching and continued to Judaize Christianity, which can be seen in the reinstitution of many Second Temple priesthood practices in Christianity at Rome.[3]

DIVORCE

One of the most significant areas that Jesus corrected by providing a new adaptation and application of Moses' law was the traditional teaching of divorce.

---

3   This is a significant claim for which detailed discussion lies beyond the scope of the present focus. In view are the Medieval cathedrals with their elaborate robes and liturgies as being the resurrection of Second Temple ritualistic ideas, but in the name of Christ.

"And Pharisees came up to him and tested him by asking, 'Is it lawful to divorce one's wife for any cause?' He answered, 'Have you not read that he who created them from the beginning made them male and female, and said, 'Therefore a man shall leave his father and his mother and hold fast to his wife, and the two shall become one flesh? So they are no longer two but one flesh. What therefore God has joined together, let not man separate.' They said to him, 'Why then did Moses command one to give a certificate of divorce and to send her away?' He said to them, 'Because of your hardness of heart Moses allowed you to divorce your wives, but from the beginning it was not so. And I say to you: whoever divorces his wife, except for sexual immorality, and marries another, commits adultery'" (Matthew 19:3-9).

The deeper significance of this story, the metastory, is not about divorce, but is about Jesus' role as a new prophetic law-giver who came to perfect Moses' law. And in order to perfect Moses' law, Jesus noted that there is a difference between God's Word or God's intention, and the written words of Moses and the Sanhedrin. Jesus challenged the sacrosanctity of the Old Testament that had grown increasingly rigid over time, which was precisely what the Pharisees didn't like. Jesus contrasted the old way or teaching with a new way or teaching—though it wasn't actually new, but only renewed, adapted for the new situation. The same kind of thing has happened again in our day as the dynamism of Jesus' way has calcified over time and new Pharisees have risen to power the twenty-first century.

The same issue continues in Matthew 19 in a slightly different way:

"The same day Sadducees came to him, who say that there is no resurrection, and they asked him a question, saying, 'Teacher, Moses said, "If a man dies having no children, his brother must marry the widow and raise up offspring for his brother." Now there were seven brothers among us. The first married and died, and having no offspring left his wife to his brother. So too the second and third, down to the seventh. After them all, the woman died. In the resurrection, therefore, of the seven, whose wife will she be? For they all had her. But Jesus answered them, 'You are wrong, because you know neither the Scriptures nor the power of God. For in the resurrection they neither marry nor are given in marriage, but are like angels in heaven'" (Matthew19:23-30).

Here we see that this aspect of Moses' law does not apply "in the resurrection." The question is not posed in order to stump Jesus. It is a serious question about how Moses' law will apply in the administration of Christ. Nor is Jesus' answer about the nature of angels, but is about the fact that the Sadducees were just like the Pharisees in that they did not know their own Scriptures or the real power of God. It was about the extent and application of Mosaic Law.

The traditional understanding is that Moses was the author of the Torah or Pentateuch, the first five books of the Old Testament. While this view has been widely criticized by various scholars over the past two hundred years, it is consonant with both Scripture and the overwhelming majority of Christian tradition, excluding the contemporary era. Rather than get bogged down in this argument, allow me to suggest that Moses served in the role of the high priest of the earliest forerunner of the Sanhedrin, which began when Jethro suggested that he gather able men to help Moses by serving as judges.

> "You and the people with you will certainly wear yourselves out, for the thing is too heavy for you. You are not able to do it alone. Now obey my voice; I will give you advice, and God be with you! You shall represent the people before God and bring their cases to God, and you shall warn them about the statutes and the laws, and make them know the way in which they must walk and what they must do. Moreover, look for able men from all the people, men who fear God, who are trustworthy and hate a bribe, and place such men over the people as chiefs of thousands, of hundreds, of fifties, and of tens" (Exodus 18:18).

Those elders eventually coalesced into seventy elders who ruled Israel and eventually became the Sanhedrin.

> "Then the LORD said to Moses, 'Gather for me seventy men of the elders of Israel, whom you know to be the elders of the people and officers over them, and bring them to the tent of meeting, and let them take their stand there with you. And I will come down and talk with you there. And I will take some of the Spirit that is on you and put it on them, and they shall bear the burden of the people with you, so that you may not bear it yourself alone'" (Numbers 11:16-17).

These elders helped Moses rule, and out of that rule the Torah or Pen-tateuch took shape as various laws and stories were written and collected. Thus, Moses was the chief editor, but had the help of those whom God had also entrusted with such responsibility. Thus, the argument about Moses' authorship of the Pentateuch has been both an unnecessary and unhelpful distraction with regard to understanding the Bible.

Jesus, then, was able to distinguish between God's communication (the Ten Commandments) and the written words and instructions of Moses (the Pentateuch). Let me say again that all of the words of the Pentateuch are God's words conveyed through Moses and the elders, and represent their faithful efforts to interpret and apply God's communication (the Ten Commandments) in the midst of the circumstances in which they lived as nomads. It's not that God's words were different than Moses' words, but that Moses' words (the Penta-teuch) comprised a faithful interpretation, understanding, and application of God's words (the Ten Commandments) that met the needs of Israel in the desert.[4] We can learn much from biblical law, and to understand Jesus correctly we must apply the light of Christ to Deuteronomic Law because engaging that process will bring Christ to light more clearly for us, for people in the current generation.

Indeed, each of the biblical covenants involved a renewed, faithful interpretation, understanding, and application of God's words (the Ten Commandments) for each new situation, historical era, covenant, or dispensation of God's people as Israel grew and matured.[5] The process stalled when Israel decided to establish a kingdom. Samuel warned them, but they persisted for centuries. Jesus, then, carried this tradition forward as He provided a model for a renewed interpretation,

---

4   God's Word is eternal, never changing. God's intention is eternal, never changing. But God's words, the words of the Bible do change according to interpretation and translation. They have changed from Hebrew to Greek to English and from KJV to RSV to ESV, etc. The words themselves change because *we* change, and in order for us to understand God's eternal Word as He wants us to understand it, we must adjust the words without changing God's intended meaning. This idea is far from new or novel in that it goes back to the transmission of the biblical text itself. And such changes have been in process for a very long time.

5   This involves the process of sanctification—growth and maturity, which happens on both the individual and social or historic levels. Individuals grow and mature, and so do societies.

understanding, and application of the Ten Commandments in His sermon on the mount.

When the Pharisees heard about what He had been saying, they rightly understood what Jesus had been doing, and they didn't like it because it meant the end of their administration. They understood that Jesus was ushering in a new covenant or a new understanding of the covenant, and they challenged Him (Matthew 19:3-9). The fact that Jesus was calling for something quite different from the Second Temple establishment can be seen in His own analysis of the problem:

> "The scribes and the Pharisees sit on Moses' seat, so do and observe whatever they tell you, but not the works they do. For they preach, but do not practice. They tie up heavy burdens, hard to bear, and lay them on people's shoulders, but they themselves are not willing to move them with their finger. They do all their deeds to be seen by others. For they make their phylacteries broad and their fringes long, and they love the place of honor at feasts and the best seats in the synagogues and greetings in the marketplaces and being called rabbi by others. But you are not to be called rabbi, for you have one teacher, and you are all brothers. And call no man your father on earth, for you have one Father, who is in heaven. Neither be called instructors, for you have one instructor, the Christ. The greatest among you shall be your servant. Whoever exalts himself will be humbled, and whoever humbles himself will be exalted" (Matthew 23:1-12).

This is the same problem that Jeremiah, Isaiah, and the prophets from old complained about. The central problem was not with the people, though the people tended to follow their leaders, which means that the central problem was—and still is—with religious leaders. One problem was exemplified by the Pharisees who were sticklers about the obedience to the law and were stuck in the past, and another problem was exemplified by the Judaizers, who presented themselves as progressives who wanted to integrate Jesus into the existing Temple system. But because the Temple system would take precedence over Jesus, these so-called progressives were also stuck in the past.

The new covenant that Jesus ushered in had been on deck since Jeremiah called for it before the destruction of the First Temple. The only thing new about the new covenant was God's impending removal of the Temple and Jerusalem in A.D. 70, which brought the

Second Temple administration to a visceral halt and birthed the New Covenant. The relationship between the Old and New Covenants was like the relationship between placenta and a child at birth.

10. Faith

... *"The righteous shall live by faith." But the law is not of faith,
rather "The one who does them shall live by them."*

—Galatians 3:11b-12

gain, to be righteous is more about being than doing. It is a
state or condition of the soul that is commensurate with God's
will. It is about intention as much as action, about attitude as
much as accomplishment, about being as much as behavior. It's not that
Christians are sinless, but that Christians ought to sin less over time.
Righteousness (from the root δίκη) is descriptive of people who fulfill
their purpose, people who are what they ought to be, are what they
were created to be, people who have integrity of thought, word, and
deed. When a person is what s/he was created to be by God, s/he is
righteous.

If we can relate it to manufacturing, a righteous thing would have
no manufacturing flaws. It would perfectly conform to the prototype after which it was designed and made. However, in the world in which
we live, no such perfect manufacturing process is possible because the
nature of the world mitigates against all such perfection. Theologically
we say that the world itself is fallen. Sin has tainted this world, skewed it
so that it can never quite measure up to mathematical perfection. So, our
righteousness is not something hard and fast, but is a quality of grada-
tion. Mathematical perfection in this world is not possible. Like a
calculus, perfection and righteousness are things that are only approxi-
mated. But neither are perfection and righteousness static, they are

dynamic, living characteristics. They exist in time because we exist in time.

Perfection and righteousness in this world grow, mature, and ripen over time. They are teleological, which means that they have a purpose which becomes increasingly fulfilled over time. Paul's statement, "ο δικαιος εκ πιστεως ζησεται," literally means that the righteous live *out of* or *from* faith. Their lives emanate from their faith. It is as much a description of a reality as it is a call to action. It simply means that genuine righteousness and genuine faith are always found together. You can't have one without the other. But their order is important: faith is the engine of righteousness, which produces justice.

Righteousness is the condition that comes from being faithful. We were created to be faithful, to befriend God, and when we believe God, trust God, and act on that belief, we prove our justification. God counts us righteous, not because of what we do or don't do, but because of our belief, which produces trust and response to His love. It's not that Christians are better than other people. Most probably aren't, but God is! So, when people believe God, trust God, and try to conform their lives to please God, they become better than they used to be.

People who don't believe or trust God are often incensed by the idea that people can become better than they used to be simply by believing and trusting God. They demand action and proof. And when believers don't measure up to the unbeliever's idea of perfection, they are accused of being full of pride, thinking that they are better than others. But this is not at all what believers think or how they see it. Believers know that God is better than they themselves are, and that their own belief and trust of God has helped them to become better than they used to be. But that doesn't mean that they are better than other people. We are not to compare ourselves with one another. We are to compare ourselves with Christ.

It is the self-righteous who think that they are better than others—and certainly better than Christians! And when self-righteous people call themselves Christian they communicate their own self-righteous attitude to others, but call it faithfulness. And this, then, leads unbelievers to mistakenly think that Christians are self-righteous snobs who think that they are better than others, not realizing that those who do this are certainly not being faithful and may not even be actual Christians. The problem is that neither the self-righteous, self-proclaimed Christians, nor unbelievers understand that *their* idea of Christianity is not actually Christianity. Nonetheless, both call it *Christianity* because they don't know any better. So, false ideas about Christianity are perpetuated.

Actually all of the ancient heresies are alive and well in the contemporary world—even in the churches. None of those errant traditions actually died out. They, too, have grown and matured. People who don't actually believe have coopted Christian language and practices to produce ideas and activities that sound Christian to the immature, but aren't. Like those in Matthew 7:21, who thought that they were Christian and even did the things that faithful Christians do, they were rejected by Christ because they were self-righteous and unrepentant.

UPRIGHT

Paul reached back to Habakkuk, prior to the destruction of the First Temple to substantiate the principle of faith in Christ:

> "Look, the one whose desires are not upright will faint from exhaustion, but the person of integrity will live because of his faithfulness" (Habakkuk 2:4, NET).

The critical elements regarding the righteousness of faith are that we first must *want* to please God, and second, we must know what actually pleases Him. Both of these things must be active, for we will not engage the time to learn about what God wants if we don't first love and want to please Him. And yet the mere desire to please Him, apart from knowing what will actually please Him, is like an empty thought, rainless clouds, a car without fuel, etc.

Faith is a source of energy and endurance. That energy comes from the Holy Spirit who inhabits the faithful. The faithful are in union with God through the Spirit. Such union is the very definition of faithfulness, and its fruit is more about character than behavior, though the two things cannot be separated.

Though we think of righteousness in terms of perfection, we must not think of it as some kind of mathematical or abstract perfection because that mindset is Gnostic, not biblical, abstract, not real. Biblical perfection (*telos*) is the goal, endpoint, conclusion, or purpose, and in order to arrive at that point it is necessary to follow the trajectory through time to that endpoint from one's present position, location, or circumstance. That trajectory is like a path or way that leads to the endpoint, the perfection. Of course, there are a variety of possible trajectories that can lead to the endpoint, so it is possible and necessary to make mid-course corrections. But the endpoint must always be active in one's mind.

In fact, the trajectory is best calculated backwards, starting from the end point and moving to the beginning or present point. It's like a laser guided missile where the laser marks the target—the end point— that the missile actively seeks. The marking of the target is separate from the mechanism of the missile. The missile cannot locate, find, or mark a target on its own, but depends on another to mark the target. The missile, then, adjusts its trajectory to hit the target. In this analogy, we are the missiles and Jesus is the targeter. He has marked the target, the endpoint, which is His righteousness, His character, and when we are on a trajectory that will bring us to that point, we are justified in God's eyes. God knows that Jesus' targeting and the power of the Holy Spirit will not fail to accomplish His purposes, to bring us to that endpoint.

NOT OF FAITH

Law does not produce faith or belief. Law is imposed on people, regardless of what people think about it or believe about it. Law in its most basic form is simply rules that are imposed by some authority by threat of force against noncompliance. It doesn't matter if the laws are good or bad, right or wrong. The law must simply be obeyed because it is the law.

Law is cultural, social. Individuals cannot make their own laws. However, faith is an individual thing. Law cannot dictate faith. People do make their own rules for behavior, but such rules do not have the force of law. Belief and faith operate at an individual level, where law, custom, and norm (νόμος) operate at the social level.

People always act in ways that are consistent with their beliefs, but not necessarily consistent with their words. Sometimes actions are consistent with weak or nonexistent faith. People often say one thing but do another, and visa versa. The *Westminster Larger Catechism* speaks to this issue of the use of the law:

> Q. 94. Is there any use of the moral law since the fall?
>
> A. Although no man, since the fall, can attain to righteousness and life by the moral law; yet there is great use thereof, as well common to all men, as peculiar either to the unregenerate, or the regenerate.
>
> Q. 95. Of what use is the moral law to all men?
>
> A. The moral law is of use to all men, to inform them of the holy nature and will of God, and of their duty, binding them to walk accordingly; to convince them of their disability to keep it, and of the sinful pollution of their nature, hearts, and lives: to humble them in the sense of their sin and misery, and thereby help them to a clearer sight of the need they have of Christ, and of the perfection of his obedience.
>
> Q. 96. What particular use is there of the moral law to unregenerate men?
>
> A. The moral law is of use to unregenerate men, to awaken their consciences to flee from the wrath to come, and to drive them to Christ; or, upon the continuance in the estate and way of sin, to leave them inexcusable, and under the curse thereof.
>
> Q. 97. What special use is there of the moral law to the regenerate?
>
> A. Although they that are regenerate, and believe in Christ, be delivered from the moral law as a covenant of works, so as thereby they are neither justified nor condemned; yet besides the general uses thereof common to them with all men, it is of special use, to show them how much they are bound to Christ for his fulfilling it, and enduring the curse thereof in their stead, and for their good; and thereby to provoke them to more thankfulness, and to express the same in their greater care to conform themselves thereunto as the rule of their obedience.

Question 95 says that the moral law applies to all humanity, saved or lost, and though it cannot cause salvation, it is useful to all. In particular that use is to show the universal need for Christ and His word for the securing of salvation for believers, who are provoked to thankfulness and inspired to obedience.

Another way to describe the use of the law is to think of it as a mirror, a bridle, and a map. The law shows us ourselves as God sees us, as helpless sinners caught in a torrent of sin. It also serves as a deterrent to steer us away from harmful behaviors. And it functions as a map to show us our proper destination. But the damnable thing about the law is that it shows us our sin and what we ought to do to escape and avoid it, but the law itself is unable to keep us from sin because it does not and cannot of itself affect our love of sin. In spite of all that it does do, it does not change our addiction to sin. The law shows us our sin, but leaves us as slaves to it because the law has no power of personal motivation because it operates at the social level. It provides a sense of duty and obligation, but not the passion, motivation, and personal desire to act on it. The motivation of the law is fear of punishment, not love of the law giver. So it makes us aware of our sin and our duty to avoid sin, and leaves us there. In the light of the law we know what we *should* do, but we still don't *want* to do it. Or we may think that we want it, but at the same time we cannot stop sinning.

11. Curse Reversed

Christ redeemed us from the curse of the law by becoming a curse for us—for it is written, "Cursed is everyone who is hanged on a tree"—so that in Christ Jesus the blessing of Abraham might come to the Gentiles, so that we might receive the promised Spirit through faith.

—Galatians 3:13-14

We are not used to thinking of ourselves as being under a curse. Nor are we used to thinking of God as cursing people. But if we believe that the Bible is true, then both of these things are also true. One of the places in Scripture to see this is Deuteronomy 27:9-10:

> "Then Moses and the Levitical priests said to all Israel, 'Keep silence and hear, O Israel: this day you have become the people of the LORD your God. You shall therefore obey the voice of the LORD your God, keeping his commandments and his statutes, which I command you today.'"

Various curses are then listed, and it is useful to review them:

> "'Cursed be the man who makes a carved or cast metal image, an abomination to the LORD, a thing made by the hands of a craftsman, and sets it up in secret.' And all the people shall answer and say, 'Amen.' 'Cursed be anyone who dishonors his father or his mother.' And all the people shall say, 'Amen.' 'Cursed be anyone who moves his neighbor's landmark.' And all the people shall say, 'Amen.' 'Cursed be anyone who misleads a blind man on the road.' And all the people shall say, 'Amen.' 'Cursed be anyone who perverts the justice due to the sojourner, the fatherless, and the widow.' And all the people shall say, 'Amen.' 'Cursed be anyone who lies with his father's wife, because he has uncovered his father's nakedness.' And all the people shall say,

'Amen.' 'Cursed be anyone who lies with any kind of animal.' And all the people shall say, 'Amen.' 'Cursed be anyone who lies with his sister, whether the daughter of his father or the daughter of his mother.' And all the people shall say, 'Amen.' 'Cursed be anyone who lies with his mother-in-law.' And all the people shall say, 'Amen.' 'Cursed be anyone who strikes down his neighbor in secret.' And all the people shall say, 'Amen.' 'Cursed be anyone who takes a bribe to shed innocent blood.' And all the people shall say, 'Amen.' 'Cursed be anyone who does not confirm the words of this law by doing them.' And all the people shall say, 'Amen'" (Deuteronomy 27:15-26).

MOSES' LAW

There are several interesting things to notice about these verses that challenge our common presuppositions. First, notice who speaks these curses, who brought them to the people. It was "Moses and the Levitical priests" (Deuteronomy 27:9). The significance of this fact is that it was not the pure voice of the Lord like the Ten Commandments. Many other times Moses had no problem quoting God, but not here. Here it was not *thus says the Lord*, but Moses and the priests who are quoted. The ESV's use of punctuation in this section is also odd, which further suggests that something different is happening here. There are quotes within quotes, which suggests second hand information.

Curses are judicial in nature. Curses are the result of a judgment, the consequence of a decision. These curses are promised as a consequence of certain behaviors. They are judicial statutes that specify that certain behaviors will be met with judicial punishments. They are loosely related to the Ten Commandments. We might even say that they are interpretations and expansions of the Ten Commandments that were directed at particular problems, which we assume were problems that Moses and the priests were trying to curb. Each one was proclaimed in public and the people attested to or swore obedience to each in turn.

Each of the specified behaviors was included in the Decalog's proscriptions, but additional specificity was then added by Moses and the seventy. No doubt Moses and the seventy had met before hand to hash out the language used here in this liturgical setting where the people pledged allegiance to the words spoken—to the words of Moses and the priests.

I don't mean to suggest or imply that God was not involved with Moses and the seventy in formulating these words—He was! But so was Moses and the seventy elders. A careful reading shows that Moses himself even made it clear that these words were not the pure words of the Lord Himself, but primarily belonged to him and the priests. Nor am I trying to take exception to any of these prohibitions. Rather, I am simply pointing out that Moses himself said that the consequences of these prohibitions (the curses) issued from him and the priests, who were endeavoring to be faithful to God's original words—the Ten Commandments. They were applying the Ten Commandments to the specific situation and needs of the people in that day. And we are well-advised to continue to honor these prohibitions and their curses. However, to honor them we must first understand them correctly, as Scripture itself intends us to. And then we are to apply the light of Christ to them, to see them in the light of Christ.

There are huge implications that can be garnered from these observations about Scripture captured in Matthew, and Jesus Himself made them. When the Pharisees pressed Jesus about His views of divorce that were in opposition to Moses' teaching, He said, "Because of your hardness of heart *Moses allowed* you to divorce your wives, but from the beginning it was not so" (Matthew 19:8, italics mine). God through Moses had said to Adam concerning marriage, "Therefore a man shall leave his father and his mother and *hold fast* to his wife, and they shall become one flesh" (Genesis 2:24, italics mine). The clear implication in Genesis is the perpetual unity of the marriage, or no divorce. Jesus distinguished between God's intention and Moses' teaching in the Old Testament.[1]

Another time the Pharisees criticized Jesus' disciples for picking corn on the Sabbath and Jesus answered them by saying that "the Sabbath was made for man, not man for the Sabbath" (Mark 2:27). Here the Pharisees thought that Jesus was violating one of the Ten Commandments, but He was not. Rather, He interpreted the Sabbath

---

1   This was not new with Jesus. The prophets of old accused the priests of old of lying, of misrepresenting God (Jeremiah 14:14, 29:8; Isaiah 3:13-15, etc.). Just because the priests said that the Lord said something doesn't mean that the Lord actually said it. The implications of this are huge! But they do not negate the veracity of Scripture.

Commandment differently than they did. They had made people slaves to the Sabbath by adding all sorts of extra language and stipulations to the Fourth Commandment. Jesus on the other hand understood the Sabbath to be an act and statement of freedom, not slavery, of rest, not rules. Jesus' understanding of the Sabbath commandment was more in line with the eighth day[2] than the seventh. Thus, Jesus did not violate the intention of Ten Commandments, though He did reinterpret their application.

As noted in *The Backstory*, Jesus was the new Moses in that His teaching trumped that of Moses. Both are interpretations of the original intent of the Ten Commandments for particular people. Jesus fulfilled the ceremonial law and the historical anticipation of Messiah, and in so doing He also provided a reinterpretation of the Ten Commandments by saying that all ten were subsumed in two:

> "You shall love the Lord your God with all your heart and with all your soul and with all your mind. This is the great and first commandment. And a second is like it: You shall love your neighbor as yourself. On these two commandments depend all the Law and the Prophets" (Matthew 22:37-40).

This, however, does not nullify the law of Moses either. The first commandment to love God means that those who love God will also love His story, and will continue to honor, value, and make good use of His story, even if that use is not the same use that His people first made, or have successively made. God's law stands as an eternal (timeless) testimony of the need for Jesus Christ. It doesn't change the value of Moses' law, but it does change our understanding, application, and judicial consequences of it.

Christ died *for* our sin, *because* of our sin. He did not die for any sin of His own, but only because of *our* sin, because of human sinfulness. He died because justice demanded it. What justice? The justice of the Mosaic Law, the Old Testament law that Moses and the Seventy

---

2   Christians worship on the Eighth Day for a variety of reasons, central to which is the fact that Christ fulfilled the Sabbath and that fulfillment inaugurated God's eternal Sabbath, which stands outside of time yet applies to time. See: Exodus 22:30; Leviticus 9:1; 12:3; 14:10,23; 15:14,29; 22:27; 23:36,39; Numbers 6:10; 7:54; 29:35; 1 Kings 8:66; 12:32,33; 2 Chronicles 7:9; 29:17; Nehemiah 8:18; Ezekiel 43:27; Luke 1:59; Acts 7:8; Philippians 3:5.

revealed and codified, the law that was in force when Jesus lived. There are a variety of legitimate ways to understand Christ's sacrifice and death. It can be understood liturgically as the fulfillment of the sacrificial system, economically as payment of the debt humanity owed to God for violation of the covenant, judicially as the human representative who received the death penalty for sin, morally as the establishment of the new Adam, the new prototype of humanity, historically as the culmination of the old age and the establishment of the new age in Christ, spiritually as Christus Victor or the conquering of Satan, sin and death, etc.

Apparently the priests during Jeremiah's day were telling people that it was enough for them to attend to the Temple sacrifices, to bring their sacrifices, pay their tithes, and not worry that they could not fulfill all of God's demands. Jeremiah differed.

> "Tell them that the LORD, the God of Israel, says, 'Anyone who does not keep the terms of the covenant will be under a curse'" (Jeremiah 11:3, NET).

Apparently, the priests in that day didn't stress the fact of the curse. It probably wasn't very popular. Jeremiah said that the priests of the First Temple could not be trusted to speak God's Word correctly, that they were deceiving the people in the name of God, they were under a curse. So, we see again that the prophets warned Israel (and continue to warn us today) that the priests who were responsible for clarifying, keeping, and preaching God's Word cannot always be trusted.

TWO PARTS

There are at least two parts of the curse that God's law brought. The one that we are used to hearing about pertains to our inability to fulfill the law. God demands that we (humanity) obey His law perfectly—fully, but we are not able to do so. No one, no human being is able to fulfill or live in perfect obedience to God's law. Thus, God demands of *humanity* what no *individual* can actually do or accomplish in and of him- or herself.

Why would God do that? In order to demonstrate something to us, in order to make a point that we would otherwise not be able to see. God makes this demand in order to demonstrate that no individual human being can do what He demands. The demand reveals some-

thing important about us by confounding us, by humbling us, by revealing a fundamental need that we cannot supply ourselves. We need
God's Holy Spirit. We are incomplete and unable to be whole (holy)
apart from God's Holy Spirit because sin has alienated us from God. In
the same way that God's Personhood is trifold, so is ours. God's individuality is tripartite, as is ours. Our trinitarian nature is not identical
to God's, but it is similar. We are like Him. And just as He would not
be God, would not be who He is apart from the Holy Spirit, neither
can we be who we are, who we were created to be, apart from God's
Holy Spirit. The curse reveals our need for God's Holy Spirit.

The second part of the curse pertains to our necessarily flawed understanding of God, of His Word, His ways, His Spirit, etc. We
cannot fully, completely, or wholly get God's Word perfectly right—
ever! His Word is timeless, and we are time bound. This means that
whatever understanding, interpretation, and application of God's
Word that we have is bound up in time. It is not, nor can it ever be,
eternal in history. Our understanding, interpretation, and application
of God's Word is limited by time, by our limited time on earth. It has
a shelf-life, a freshness date. It needs to be refreshed every so often or it
goes bad. First it gets stale, then it goes sour, and finally it rots because
God's Word itself is living. However, this time-bound factor is not
part of God's Word, God's will, but is endemic to time, not to God.
It's not that God's Word or God's will goes bad, but that our time
bound understandings, interpretations, and applications restrict our
abilities to adapt to the ongoing dynamism of life, of the ever changing circumstances in which life finds itself. And when we hold on to
old, stale, and/or rotting ways of understanding, interpreting, and/or
applying God's Word, God's will, we are unable to adapt to the dy-
namics that life actually presents to us.

While it is true that the Ten Commandments are timeless in their
intention and expression, much of the application of these commandments that were derived by the seventy elders and codified in
Deuteronomy and elsewhere are time-bound. Application is necessarily directed to a specific situation and context, and when that situation
and context changes the application must also change. But when it
does not change, and when an inappropriate application is provided
for a situation or context that it was not designed for, or when past ap-

plications are woodenly understood in their past codifications, problems ensue. Yesterday's solutions, yesterday's ideas and understandings, are inadequate for today's problems. God's church has always been awash in this difficulty, and this is why revival and reformation are in continual need. God's Word, His intention in the Ten Commandments, needs to be continually refreshed, owned, and applied in the immediate context of the arc of human history.

Thus, every so often we (individuals, churches, societies) need to rethink, reevaluate, and reconsider our understanding, interpretation, and application of God's Word, God's will. And we cannot do this by ourselves. Actually only God Himself can do this, and He does it through His Holy Spirit, who inhabits the lives of believers. This process is part of the curse of the law. It is a curse because it requires the shaking of human foundations, and such shaking is not only disconcerting, it is dangerous. Our sin nature does not like change. We naturally resist it and are suspicious of those who suggest it.

But change is essential for life. Life is a dynamic process, a verb not a noun. Though God Himself does not change, we do. God then adapts to our changes, our growth and maturity by reissuing His covenant intentions every so often. Each instance of this reissued covenant is different yet the same. God restates His original intention and reapplies it to our dynamic conditions, often following some significant historic event that marks a new chapter in human maturity.

The Noahic covenant promised a new start apart from unredeemable sin. The Abrahamic covenant promised a new religion of grace and faith apart from the ancient religion of coercion, domination, and revenge. The Palestinian covenant promised a new home for God's covenant people who were homeless, landless. The Mosaic covenant promised a new culture based on love, respect, and freedom apart from the ancient culture and laws of domination, slavery, and revenge. The Davidic covenant promised that God Himself would guide and dwell among God's covenant people, even in their sin. God would be present, not distant. And the New Covenant in Christ promised the presence and power of God's Holy Spirit to nurture, guide, and protect God's covenant people.

THE BLESSING

Why was Christ crucified?

'...so that in Christ Jesus the blessing of Abraham might come to the Gentiles, so that we might receive the promised Spirit through faith" (v. 14).

Paul said that Abraham was the model, that he believed with no evidence, nothing other than God's promise to make him the father of many. Abraham had faith that God would do what He said He would do. He simply trusted God's Word, a word that came to Abraham audibly, as a voice or idea or however that worked. At that point Abraham did not have the Bible or the tradition of a long established culture. He only had a personal relationship with God through the Holy Spirit. We are to follow Abraham's example, his simple trust of God, of God's Holy Spirit.

But this does not mean that we are free to ignore history or the long biblical tradition that has preserved God's Word, God's will, and God's way through the ages. Abraham did not have these things, but we do. We have so much more than Abraham ever had! This accumulation of tradition makes it both easier and more complex, both simpler and more difficult for us to exercise faith than it was for Abraham. On the one hand, we have an abundance of tradition and witnesses to follow; but on the other hand, we cannot and must not ignore the general accumulated tradition. So many very wise and faithful people have preceded us and left us a great wealth of literature and tradition—and we are obliged to become familiar with it because God's Word, God's will, and God's way inhabits it. God has spoken through it and speaks through it still. Just as God's Word was with the seventy elders as they applied the Ten Commandments to their situation, God continues to guide His church and His people throughout history. But this does not mean that the Bible does not hold a very special place in the process of interpreting and understanding God's Word, nor does it mean that every application God's people try has the same weight of authority as the Bible. Great care must be taken in the handling of God's Word.

Nor does this mean that we must be slaves to what has preceded us, either. God is alive and well. God still speaks. He still speaks through His accumulated tradition, and He still speaks beyond it. God is always saying the same old things in new ways. God speaks from His eternal purpose, His *telos*, not merely from this or that point in the past. He speaks from the future accomplishment of His purpose, and draws people into it, into Himself, into Christ, who is the manifestation of His eternal purpose. God is alive. He is both in time and beyond time.

Those who invest in the stock market are often advised that past performance is not a guide to or a guarantee of future performance. What happened in the past is not necessarily a guide for what will happen in the future. Yet, financial people study past performance carefully and continually. The same caution applies to God. We can trust that God will always be faithful to His covenant, His intent, but not that God will always do the same things in the same ways. It is very useful to know about God's past performance because God doesn't change. But the fact that He Himself doesn't change doesn't mean that He doesn't change how He says things or does things. God is in active relationship with His people, who do change. So, He adjusts to meet our varying needs. When we need encouragement, He encourages us, and when we need discipline, He disciplines us, etc.

Here Paul said that God's ultimate purpose throughout history is to provide "the promised spirit through faith" (v. 14). God neither withholds nor forces the spirit upon anyone. But neither is the spirit separate from faithfulness. They are one and the same thing, like two sides of a single coin. The spirit is manifested through faithfulness, in faithfulness, by faithfulness. Faithfulness is both the root and the fruit of the spirit. And the spirit is both the root and the fruit of faithfulness. It doesn't work one way, it works both ways simultaneously—both/and not either/or. Both sides are necessary for the coin to be a coin.

12. Not Imposed

To give a human example, brothers: even with a man-made covenant, no one annuls it or adds to it once it has been ratified. Now the promises were made to Abraham and to his offspring. It does not say, "And to offsprings," referring to many, but referring to one, "And to your offspring," who is Christ. This is what I mean: the law, which came 430 years afterward, does not annul a covenant previously ratified by God, so as to make the promise void. For if the inheritance comes by the law, it no longer comes by promise; but God gave it to Abraham by a promise. —Galatians 3:15-18

The idea that Paul was trying to convey here is quite simple once it is understood. It's not a new idea, but goes back into antiquity. The Old Testament prophets were well aware of it when they called for a new heart (Ezekiel 36:26, Jeremiah 31:33, etc.). But in Christianity, centuries of confusing exegesis about Paul's letter to the Galatians has taken its toll. And because this argument is at the very heart of the gospel, Satan has spared no quarter in his prosecution of confusion. Paul's idea is that God's blessing or inheritance comes as a gift, not as a reward, nor a wage. It is bestowed not earned. In order for grace to be grace it must be pure gift—unanticipated, unwanted, unearned, and in this case, unconceived (not originated) by human thought.

Paul's larger argument was that Christ came to correct by providing a new adaptation and application of Moses' law, as previously indicated. It is this larger argument that he was working to illustrate here. So, he began by posing an analogy to human law. The idea is that once a man-made human agreement has been ratified or signed it becomes law and cannot be changed. Of course, we know that laws can be changed.

Nonetheless, Paul's intention was to suggest the stability of legal documents. We must not press this analogy too far lest it lose its usefulness.

In contrast to this comes the next verse, which discusses a promise. A promissory agreement is more flexible, easier to change because it does not have the character of law. Abraham's covenant was a covenant of promise, whereas Moses' covenant was a covenant of law. Moses was a law maker, but Abraham received a promise, which was for Abraham and his σπέρμα (*sperma*). It is quite understandable that the Jews thought that this meant his physical children or offspring—and it does. But that is only one of the definitions of the Greek word.

The problem is that if the original gospel (Genesis 12:3) was to include the gentiles, there would have to be a different understanding of this word because gentiles were gentiles because they were not in the Jewish bloodline. This would necessitate a different understanding of the word or idea of Abraham's progeny. The Hebrew word in Genesis 12:3 is מִשְׁפְּחֹת, which literally means *families* or *clans* and implies *nations*. So, if it includes all of the families, clans, and nations of the world, it cannot mean that all of them belonged to the same family, clan, or nation unless we understand all of humanity to have come from the family of Adam, which God does. Nonetheless, it cannot simply mean blood lineage issuing from Abraham as ancient Israel had calculated it.

The best alternative reading comes from typology. Each of the central covenant partners—Adam, Noah, Abraham, Moses, David, and Jesus Christ—can be understood representatively as types. Of course, the two primary types are Adam and Christ. The typological progeny of these types include those who are modeled after their respective spiritual prototype. This is how Paul had come to understand the lineage of humanity. People were either in the line or type of Adam or in the line or type of Christ. It was about character not clan, grace not race.

To indicate this Paul made much ado about the singularity of the word σπέρμα in order to suggest that he was using the term in a different or special way. Similarly, farmers use the word *seed* as a plural noun to represent many individual seeds that share a common type. This is not a complicated idea and would make immediate and clear sense to people familiar with farming. However, the farther away from farming that people are, the more difficult the idea seems to become. The singularity of the seed refers to Christ because He is the prototype, the model for many.

DIVERGENCE

We must not miss the significance of the fact that Moses was in charge of Israel during their forty years in the wilderness, nor that God's residence with Moses in the wilderness was in a tent, a tabernacle—a temporary dwelling. It could be moved when the people moved. It was never intended to be a permanent dwelling. And the story about Moses' and Israel in the wilderness is a story about their lostness, their diversion on the way to the promised land, as a temporary affliction. God provided for and protected them during those lost, nomadic years. Like manna, the Tabernacle was supposed to be a temporary thing.

During that time God told Moses that he would not be able to enter the promised land himself (Deuteronomy 1:31). Why not? The traditional understanding is that in the midst of the people complaining against Moses and Aaron for bringing them out into the wilderness, God instructed Moses about how to provide them with water from a rock. Moses was to speak to the rock and it would yield water. But when Moses gathered the people, he did not carefully follow God's instructions. Rather than speak to it, he hit the rock with his staff, and then took credit for the miracle. He was not careful in his obedience. He didn't do exactly as he had been instructed. He had not been careful with God's Word—and this story provides a very important understanding about Moses. Moses had inserted himself into the interpretation and execution of God's Word, and doing so he limited its application to his own time, which makes sense. What else could he do?

We should not assume that this was the only time that Moses ever did such a thing, that this one event warranted his exclusion from the promised land. Rather, this event illustrated a pattern in Moses' life. The highlighting of this story, of setting such a significant consequence for such an apparently trivial matter, suggests a deeper issue, a pattern of behavior illustrated by this story. Moses inserted himself into his interpretation and execution of God's Word regularly, which is the same kind of understanding that Jesus communicated about Moses in His response to the Pharisee's question about divorce. Moses' laws of divorce factored in the hardness of heart in Jewish culture at that time, during their wilderness wandering. That hardness of heart was not supposed to continue.

Moses' teaching about divorce was set in terms of permission rather than prohibition, as the Ten Commandments were. Moses turned God's model of marriage into a kind of limited permission for divorce. By setting up rules about when they could divorce, Moses drew a line in the sand, which focused attention on the line, on the rules of divorce rather than on the ideal model of marriage. In order to be a faithful husband, then, husbands would need to keep their wives from crossing that line, from breaking the rules. Rather than husbands focusing on their own relationship with God and with their wives, they focused on keeping their wives away from the forbidden line as a matter of *their* responsibility. Rather than being a partner in covenant marriage, husbands became marriage referees. By giving permission to divorce in some situations, Moses focused on divorce rather than marriage, on keeping the marriage from divorce, rather than making the marriage all that it could be.

Moses was forbidden from entering the promised land because of his tendency to insert himself into the interpretation and execution of God's Word. This is the very thing that was on Jesus' mind during his sermon on the mount, when He kept saying, "You have heard that it was said," followed by, "But I say to you," in Matthew 5. That sermon served as a new adaptation and application of God's Word for life in Christ.

These biblical facts about Moses suggest to the careful reader that his administration, the laws and customs Moses developed, were intended to be temporary measures to minister to Israel during her wilderness wanderings. This does not mean that everything Moses did, all of his laws and statutes, had no application at any other time. Not at all! But it does mean that they cannot simply be imported into future eras without careful, prayerful, and faithful attention to God's intention in the light of Christ.

However, what we see in the Bible is the desire to return to an imagined time when Israel supposedly functioned as a faithful, well-oiled, worship machine, when people lived according to Moses' laws and all was well. But such a time never actually existed, so the desire to return to such a time issues from our feeble imaginations, not from God's Word. It is a pipe dream! Consider two of the best Old Testament kings: Hezekiah and Josiah.

HEZEKIAH

> "And he did what was right in the eyes of the LORD, according to all that David his father had done" (2 Kings 18:3).

Hezekiah witnessed the destruction of the northern kingdom of Israel by Sargon, king of Assyria in 720 B.C., and was king of Judah during the invasion of Jerusalem by Sennacherib in 701 B.C. He carried forward the reforms of King David by bringing sweeping religious reform that included a strict mandate for the worship of Yahweh alone and a prohibition of worshiping other deities within the Temple in Jerusalem.

However, part of his reform effort changed one of the central teachings of Moses. Don't neglect the significance of this little touted fact.

> "And he broke in pieces the bronze serpent that Moses had made, for until those days the people of Israel had made offerings to it [it was called Nehushtan] (2 Kings 18:4).

Moses had established the bronze serpent in the desert (Numbers 21:9), and we know it as a prefiguration of Christ, which means that it was a very important element of Old Testament worship. And apparently David had continued worship of the Nehushtan in the Temple. So, when Hezekiah destroyed it, he altered a Temple worship practice that had been established by Moses and carried forward into the Temple by David. By what authority did he do this?

> "He trusted in the LORD, the God of Israel, so that there was none like him among all the kings of Judah after him, nor among those who were before him (2 Kings 18:5).

Here we see that Hezekiah was recognized as being greater than David, if we are to understand the plain reading of this verse. And that greatness would have been necessary in order for him to correct the teaching of Moses and David regarding the Nuhushtan. To review: Hezekiah changed an established worship practice established by Moses and confirmed by David.

The general emphasis of Hezekiah's reform was for ritual, purity, accomplished by destroying idols, reforming the priesthood, abolishing idolatry, and centralizing worship in the Temple. He also reestablished the Passover pilgrimage and the tradition of inviting the scattered tribes of Israel to take part in a Passover festival. Thus, he sent messengers to Ephraim and Manasseh inviting them to Jerusalem for the celebration of the Passover. Again, it was the *king* who authorized all of this, not the priests, though the priests were probably involved. However, the king's messengers were ignored and even scorned as they spread this word to the people (2 Chronicles 30:10). Nevertheless the Passover was celebrated with great solemnity and such rejoicing as had not been in Jerusalem since the days of Solomon.

Note that Hezekiah's reforms were deemed by the Bible to be good and necessary, that Hezekiah had corrected some of the teachings and practices established by Moses and David, and yet the people in the countryside scorned him. His reforms were not universally accepted. Why not?

During Sennacherib's invasion, Hezekiah had made a deal with Sennacherib to pay him tribute (2 Kings 18:14), which means that in some sense Hezekiah became a vassal of Sennacherib. Sennacherib then engaged in what we might call psychological warfare in the court of Hezekiah. The Rabshakeh, an Assyrian vizier attached to Sennacherib, now held a position in Hezekiah's court and began to "advise."

> "And the Rabshakeh said to them, 'Say to Hezekiah, "Thus says the great king, the king of Assyria: On what do you rest this trust of yours? Do you think that mere words are strategy and power for war? In whom do you now trust, that you have rebelled against me? Behold, you are trusting now in Egypt, that broken reed of a staff, which will pierce the hand of any man who leans on it. Such is Pharaoh king of Egypt to all who trust in him. But if you say to me, 'We trust in the LORD our God,' is it not he whose high places and altars Hezekiah has removed, saying to Judah and to Jerusalem, 'You shall worship before this altar in Jerusalem'? Come now, make a wager with my master the king of Assyria: I will give you two thousand

horses, if you are able on your part to set riders on them. How then can you repulse a single captain among the least of my master's servants, when you trust in Egypt for chariots and for horsemen? Moreover, is it without the LORD that I have come up against this place to destroy it? The LORD said to me, Go up against this land, and destroy it'" (2 Kings 18:19-25).

He began to undermine the teachings and trust of Yahweh, suggesting that God had honored Sennacherib by causing him to win on the battlefield. Again, note that Hezekiah's reforms and emphasis on religious purity were at best a mixed bag. The purity of Hezekiah's reforms was tainted.

Into this mix we must also note that Isaiah and Micah prophesied during Hezekiah's reign. It is too often thought that the prophets spoke against the sins of the people, and of course they did. However, they primarily spoke against the sins of the kings and priests, and it is important to realize that *during* one of Israel's periods of reformation, Isaiah and Micah prophesied *against* the king and the priests who were bringing about that reform. The reforms actually came to Judah, but because the Northern Kingdom had just fallen, Hezekiah's kingship was understood to be a continuation of the faithfulness of Israel.

History is messy, and its messiness mitigates against our desire to create a neat story about faithful Israel holding their own against the forces of evil and darkness, or the power of religious purity to stand against the corrupting powers of Satan. While such stories make compelling moral tales, life is not so simple.

JOSIAH

The preeminent model for such a return to some former supposedly golden era was Josiah. King Josiah (641-609 B.C.) is credited with the Deuteronomic Reform.[1] Josiah became king of Judah at the age of

---

1 A reformation instituted in the reign of King Josiah, so called because the book of the Law was found in the Temple and served as the basis of the reform, is considered by scholars to be the same as the law code in the book of Deuteronomy (chapters 12–26). The reform consisted of removing pagan altars and idols from the Temple, destroying rural sanctuaries and fertility cults, and centralizing worship at the Temple of Jerusalem. For an alternate view of this reform see: Barker, Margaret. *Temple Theology: An Introduction*, Society For Promoting Christian Knowledge (SPCK), 2004, p. 76, "Josiah's Purge." Barker is off base in so many ways, but there is a nub of truth to her argument.

eight, following the assassination of his father, King Amon, and reigned for thirty-one years. Eight! Surely some oddities and skullduggery were afoot in the king's court. How could it be otherwise! To date, there is no information about Josiah other than the biblical texts, no other archeological or historical references have been found.

In the eighteenth year of his rule, Josiah ordered the High Priest Hilkiah to renovate the temple with tax money that had been collected. Hilkiah then discovered the "Book of the law" (2 Kings 22:8), which is understood to be what we call the *Book Of Deuteronomy*. The focus of the find was on the *law*.

> "Then Shaphan the secretary told the king, 'Hilkiah the priest has given me a book.' And Shaphan read it before the king. When the king heard the words of the Book of the Law, he tore his clothes. And the king commanded Hilkiah the priest, and Ahikam the son of Shaphan, and Achbor the son of Micaiah, and Shaphan the secretary, and Asaiah the king's servant, saying, 'Go, inquire of the LORD for me, and for the people, and for all Judah, concerning the words of this book that has been found. For great is the wrath of the LORD that is kindled against us, because our fathers have not obeyed the words of this book, to do according to all that is written concerning us" (2 Kings 22:10-13).

Hilkiah then took a cadre to visit Huldah the prophetess, who was "keeper of the wardrobe" (2 Kings 22:14) for advice. She prophesied:

> "Thus says the LORD, Behold, I will bring disaster upon this place and upon its inhabitants, all the words of the book that the king of Judah has read. Because they have forsaken me and have made offerings to other gods, that they might provoke me to anger with all the work of their hands, therefore my wrath will be kindled against this place, and it will not be quenched" (2 Kings 22:16-17).

Note that the Lord intended to bring future disaster upon Israel, to fulfill the curses specified in Deuteronomy 28, presumably (perhaps) because of the apostasy that had preceded Josiah. The book of the law had been lost, which means that it had not been followed. Yet, in spite of the fact that Josiah intended to reinstate the law, Huldah prophesied *future* calamity. But Josiah was trying to avert future calamity by reinstating the law because he believed that obedience to the law would bring God's blessing.

This is the model for all religious reform ever since. The call for revival, reformation, reconfiguration, reconstruction, etc.—is a call to return to some previous time when things were better, to the beginning. But it is a false model because, as Paul was teaching, obedience to the law cannot bring about God's blessing because the law cannot remove sin. Yet, here was Josiah hoping to do just that! Josiah's Deuteronomic Reform was an attempted return to the law for salvation, for safety or deliverance from God's curse for disobedience. While it is possible to argue that the Jews did not use the law as a means of salvation, Christians have often turned to Josiah's law-based reform as a model for religious and social reformation.

And Huldah's prophecy of God's wrath was a response, not simply to Israel's previous forgetfulness of God's law, but to Israel's future efforts of reformation through the *law*. Josiah's rekindling of the law in apostate Israel would only serve to reveal more sin and facilitate more of God's wrath, which it did.

At the very time that Josiah's reform was in full swing, Jeremiah was preaching about the futility of that very reform. Jeremiah's ministry was active from the thirteenth year of Josiah's reign, and included several kings who followed in rapid succession before the Northern Kingdom was sacked. And what was Jeremiah preaching to Josiah's reform?

> "Hear, O earth; behold, I am bringing disaster upon this people, the fruit of their devices, because they have not paid attention to my words; and as for my law, they have rejected it. What use to me is frankincense that comes from Sheba, or sweet cane from a distant land? *Your burnt offerings are not acceptable, nor your sacrifices pleasing to me.* Therefore thus says the LORD: 'Behold, I will lay before this people stumbling blocks against which they shall stumble; fathers and sons together, neighbor and friend shall perish'" (Jeremiah 6:19-21, italics mine).

> "For in the day that I brought them out of the land of Egypt, *I did not speak to your fathers or command them concerning burnt offerings and sacrifices.* But this command I gave them: 'Obey my voice, and I will be your God, and you shall be my people. And walk in all the way that I command you, that it may be well with you.' But they did not obey or incline their ear, but walked in their own counsels and the

stubbornness of their evil hearts, and went backward and not forward" (Jeremiah 7:22-24, italics mine).

Note that Jeremiah said that God had *not* given them their ceremonial laws, but had given them moral law. In fact, God said, "Obey
my *voice*" (קוֹל, Jeremiah 7:22). The Hebrew word refers to sound,
not sight, to what is audible, not to writing. It was a call to follow
God's Holy Spirit, and not just the letter of God's law (2 Corinthians
3:6). Again, in view is the distinction between the Ten Commandments or God's intention and Moses' laws. Moses and the seventy
elders gave them commands concerning burnt offerings and sacrifices.
So, at the very time that Josiah was bringing about the Deuteronomic
Reform, Jeremiah was preaching against much of Deuteronomy's ceremonial commands, which had been authored by David. The Temple
establishment did all they could to ignore Jeremiah and double down
on their Deuteronomic Reform. And the result was disastrous, the
Temple ended up being destroyed. Twice!

Jeremiah was preaching for new hearts, which come only through
God's grace. But the Temple establishment, with its new found enthusiasm for the law had the support of the king and the Temple
establishment. No doubt much of the revival enthusiasm was actually
motivated by fear of God's retribution, fear of God's curse. This whole
event was an instance of the struggle between law and grace as Paul
was fashioning it in Galatians.

Indeed, Paul's argument about law and grace was not new, but has
been the central argument of the Bible for a very long time. What was
new in Paul's argument was the advent of Jesus Christ. Paul saw, perhaps more clearly than anyone else in history at the time, that Jesus
Christ was the fulfillment of God's law. The advent of Jesus Christ
would bring about the end of Satan's reign, the end of Adam's type as
the model for human being. A new model for being human had manifested in the Person of Jesus Christ.

The fact that the law cannot fulfill the promise of God's restitution
does not void God's promise. The law and the Tabernacle/Temple go
together. What was true of the Tabernacle was true of the law. The
law was for the Tabernacle/Temple of God. It served a purpose for a
time, and now serves a different purpose in Christ. While we are not
obligated to its performance, there is much we can learn from it. Thus,

the institution and application of Moses' law was always intended to be both temporary and dynamic. It was designed to meet particular needs at a particular time, and to demonstrate that salvation through the law, or perfect obedience to God's demands, is impossible apart from Christ.

Once that was historically demonstrated in A.D. 70 with the destruction of Jerusalem and the Second Temple, which ended the Temple administration and scattered the Jews across the globe, there was no more need to perform Moses' Tabernacle/Temple based law. Yet, that law and its history must continue to stand as an historic lesson for all of humanity about the God of the Bible and His law. The law is no longer in effect as it was prior to A.D. 70, in part because the instituted authority which applied and adjudicated that law has been destroyed. The legal authority that authorized and administered that law no longer exists. But this does not mean that the history of that administration is without value. On the contrary, it is of great value. But it does not operate as it did prior to A.D. 70. Now it yields to the administration of Jesus Christ.

13. In The Midst

Why then the law? It was added because of transgressions, until the offspring should come to whom the promise had been made, and it was put in place through angels by an intermediary. Now an intermediary implies more than one, but God is one. Is the law then contrary to the promises of God? Certainly not! For if a law had been given that could give life, then righteousness would indeed be by the law. But the Scripture imprisoned everything under sin, so that the promise by faith in Jesus Christ might be given to those who believe.
—Galatians 3:19-22

Paul's use of *law* (νόμος) assumes knowledge of the difference between the Ten Commandments, Moses' law, and the Torah, which is responsible for much confusion about what he meant. The distinctions are there, but seeing them requires us to see through Paul's eyes, and understand the transformation that Christ brought to Second Temple Judaism, as I have argued. Then again, what Paul was saying about law and gospel actually applies to each category of law in the sense that the law—any law—cannot be used to achieved salvation. The unsaved and unregenerate don't care about God or His law—or salvation. It's not that they cannot obey any of it. Clearly, they can—not perfectly, of course. They could if they would, but they don't care about it. They don't love God, nor are they motivated by the love of God.

Loving God, caring about God, being motivated by the love of God means *wanting* to do what God wants you to do. That desire is a critical element, and it is given or received, not taken or achieved. God gives it through Jesus Christ and we receive it through His Holy Spirit. So, each member of the Trinity—Father, Son, and Spirit—are involved in our salvation. And it is essential that each Person of the Godhead is involved because of the unity and wholeness of God's character. It is the unity and wholeness of God's character that provides for the unity and wholeness of our character as Christians.

Adam's transgression in the Garden followed very quickly after God's initial gift of life. That transgression produced an historic wake, and the ripples of that wake continue to unfold as real consequences. God's first response to that transgression was judgment, by which is meant that God evaluated the transgression. And following His evaluation came the consequence—His curse. God's judgment or evaluation was that Adam's desire to follow the advice of the Serpent (to eat of the tree), and to disregard God's command (not to eat of the tree), would lead to ultimate death.

The domination of self-concern that was introduced by the Serpent would flower into selfishness, envy, greed, and aggression that would tear all future societies apart. Whereas God's counsel of obedience that issues out of self-deprecation, charity, and contentment would bind people in mutual service that would flower in abundance for all. The one would be a force for death and destruction, and the other would be a force for life and abundance. The one requires trusting the Serpent, which is actually a form of self-trust and self-reliance, and the other requires trusting God, self-doubt, and trusting others. The difference is subtle, not hard and fast.

SEED

Again, Paul made much ado about σπέρμα (*sperma*), which is a plural noun used in the singular. Understanding how Paul used this term and what he meant by it is essential to understanding Paul's message to the Galatians. The law was added, "until the offspring should come to whom the promise had been made" (v. 19). The original promise was made to Abraham:

> "And God said to Abraham, 'As for you, you shall keep my covenant, you and your *offspring* after you *throughout their generations*. This is my covenant, which you shall keep, between me and you and your *offspring* after you: Every male among you shall be circumcised'" (Genesis 17:9-10, italics mine).

Because Isaac was *not* the only faithful person to follow Abraham, and because Isaac was the only son Abraham fathered, then this command was *not* about strict blood lineage. To put the same idea positively, this command pertained to blood lineage only if Isaac was the only faithful person to follow Abraham. But he was not! To put it differently, because the clan of Abraham itself divided into warring camps, the emphasis on blood lineage as developed by Israel cannot be God's intent. Notice that *every* male in Abraham's retinue was to be circumcised as part of this covenant, not just a particular family. Did this mean that every circumcised male would be a faithful follower of Abraham? Of course not. From what we know about Jacob and Esau, and later from Israel's wilderness wanderings, we definitively know that every circumcised male following Abraham, his seed or progeny, was not faithful because a whole generation who followed Moses were forbidden to enter the promised land because of their faithlessness. All of this means that we must take care to read and understand God's Word carefully. There is more to it than what first meets the eye.

At first the promise to Abraham appears to be to him and his biological children, yet that promise goes only to one child, Isaac (not Ishmael), and then to Jacob (not Esau), who becomes Israel. The command to circumcise all of the males in Abraham's camp cannot be a command for blood purity because they would not have been from one biological family, and even if it does, that family further exclusivefies the covenant. That group has been identified to be of the lineage of Shem, so the oneness suggested here must be like the oneness of the Shemites or any other people group. And as noted, biblical history is the story of significant divisions between members of the same family —Cain and Abel, Isaac and Ishmael, Jacob and Esau, etc. Over and again, the families of the Bible fight and war against one another, while Israel works to maintain familial bloodline purity for the inheritance of God's blessing. Israel argues that God's inheritance belongs to *them*, to the clan of Jacob, against the sea of pagan gentiles. Yet, the Bible teaches over and over that God's chosen people are both unwilling and unable to adhere to God's law as provided by Moses apart from the Holy Spirit which Christ unleashed.

Therefore, in the light of history we must surmise that God did not choose them to be a model for the rest of the world to emulate, but chose them to demonstrate that, even with the help of the law provided by Moses, they would be unable to conform to God's dictates.

And yet, in spite of their foolish hardheadedness and disobedience, God would bless them. Both of these things are clearly shown in Scripture. The nation of Israel failed to manifest God's blessings through obedience to His law, and yet the Jews as a people were blessed. They prospered in spite of their faithlessness. This story is a demonstration of God's great grace and mercy in the face of human disobedience and failure. It is a story of grace from beginning to end.

This is a great example of why we must not limit our understanding of Scripture to the understanding of those to whom it was first directed. Neither Jesus nor Paul did that with the Old Testament. Sure, it is important to understand how people contemporary to the biblical writings understood them. But to limit ourselves to their perspective as being the only meaningful perspective, or even the best perspective, robs us of the accumulated treasure of historical insight. Rather, because the perspective of Scripture itself is teleological, projecting the *eschaton* into and beyond each present epoch, we are called in each generation to adjust ourselves to the trajectory of God's purpose in the light of Christ and the accumulated light of history. Scripture is for each successive generation, not just for those who originally heard it.

In the light of Christ the offspring or seed (σπέρμα) mentioned in verse 19 refers to both Jesus and to the harvest of souls He would gather into God's kingdom throughout history. It has both singular and plural meanings because Christ manifested a human typological model for people to conform to. Or another way to say the same thing is that Christ lives through His Holy Spirit in and through the ongoing lives of His people. Thus, God's promise to Abraham was that Christ or Messiah would redeem His people in human history. God's promise was to the coming of Christ and through Christ to the coming of Christ's people.

We must take care here not to limit God's promise to words alone, by which I mean that God's promise is about reality and not simply to the words that point to reality. God's promise is to the actual manifestation of the character of Jesus Christ in the lives of actual individuals, and not merely to those who use the right language to describe the reality or right liturgical worship, but fail to manifest it themselves. In addition, we must not limit God's promise to the immediacy of some particular historical epoch, but grant God the vision to see the end from the beginning.

> "Remember this and stand firm, recall it to mind, you transgressors, remember the former things of old; for I am God, and there is no other; I am God, and there is none like me, declaring the end from the beginning and from ancient times things not yet done, saying, 'My counsel shall stand, and I will accomplish all my purpose,' calling a bird of prey from the east, the man of my counsel from a far country. I have spoken, and I will bring it to pass; I have purposed, and I will do it" (Isaiah 46:8-11).

God writes history from the future by drawing the present into the future He envisions. We do the same thing by drawing up plans according to some particular future vision and working to fulfill those plans. God acts from the future to draw the present forward into reality. Satan acts to push the present into some imagined future from the past, to push the present off God's trajectory, out of God's reality. Thus, God's impetus is forgiveness of the past, and Satan's impetus is revenge for the past. God's intention is to replace the old religion of vengeance that focuses on the past with Christ's new religion of grace and mercy that focuses on the future.

GOD'S ANGELS

Paul said that angels or messengers from God had foretold about a mediator who is of God but not identical with God. That is to say that prophets and other biblical writers had written about God's promise to send someone to fix this broken world—the long awaited Messiah. That promise goes back to the protoevangelium of Genesis 3:15:

> "I will put enmity between you and the woman, and between your offspring and her offspring; he shall bruise your head, and you shall bruise his heel."

God was speaking judgment to the Serpent here. The enmity would be between the children of the Serpent and the children of the woman (Eve, or God's family). God's curse of the Serpent to go on his belly suggests an inability to become upright or righteous, and the eating of dust suggests dryness or fruitlessness. The enmity between the Serpent and the woman, and between their respective progeny, meant war between Satan and humanity, or war between two opposing ways of existence, of being human. The way of the Serpent included all who followed his advice—Adam and Eve, and their offspring.

In this war between the Serpent or Satan and humanity there is the implication that the offspring of the woman would strike at the head of the Serpent and the Serpent would strike at the heel of the other. A strike at the head is a direct attack, where a strike at the heel is a hidden attack, a stealth attack. This struggle is seen again in the relationship between the twins, Jacob and Esau.[1] The child(ren) of the woman would eventually crush the headship of the Serpent, but the Serpent had already bitten the heel of humanity as Adam and Eve bit the forbidden fruit. The Serpent's poison had already infected the heel of humanity. That poison was Eve's understanding of the forbidden fruit, that it was "good for food, and that it was a delight to the eyes, and that the tree was to be desired to make one wise" (Genesis 3:6). All humanity followed Eve's judgment rather than God's. But Christ did not follow Adam and Eve. He has a different Father, so He was able to fulfill the law of God. Thus, John testified:

> "The reason the Son of God appeared was to destroy the works of the devil" (1 John 3:8).

Jesus was the mediator who would bring this destruction about. He intervened on our behalf to reconcile believers to God in order that those believers would eventually supplant or overtake the headship or authority of the world. However, we must remember that God's ways are not our ways. We must remember that when Israel went to Samuel to ask for a king, God told Samuel to tell the people that what they wanted was evil and it would not work out well for them. But they insisted, so God relented. And the Bible is the story of how that kingship ended in disaster in A.D. 70.

This means that God's way of ruling is different than that of worldly kingships. The kind of top-down imposition of the king's will on the people is not God's way. That's not how God works, and to think that Christians want to capture Satan's centers of power and in-

---

1　The biblical example is Jacob who was born holding Esau's heel (Genesis 25:26), which prefigured Esau selling his birthright or inheritance to Jacob for a bowl of stew. Jacob, whose name means *supplanter*, supplanted Esau's inheritance right.

fluence for themselves and impose Christianity on the world is completely wrongheaded. Christians are not to desire to capture the top-down centers of worldly power, we are to want to convert or supplant them with a better way. Just as God is not out to destroy the world, but to remake it in the image of Christ,[2] so Christians are not out to destroy the world or the things of the world, but to convert or supplant them into the service of Jesus Christ for the benefit of all humanity.

2 For more on this see Ross, Phillip A. *Peter's Vision of Christ's Purpose in First Peter*, 2011, and *Peter's Vision of The End in Second Peter*, Pilgrim Platform, Marietta, Ohio, 2012.

14. The Tutor

Now before faith came, we were held captive under the law, impris-
oned until the coming faith would be revealed. So then, the law was
our guardian until Christ came, in order that we might be justified by
faith. But now that faith has come, we are no longer under a
guardian, for in Christ Jesus you are all sons of God, through faith.
— Galatians 3:23-26

To understand this verse we equate *faith* with *Christ* because Paul understood Christ to be the manifestation of faithfulness. This would make it read: *Before Christ came we were held captive under the law, imprisoned until the coming Christ would be revealed.* That's what Paul was saying.

God promised to bless the world through Abraham, but Egypt first saved, then captured and oppressed, Israel. So, Moses led them into the wilderness to start over, to begin again with a clean slate. However, Moses found that it was much easier to get the people out of Egypt than to get Egypt out of the people. The transition was not smooth. The people needed help, which Moses tried to supply but he alone wasn't able. Their troubles were too much. So, Moses took Jethro's advice and got help. Finally, the law was born in the wilderness from their efforts. And the first order of the law was to build the Tabernacle to focus the social order. The Tabernacle, a temporary institution, never intended to be a permanent fixture, was designed to help Israel in the wilderness. The law that Moses and his helpers fashioned under God's tutelage brought order through service to the Tabernacle in the hope of forging a people dedicated to God. However, neither the Tabernacle nor the Mosaic law was able to get Israel to the promised land. So Joshua endeavored to take it by force, with God's blessing and calling.

From the rotten failure of the Tabernacle, the people then called for a king, like the kings of the world. God told them that such an idea would not work out well. Again, they insisted, so God relented. And soon the Temple was built to replace the Tabernacle. It was even modeled after the Tabernacle. King David drew up the plans, and King Solomon, his illegitimately conceived son of sin, completed it. Solomon's children then took the kingdom of Israel into civil war that did not end until the destruction of Jerusalem and the Temple in A.D. 70. Christ had come and the church was born.

Moses' law served a temporary function between the promise and the fulfillment. It was a teacher. Teachers teach people how to learn by modeling learning behavior. The law provided a model, but it was a dead model not a living model. It was static and petrified, not dynamic and living. Law is necessary, but not sufficient. The general principles of the Ten Commandments became particular laws, rules, and judgments aimed at specific situations as Moses and the elders sought to bring help to Israel in the wilderness.

JUSTIFIED

Much ink has been used in the effort to understand what justification means and how it works. The usual explanations of δικαιόω focus on the idea of making or declaring people righteous or right with God, in obedience to God's commands and will. People often misunderstand it to mean that they get off the hook for some previous behavior. Little emphasis has been given on its meaning as showing, exhibiting, or evincing righteousness, but that is the literal meaning of the root word, δεικνύω, *to provide evidence or proof of a thing.*

We have been taught that it is God who provides the righteousness, that it is He who declares it—and rightly so. But by focusing on God's role in our righteousness we tend to neglect our role. While it is true that God does it, He does it in and through willing believers. So when Paul says that believers are "justified by faith" (v. 24) he means that our faith is the evidence or proof of God's presence in our lives. Paul was not talking about two different things: God's justification, and our faith. He was talking about one process that has two elements, like cause and effect: God's justification, and our faithfulness. Our faithfulness proves, shows, and demonstrates our rightness with God.

The two sides of the coin are always necessary parts of the coin, and they always appear together. The coin cannot exist without the two sides. It is easy to get so lost in the analysis that we lose sight of the reality, of the actual thing being analyzed. Our faithfulness vindicates God's justification, God's presence in our lives.

Justification is not a thing or a quality, it's an activity that produces faithfulness in the lives of people. It is God's activity in people's lives. To be justified by God's grace means that God's grace is the source of faithfulness in someone's life.

IMPRISONED

It is the nature of law to guard, protect, and control people by limiting behavior. Laws either encourage or forbid certain behaviors. And this is exactly what God's law does. The first instance of God's law provided for our proper diet. This law came in two parts: one positive and one negative. We had permission to eat the fruit of every tree except one, the tree of the knowledge of good and evil (Genesis 2:16-17).

The translation of φρουρέω as *imprisoned* strikes me as a bit biased because the purpose and function of law is to both to protect and to forbid, to free and to limit. The observance of law protects people from anarchy by forbidding the kinds of behaviors that tear societies apart, leading to a cycle of violence and revenge. Societies cannot progress above a most rudimentary level until such a cycle has been eradicated.

But anarchy is not the only danger that societies face. The laws needed to suppress anarchy can and often are conscripted for exploitation by the group in control of the law, leading to authoritarianism where one group takes unfair advantage of another group. It appears that such was the case in ancient Israel with the Temple establishment. Yet we need not think of the Temple establishment as being particularly unusual, rather, this kind of exploitation is very common throughout history and throughout the world because it is a function of sin.

Nonetheless, Paul said that Israel had been imprisoned, confined, and/or shut up by the law. Again, it appears that Paul made an assumption regarding the word νόμος (law) that increases the ease of our

misunderstanding of what he was saying regarding the differences between the Ten Commandments, Moses' law, and the Torah. The role
of the Ten Commandments is to protect people by instituting a standard of behavior designed to eliminate the cycle of violence and
revenge. Moses' law involved the application of that standard to the
wilderness situation of Israel, which like the Tabernacle was intended
by God to be temporary. And the Torah in its widest meaning provided ongoing commentary and adjustment to the tradition of law,
which included both the Ten Commandments and Moses' laws. Thus,
the three parts of the law (νόμος) are: a particular standard (Ten Commandments), specific applications (Moses' law), and ongoing
commentary and adjustments (Torah).

UNVEILED

Paul said that the law was a temporary institution until faith (or
faith that Christ is the long expected Messiah) could be revealed or un-
veiled. But why couldn't Christ have been revealed in the first place,
which would have circumvented the need for the temporary institution of the law? Why did the people of God need to endure the veiling
of God's whole truth? The short answer is not about God's inability,
but about ours. The lesson that comes from frustration with the inade-
quacy of law to change hearts and minds is necessary because we
(humanity) have been habituated to use law to try to do this very
thing. We still do it today. More than ever!

The establishment of law may produce compliance but it cannot
change hearts and minds—or can it? In order to understand the inter-
relationship between law and grace, and see that they are not actually
opposed to one another, it is necessary to refrain from jumping to premature conclusions based on old habits, old thinking. Sometimes it
seems that Paul taught the complete opposition of law and grace, and
at other times he seems to abandon that opposition by upholding both
of them. And this is the central theme of this study and it is intimately
intertwined with the Temple veil (Exodus 26:31-35), which was a
symbol of Moses' veil, which was a symbol of Israel's blindness.

Paul's treatment of the doctrine of the veil provides the foundation
for understanding the relationship between law and grace. That story
begins with Moses on the mountain receiving the tablets of the Ten

Commandments (Exodus 20). God called Moses to come up to the mountaintop alone to receive the Commandments. Moses met with God *panim el panim* (פָּנִים אֶל־פָּנִים), face to face, an idiom that means *personally,* person to person. This fact is critical because the fulfillment of God's mission is to "put my law in their inward parts, and write it in their hearts; and (I) will be their God, and they shall be my people" (Jeremiah 31:33, Proverbs 3:3; 7:3).

God gave Moses the Ten Commandments (Exodus 31:18), but they were not for Moses alone. Again, this fact is also critical because law by nature is both personal and social, and neither of these aspects of law can be denied or ignored if law is to fulfill its own definition. Law is both personal and social. The story continues with Moses being delayed returning from the mountain.

> "When the people saw that Moses delayed to come down from the mountain, the people gathered themselves together to Aaron and said to him, 'Up, make us gods who shall go before us. As for this Moses, the man who brought us up out of the land of Egypt, we do not know what has become of him.' So Aaron said to them, 'Take off the rings of gold that are in the ears of your wives, your sons, and your daughters, and bring them to me.' So all the people took off the rings of gold that were in their ears and brought them to Aaron. And he received the gold from their hand and fashioned it with a graving tool and made a golden calf. And they said, 'These are your gods, O Israel, who brought you up out of the land of Egypt!'" (Exodus 32:1-4).

This is sometimes referred to as Israel's original sin. In the shadow of God's promise to provide for Israel, Israel turned her back on God, engaging in the very thing that God first forbade!

While this was happening at the foot of the mountain, God told Moses about it and threatened to annihilate them (Exodus 32:7-10). But Moses made three appeals to the LORD on behalf of Israel. First he appealed to God's program of salvation itself (Exodus 32:11). He asked why God would not complete what He had begun with them. Then he appealed to God's character and reputation among the nations (Exodus 32:12), asking what people would think of such a God. And lastly he appealed to God's promises made to the patriarchs, when He said, "I will multiply your offspring as the stars of heaven, and all this land that

I have promised I will give to your offspring, and they shall inherit it forever" (Exodus 32:13). And because of these appeals, the LORD repented, choosing to work with Israel rather than destroy them.

Moses went down from his mountain meeting with God, tablets in hand to share God's redeeming grace, but at this point "*Moses'* anger burned hot, and he threw the tablets out of his hands and broke them at the foot of the mountain" (Exodus 32:19). God had relented His judgment, but Moses was not able to be as charitable. Notice how God's law and grace are intertwined with Moses' ability to mediate both. Law, gospel, God, and Moses are all bound up together in this story, and they cannot be neatly separated. Moses then instituted his own penalty for their idolatry, without God's direction.

> "He took the calf that they had made and burned it with fire and ground it to powder and scattered it on the water and made the people of Israel drink it" (Exodus 32:20).

God had not given this order. Rather, Moses, in his anger, instructed the people in what *he* thought to be just and right, which prefigured something important about Moses. He was not as careful as he needed to be in handling the Word of God. *Moses* then set up what would become the pattern for Old Testament worship.

> "The next day Moses said to the people, 'You have sinned a great sin. And now I will go up to the LORD; perhaps I can make atonement for your sin.' So Moses returned to the LORD and said, 'Alas, this people has sinned a great sin. They have made for themselves gods of gold. But now, if you will forgive their sin—but if not, please blot me out of your book that you have written.' But the LORD said to Moses, 'Whoever has sinned against me, I will blot out of my book. But now go, lead the people to the place about which I have spoken to you; behold, my angel shall go before you'" (Exodus 32:30-34).

God's angel or messenger would lead them, but God Himself would not be with them. God would not put up with their stubbornness, their old habits. God knew that they would need to be weaned away from their old habits, superstitions, and religion.

> "Go up to a land flowing with milk and honey; but I will not go up among you, lest I consume you on the way, for you are a stiff-necked people" (Exodus 33:3).

Again God met personally with Moses (Exodus 33:11). Moses' intercession (Exodus 33:12-19) is filled with expressions of God's grace. Thus, the story of Moses getting the law from God is permeated with God's grace. In fact, God's giving of the Ten Commandments itself is first and foremost an act of His grace and mercy. The Lord then told Moses to carve two more stone tablets to replace the broken ones. So, he did and ascended the mountain again for the Lord to inscribe them.

> "The Lord passed before him and proclaimed, 'The LORD, the LORD, a God merciful and gracious, slow to anger, and abounding in steadfast love and faithfulness, keeping steadfast love for thousands, forgiving iniquity and transgression and sin, but who will by no means clear the guilty, visiting the iniquity of the fathers on the children and the children's children, to the third and the fourth generation'" (Exodus 34:6-7).

Again we see that the Lord leads with mercy and grace, but does not neglect justice. And Moses responded,

> "If now I have found favor in your sight, O Lord, please let the Lord go in the midst of us, for it is a stiff-necked people, and pardon our iniquity and our sin, and take us for your inheritance" (Exodus 34:9).

Remember that this occurred during the giving of the law, the Ten Commandments. God's dispensation of the law is bathed in His grace and mercy from beginning to end. Clearly law and grace are not opposed to one another. Rather, the Ten Commandments are the fruit of God grace. God's response to Moses' humility was to renew the covenant.

> "And he said, 'Behold, I am making a covenant. Before all your people I will do marvels, such as have not been created in all the earth or in any nation. And all the people among whom you are shall see the work of the Lord, for it is an awesome thing that I will do with you'" (Exodus 34:10).

God then said he would drive out the nations before the Israelites and warned them not to make covenants with them. The Jews were to tear down their pagan altars and destroy their Asherah poles because God is a jealous God (Exodus 34:14), which means that the *Jews* had pagan altars and Asherah poles. The people were to abstain from all forms of idolatry (Exodus 34:17) and keep the various festivals and

Sabbath days (Exodus 34:18-26). Moses was then instructed to write for himself the terms of the covenant, now renewed (Exodus 34:27). According to Jewish tradition God's giving of the Ten Commandments ended with Yom Kippur, the holiest day of the year. This was the key event that shaped Judaism, its most important memory to preserve.

15. Putting On Heirs

For as many of you as were baptized into Christ have put on Christ. There is neither Jew nor Greek, there is neither slave nor free, there is no male and female, for you are all one in Christ Jesus. And if you are Christ's, then you are Abraham's offspring, heirs according to promise. —Galatians 3:27–29

What does it mean to wear Christ? βαπτίζω means to overwhelm, and should not be confused with βάπτω, both are translated as *baptize*. The best example of the difference between them is a text from the Greek poet and physician, Nicander, who lived about 200 B.C. It is a recipe for making pickles, and is helpful because it uses both words. Nicander says that to make a pickle, the vegetable should first be *dipped* (βάπτω) into boiling water and then *baptised* (βαπτίζω) in vinegar. Both words are about the immersing of vegetables. The first is of short duration in hot water. The second, the act of baptizing the vegetable, is of long duration in vinegar and produces a permanent change of character. In the New Testament, βαπτίζω more often refers to our union and identification with Christ, and βάπτω refers to the initial shock of contact with the Holy Spirit and the ceremony of our water baptism.

The word in this verse is βαπτίζω, which indicates a permanent change of character over a long duration. So, this putting on of Christ is not a temporary thing such that Christ can be put on and put off at will. When Christ is put on everything changes forever. Where the ceremony of water baptism is a public announcement that the person being baptized belongs to Christ, the person's baptism involves stewing in Christ and living out the change of character that results.

To say that baptism in Christ is a matter of putting on Christ suggests the long process of getting pickled in the Holy Spirit, of being progressively changed by conforming to the character of Jesus Christ. To put Christ on is to wear Him such that when people see you, what they mostly see are the clothes you are wearing, which is Christ.

Verse 28 jumps to the first consequence of wearing Christ. Because all Christians are to wear Christ, they all wear the same clothes. It's like wearing a uniform. *Uniform* means always the same; showing a single form or character in all occurrences. Christian unity is a matter of wearing Christ. And where Christians wear Christ they are in uniformity or unity, and where they don't they aren't.

> "There is neither Jew nor Greek, there is neither slave nor free, there is no male and female, for you are all one in Christ Jesus" (v. 28).

This is the condition of all baptized Christians according to Paul. It is an existing reality, not a future hope. Christian unity is not a future condition of the church but is a present reality. The failure of Christian unity is a failure to put Christ on.

The role of the church in baptism is similar to the role of the state in marriage. That role is to facilitate the official recognition of an existing reality, not to be a cause of the reality. John the Baptist said that Jesus "will baptize you with the Holy Spirit and with fire" (Matthew 3:21). Baptism is of the Holy Spirit. He does it, we conform to it. Our job is to realize it, to live as if it is real—because it is. The calling and charge of all baptized Christians is to live into the reality of baptism, to be pickled in Christ.

FALSE CATEGORIES

Verse 28 acknowledges various categories of humanity that are not of concern to God—nationality, ethnicity, financial status, and sex. At that time nationality was tied to ethnicity much more than it is today. Today modern travel technologies have allowed much more ethnic mixing among the nations than what happened during Paul's day. At that time nationalities were essentially blood kin groups. Thus, Paul meant that ethnic and genetic differences, what we often call different *races*, are simply insignificant. There is only one race—the human race. The biological differences between the various ethnicities are simply meaningless to God and should be meaningless to Chris-

tians as well. They are far less significant than breeds are to dogs or
horses.

The real differences between human beings and human societies
are cultural, habitual, and ethical. The significant differences between
people and cultures are religious, philosophical, presuppositional, and
moral. The significant differences are about beliefs, attitudes, values,
and religions, the very things that we have been taught not to discuss
in polite company—which is completely absurd because discussion is
the only way to mitigate our differences. Such discussions promote our
growth, maturity, and sanctification. Our very survival depends on our
ability to discuss such things, and to do so without force, manipula-
tion, deception, or rancor. We must learn to differentiate between
people and ideas, and not get defensive when our ideas, values, and beliefs, are challenged. We must also learn to not attack people because
their ideas, values, and beliefs are different than ours. Rather, let us all
engage in civil and rational discussion in order that the best ideas and
the greatest truths can be integrated into our various cultures.

Paul also said that God is not concerned about whether we are
slave or free. But what does that mean in today's world? I have suggested above that it pertains to one's financial status because that was
one of the primary differences between being slave or free in Paul's
world. Our financial differences are meaningless to God. He doesn't
consider them in His judgment. Yet, the Bible is full of concern about
care for the poor by the rich (Psalm 34:6; Proverbs 22:9, 31:20, Daniel
4:27, Matthew 19:21, Galatians 2:10, James 2:5). God wants us to be
mindful of one another's needs, and not to be selfishly focused on ourselves to the neglect of others.

Another element of this pertains to freedom or what we call *human rights*. Paul's use of the ideas of slave and free also suggests a
difference of rights. In the same way that God is not concerned about
our financial assets, He is also not concerned about our human rights
in the same way that we are. But this does not mean that God is not
concerned about money and wealth, and what we do with it, or about
how we allocate human rights, or about justice. Rather, God's concern
is about our self-created disparities between rich and poor, between
slave and free. Thus, His plan is to reduce and eliminate those disparities that rob people of life, broadly considered. All people should have

access to the basic necessities of life: food, shelter, and worship. This does not mean that everyone ought to eat what they want, or live where they want, or worship as they want. Rather, people should not be starved or homeless. But neither should they be bound to religious forms of worship that do not provide for them what true worship provides.

My inclusion of worship here is not simply about the freedom to attend worship services, but neither does is exclude this. Rather, I am defining worship in its widest definition: to bring glory to God. To understand this we need to understand what brings glory to God. Usually this kind of discussion goes to worship services, and that's fine —but I don't want to go there or to leave the discussion there. Rather, I want to pick it up at that point because worship is about much more than what happens at a local church on a Sunday morning. Real worship is about our lives, about putting on Christ, about conforming ourselves to the character of Christ twenty-four-seven. This is what we are to do with our freedom in Christ. We are not to do what *we* want to do, but to do what *God* wants us to do. We are to *want* to do what God wants us to do, which is only possible in Christ.

Paul also put sex in this category of concerns. The differences between male and female cannot exclude one from being whole in Christ. Again, God is not concerned about our sex with regard to our calling or salvation. But this does not mean that God is not concerned about sex. We are to be what and who God created us to be, and He created us male and female, one or the other. It's not that one's sex is not important. To the contrary, it is very important. However, it is not to be an impediment to our calling, our sanctification, or our salvation.

Paul's admonition here is to not focus on these differences—Jew vs. Greek, bond vs. free, male vs. female—with regard to our inclusion and personal wholeness in Christ. Rather, he said that we should focus on the reality of baptism, putting on Christ, living in Christ, etc. All of these categories were traditionally used to determine who was "in" and who was "out" of fellowship with God. *Not any more!* said Paul. In Christ, fellowship with God is determined by actual fellowship with God.

ONE IN CHRIST

Our oneness in Christ is a plural unity, or a unified plurality because Paul was speaking to them all, not to an individual. Thus, Christian unity is a group thing as well as an individual thing. Unity is necessarily tied to Set Theory and wholeness.[1] While these ideas are abstract in their considerations, they have very practical and ordinary implications and applications that directly pertain to Christianity and Christ's church.

In order to consider such implications and applications we need to think beyond what has passed for conventional Christian unity in the popular imagination, the institutional unity of various denominations. The effort to unify the various denominations falls far short of the mark for many reasons. First of all, the denominations themselves are structured to oppose unity in that they are defined by what sets them apart from other Christians. And to try to unify what by definition differentiates and separates Christian wholeness is fruitless. It starts on the wrong foot, dances to the wrong music, and barks up the wrong tree. Paul explicitly told us not to engage in subgroup structures like our current denominations.

> "For when one says, 'I follow Paul,' and another, 'I follow Apollos,'
> are you not being merely human?" (1 Corinthians 3:4).

The goal of Christian unity is not simply to be in unity with other Christians or their churches, but primarily to be in unity with Jesus Christ first and foremost. Christian unity is not something to be found in the churches, nor among various Christians. Christian unity is not built or achieved by us. Rather, it is given by God, and has already been given in Christ. It is not a long hoped for ideal to aspire toward, it is a living reality. It does not depend on church pronouncements or corporate documents. It depends upon God in Christ. Christian unity is organic, not primarily institutional.

ABRAHAM'S SEED

Paul's previous comments about Abraham's seed being one[2] (Galatians 3:16) does point to Christ, but it doesn't simply point to the man,

---

1   https://en.wikipedia.org/wiki/Set_theory. Also, Bohm, David. *Wholeness and the Implicate Order*, Routledge, 2002, for a higher order treatment of this idea.
2   Seed, p. 142.

Jesus Christ. Rather, it points to Christ's role in the Trinity, in the wholeness of God, and in the wholeness or unity of Christians in Christ.[3]

While it is possible to differentiate Jesus Christ from the other members of the Trinity, it is not possible to separate them. They always appear together in the Person of Jesus Christ because of Christ's role as Messiah or mediator between God and man. Thus, to speak of Abraham's seed as being Jesus Christ involves the wholeness of Jesus Christ, which includes all those who are in Christ throughout history. It is this wholeness of Christ that constitutes Christian unity, and this wholeness or unity, like Christ, cannot be broken or separated, though various parts of it can be differentiated. That differentiation always belongs to thought and discussion, and not to reality.

Christ is not like a manufactured thing than can be assembled from and disassembled into its constituent parts. Jesus Christ is a Person, and just like other human persons He is always whole—and His wholeness includes the Father and the Spirit. Life is always a function of wholeness; each instance of life, whether cellular or macro, is whole. Each instance, each cell or critter exists as a functioning whole. And that wholeness is essential for life to exist.

Thus, Paul's comment about Abraham's seed does indeed refer to Jesus Christ, but it also refers to Christ's church in the same way that a farmer thinks of a hybrid seed in terms of the crop(s) it can produce. Yet, the farmer also refers to the hybrid seed in the singular because it is a *type* of seed. Paul's comment about Abraham's seed involves typology, and refers to Christ's church, Christ's people, those who are in Christ. That's the type of people they are.

And yet to mention Christ's church is for us today to invite misunderstanding because of the long history of misunderstanding among Christ's church(es). That misunderstanding issues from the many churches themselves, which have endeavored to define and create themselves as various cultural institutions or cultural subgroups. Of course, such definition and creation was a necessary part of the development and growth of Christ's church, Christ's people, those who are in Christ. But as Christ's church, Christ's people, those who are in

---

3   Ross, Phillip A. *Colossians—Christos Singularis*, Pilgrim Platform, Marietta, Ohio, 2010.

Christ grow as a group and over time begin to dominate culture. Those divisions that were once important in the beginning become less important until at last they become impediments to the later development of Christ's church, Christ's people, those who are in Christ.

In the beginning of Christian history it was essential to differentiate and separate Christ and Christ's way from Satan and Satan's way in order to produce interest and cultural momentum to replace Satan's way with Christ's way. The initial focus was on the differences. But as Christ became increasingly effective and more and more people began following Christ's way, the more important it becomes to abandon the focus on the differences between Christ's way and Satan's way, and the more important it becomes to focus on the extant unity of Christ and His people. In the beginning it is important to distinguish between the spirit and the flesh, for instance. But over time we need to give more attention to the spirit and less to the flesh.

To continue focusing on the differences gives Satan more attention than he deserves, and leads to various legitimate differences among faithful Christians to be falsely attributed to Satan. In the end, for any group to continue to focus attention on group differences rather than group unity in Christ will tend toward group division rather than group cohesion. Groups, like individuals, have stages of growth and maturity, and what is needed in the early stages is not what is needed in the later stages. Thus, to attempt to return to first century Christianity in the twenty-first century is like an adult individual reverting to baby food and diapers. It is madness.

I am aware that this cuts across the grain of the common understanding about reformation and revival in the churches. The usual understanding of renewal is for the church to return to some former era of church glory and perceived success. Some want to return to the first century, some to the fourth, others to the sixteenth, and some to the nineteenth. And what is usually meant by such a return is to return to the practices, beliefs, and/or theology that was active at that time.

This desire is thought to be faithful to Jeremiah's admonition:

"Thus says the Lord: 'Stand by the roads, and look, and ask for the ancient paths, where the good way is; and walk in it, and find rest for your souls.'" (Jeremiah 6:16).

Jeremiah called for a return to the ancient paths, and we might wonder what paths he had in mind since he was preaching in opposition to a reform movement during the First Temple period. Did he have in mind to return to the Tabernacle[4] period? Or perhaps the giving of law to Moses on Mt. Sinai? I suspect Jeremiah had the latter in mind, the giving and receiving of the Ten Commandments, which provide the basis for God's mission to humanity.

But also note that Jeremiah called for a return to the ancient paths, not to some time of former glory, nor to some former application of the Ten Commandments. Rather, he called for a return to the source, for a fresh application of the Ten Commandments. Note also that the source he referred to is not a point but a path. That source is what I have referred to elsewhere as a trajectory.[5] A path is a way, a direction, a route. He was not calling for a return to a former doctrine, but to the old path, the old way, the old trajectory.

Church renewal, reformation, or revival is always a social thing and never merely an individual thing. It is a revival of social values and norms, a reformation of culture. Of course, it involves individuals, but to constrain it to nothing but individuals is to rob it of its greater effectiveness. Genuine church renewal always spurs on genuine cultural renewal, and by renewal I mean the fresh engagement of the Ten Commandments in the broader culture. Where the broader culture is not reached, the efforts of renewal flounder because they cannot get any traction on the path. The wheels of reformation spin, heat is generated, but the church—God's people, those in Christ—go nowhere for the lack of traction. Genuine reformation and revival is never a simple return to some previous time, practice, understanding, or theology, but rather involves a fresh, serious, and sustained engagement of God's Ten Commandments from the contemporary perspective of the larger culture. Though genuine reformation and revival begins in the church, it cannot be contained to the church because it expands the church through renewal, reconsideration, and conversion. This is how the church, Abraham's seed, grows into a fruitful harvest.

---

4   *The Tabernacle*, p. 15
5   Ross, Phillip. A. *Peter's Vision of The End in Second Peter*, Pilgrim Platform, Marietta, Ohio, 2012, Index: trajectory.

HEIRS

God promised Abraham an heir, and that heir was Isaac. But it was not Isaac alone. Rather, Isaac was the representative head of God's chosen lineage. But was that lineage a function of being born of Abraham's flesh, or of Abraham's spirit? We know the answer today, but the Jews of Abraham's day did not divide flesh and spirit as we so often do today. At that time God used the Jews to develop a sustainable culture that could carry God's spiritual message of grace into the far distant future. And the most effective way to do that was the develop historical institutions that would carry over generation to generation. Ancient Israel's understanding of circumcision contributed to that project.

That was what God's church needed at that time, but today we are not called to revert to the practices of Abraham's day. Thus, we have Paul's various messages about circumcision being unnecessary. The practice of circumcision had a purpose, but in Christ that purpose has been fulfilled. It's fulfillment means that it is no longer necessary to practice circumcision. However, just because a thing is not necessary does not always mean that it should be abandoned. Rather, it means that it *can* be abandoned without consequences. It may still have some value other than its original value in its original historic setting.

Understanding this about circumcision helps us understand Paul's more general teaching about law that has been so misunderstood. At its inception circumcision was part of the law. God instituted it, and it needed to be a sustainable practice from generation to generation. With the advent of Christ the practice of circumcision and other elements of the law had produced the needed historic institutions in Jewish culture for the next phase of God's revelation of truth in Christ to bloom. It bloomed in the birth, death, and resurrection of Jesus Christ, which set in motion a new phase or covenant of God's revelation of truth. This was God's promise from the beginning. Abraham's seed, Abraham's heir—the crop that would grow as a result of God's grace and mercy—entered a new season. And that season began more than two thousand years ago. That crop has been growing in God's field, increasing its yield and dominance in the field over time. That crop is now coming to a new harvest, just as God promised it would. That crop is us!

16. Fullness Of Time

I mean that the heir, as long as he is a child, is no different from a
slave, though he is the owner of everything, but he is under guardians
and managers until the date set by his father. In the same way we
also, when we were children, were enslaved to the elementary princi-
ples of the world. But when the fullness of time had come, God sent
forth his Son, born of woman, born under the law, to redeem those
who were under the law, so that we might receive adoption as sons.
And because you are sons, God has sent the Spirit of his Son into
our hearts, crying, "Abba! Father!" So you are no longer a slave, but
a son, and if a son, then an heir through God.   —Galatians 4:1-7

Paul notes that there is a difference between children and adults, that maturity is a process that requires different things at different times, and that complete freedom is not granted to children. Freedom can and will be abused by the immature. So, learning how to find satisfaction in serving others is a key element for growth into mature, responsible adulthood. Children are no different than slaves in this regard, said Paul.

Such a statement offends our contemporary sensitivities because we have been taught to eschew everything associated with slavery. We think that because we are on the other side of the Civil Rights legislation of the 1960s we are or we ought to be completely free from every vestige of slavery. However, the biblical word translated as *slavery* (δοῦλος) can also be translated as *service*. The word can mean slavery, but it can also suggest one who gives himself up to another's will, those whose service is used by Christ in extending and advancing His cause, to be devoted to another to the disregard of one's own interests.

It is an error to think that the Western institution of slavery practiced by the American Southern states prior to the Civil War was exemplary of the kind of slavery practiced in Paul's day by Christians. Or to think that there was no difference between slavery practiced by Romans and that practiced by Christians in Paul's day. Paul's letter to Philemon serves as a guide for Christian slavery.

Part of the difficulties that cloud our understanding of the slavery issue pertain to the intensity of the prosecution of the Civil Rights Movement that was necessary to break the grip that sin held on the American experiment. While that legislation was passed in 1964 we are still struggling with civil rights issues, and the intensity of our passion tends to cloud the sensitivity of our judgment. So, it will be difficult for many people to hear what Paul was trying to say. Please don't rush to judgment.

Paul's point was that the value of learning Christian service is essential to mature Christian growth and sanctification. The great difference between slavery and service, of course, is the willingness of the servant. Clearly, forced slavery should never be practiced or instituted. But voluntary selfless service of others is a noble and worthy calling that should be encouraged. And it actually is very much encouraged in contemporary society. Consider the idea of servant leadership[1] in the corporate world. Of course, this idea is not new to modernity, but is quite ancient. It is what has always defined good leadership, and has always been abused by too many sinful, selfish leaders.

Paul used the word δοῦλος (*slave* or *servant*) to describe the proper attitude of faithful Christians, those who engaged in voluntary selfless service of others. Societies function best when people are not committed to selfish concern for one's own welfare, but when people are committed to selfless concern for the welfare of others. Thus, Paul refers to Christians as slaves to Christ.

> "For he who was called in the Lord as a bondservant (δοῦλος) is a freedman of the Lord. Likewise he who was free when called is a bondservant of Christ" (1 Corinthians 7:22).

---

1   Greenleaf, Robert K.; Spears, Larry C. *Servant Leadership: A Journey into the Nature of Legitimate Power and Greatness*, Paulist Press, 2002.

This double meaning of the word causes much confusion for the immature who are naturally self-centered. Overcoming self-concern and the rush to judge others is a mark of Christian maturity.

ELEMENTARY

Paul's underlying presupposition, following a major theme of the Old Testament, was the reality of historical development. Humanity as a whole is like a human individual in that humanity itself, the corporate whole, grows and matures over time. One way to understand this is to consider history, which consists of the writings of various people over time. Those writings accumulate as each new generation reviews and adds to the collective story as it unfolds over time, adjusting to the trajectory of historical understanding. The mere volume of literature increases over time as it accumulates, adding depth, insight, scope, significance, etc. to the arc of the story. Of course, the momentum of history is both progressive and regressive, in that some lessons are learned and mistakes are corrected, and at other times lessons are not learned and mistakes repeated. Whatever else it is, history is dynamic, not static. It may not always move forward, as it sometimes stagnates, but it cannot move backward. Time unfolds like a unidirectional arrow.

So, the elementary principles Paul mentioned can be thought of as being analogous to childhood ideas that necessarily precede more mature lessons of life. Some of the more basic, *elementary* things must be assimilated before other more complex and advanced lessons can even be considered. There is an order of learning that precedes from the simple to the complex, from the shallow to the deep. Think of the progress of learning math. First we must learn addition and subtraction, then multiplication and division, then geometry, where we learn various mathematical facts and relationships that exist in the world. Mastering geometry requires knowledge of trigonometry, which leads to calculus. The order of progress is necessary. And so, said Paul, is the unfolding of human maturity over time.

Individuals always exist in a specific historical context, and their self-understanding and identity cannot be separated from that historical context. Early in human development the accumulation of history was small, and that accumulation contributed significantly to the context of the individuals who lived during that particular time. As time passes the accumulation of history grows, which enlarges the context of later individuals. This does not necessarily mean that contemporary people are always smarter than their predecessors. But it does mean that the potential to be smarter is there, where smarter means access to a greater volume of history. Of course, access does not necessarily mean mastery thereof. Contemporary people are *potentially* smarter than their predecessors, but the degree of individual realization of that potential can be quite varied.

Yet, we are not just talking about our progressive maturity over time and history. We are also talking about the fact that over time our understanding of Christ increases as more people seriously consider and study Him. And as more people are in unity with Him, the brightness of the truth that He has revealed about God and Himself also increases. The very light of Christ increases over time.

Another aspect of this phenomenon is related to what we call *big data* and *data-intensive computing*. I'm suggesting the contemporary insight that individuals who compute data become exponentially more powerful when they are networked into data sharing groups—societies. We see the same sort of phenomenon with fire. A group of logs will burn exponentially hotter than a single log burning alone. The combination grows exponentially rather than arithmetically. And the same kind of thing happens with people, or I should say with populations that can share data contemporaneously, that are networked through modern communication technologies. The wealth of information and computational power increases with technologically networked populations, which produces new and expanded technologies, which allow for larger networks.

We can also think of this phenomenon as an increase in consciousness or awareness of more raw information as a result of technologically networked populations. This does not mean that every individual takes or is able to take advantage of these increases. It only means that the increases are available to those who are able to pursue them. A similar thing happened with the invention and spread of the printing press as ideas began to be shared among more and more people. More books were available to more people, but again, that does not mean that everyone had the same access, opportunity, or ability to read them. But many did!

One more analogy comes to mind. The average individual living in the first century, for instance, would interface directly with nature much more often than the average individual living in the twenty-first century. Those living in the twenty-first century would interface much more with the technological world created by humanity than with raw nature in the wild. Living in modern cities is quite different than living on an ancient farm. Thus, first century individuals would better master life in nature, while twenty-first century individuals would more likely flounder in nature because their energy and attention is spent on mastering life in a technological world. The point is that their experiences of life, their contexts, are quite different, and in many ways incommunicable to previous generations in a similar way that many elements of adult life are incommunicable (not understandable) to the young. The young just don't have the accumulated experience from which to draw big data patterns and relationships. But neither do the old live in the same world as the young, particularly as the speed of technology has increased. Thus, human growth and maturity is progressive. It unfolds in a particular order, which is part of Paul's point.

FREEDOM

Children should not be granted complete freedom until they have learned the value of selfless service of others. Granting premature freedom usually fuels the growth of pride and selfishness. This is such common sense that it hardly needs to be said, but this is exactly what Paul was saying here. Paul was speaking analogously, suggesting that that history itself was like an individual in that early history was like the childhood of man, and that the advent of Christ marked the beginning of humanity's maturity. Or we might argue that Paul did not refer to humanity in general, but to Israel as God's chosen people. Nonetheless, the point remains.

However, while this argument is true, it falls short of God's intention for all of humanity, in that the gospel of God's grace was always intended to be a blessing to all humanity. Part of Paul's point was that the manifestation of God's original intent had been delayed, it was not fully manifest instantly in early human history, partly because humanity exists in time. And existence in time always involves process, a course of action, of maturity, and not simply an instance. It takes time to send and to receive a message. It takes time to learn. Often it requires time and repetition to learn what we need and how the world works.

During this time of childhood or adolescence humanity was "under guardians and managers" (v. 1)—rules, Moses' elders and laws. God gave Moses the Ten Commandments to give to the people, which he did. But they could not rightly utilize them. They were unable to appropriately apply them to their nomadic existence. God was ready and willing just to kill them all for their inability, but Moses intervened. So God led Moses and his seventy elders to help apply them to their various circumstances. That was good and helpful, so these laws became codified over time. However, we now clearly know because Christ has come, that all of those laws were not intended to be eternal. We see in Christ's teaching that He reinterpreted the Ten Commandments to better guide His people into the future of His making. Various laws of Moses were fulfilled by Him, others were abrogated, others became unnecessary. And we are still in the process of coming to grips with these changes.

FULLNESS

The fullness of time refers to the completion of Israel's history that led to the manifestation of the long awaited Messiah. Moses had foretold of His coming (Deuteronomy 15:18), and the history of the Old Testament was then fulfilled by His coming. Matthew 1:1-17 provides an overview of that story from the perspective of Christ's genealogy, concluding:

> "So all the generations from Abraham to David were fourteen generations, and from David to the deportation to Babylon fourteen generations, and from the deportation to Babylon to the Christ fourteen generations" (Matthew 1:17).

The deportation of ancient Israel to Babylon, which followed the destruction of the First Temple, provided the fulcrum or the midpoint in Matthew's historical analysis. Matthew considered all that led to the building, corruption, and destruction of the First Temple to be the first half of that history, and all that led to the building, corruption, and de-struction of the Second Temple to be the second half—and the two halves make a whole, a fullness. The history of the Temple was full be-cause it had been fulfilled. God sent His Son, not as a substitute for the Temple, but as the real Temple. If anything, the Temple(s) of the past had been used as a substitute for the Son.

HUMAN SON

Paul specified three things in v. 4. First, that God sent His Son, second, that He was born of a woman, and third, that He was born under the law. These things are important.

To understand the first point, allow me to digress into prenatal medicine as an analogy. The blood that flows in a fetus' arteries and veins is only produced within the body of the fetus itself. It is different from the blood of the mother. And that process begins only after the introduction of the male sperm to the ovum. An unfertilized ovum cannot develop blood because the unfertilized female egg does not contain the elements essential for the production of blood. It is only af-ter the male sperm has entered the ovum that blood is able to develop.

The mother provides the unborn fetus with the nutritive elements for the building of the baby's body through the placenta.

> "The fetal heart pumps blood through the arteries of the umbilical
> cord into the placental vessels, which, looping in and out of the uter-
> ine tissue and lying in close contact with the uterine vessels, permit a
> diffusion, through their walls, of waste products from child to
> mother and of nourishment and oxygen from mother to child. As has
> been said, this interchange is effected by the process of osmosis, and
> there is no direct mingling of the two blood currents. In other
> words, no maternal blood actually flows to the fetus, nor is there any
> direct fetal blood flow to the mother."[2]

In the language of the Bible, because Adam was the federal head of the human race, it is his blood that carries Adam's sin through the generations. Therefore, in order for a sinless man to be born a son of Adam, God needed to provide a way for that man to have a human body derived from Adam—Eve's body was derived from Adam, but not contaminated by Adam's sinful blood, his sperm. Thus, Mary's vir-

---

2   Zabriskie, Louise R.N. *Nurse's Handbook of Obstetrics*, Fifth Edition, 1937, p. 82.

gin birth accounts for the sinlessness of Jesus Christ because Jesus' blood was begun by the Holy Spirit, by God Himself—who is not a child of Adam.

An old answer to the issue of Christ's sinlessness in conjunction with His human birth involved making Mary into an "Immaculate Virgin." But her virginity alone does not solve the problem of how Jesus was sinless, because the bloodline runs through the male. The mother is not responsible for the blood of her fetus, the father is. The concern is not even whether Mary had premarital sex or not. The issue is the father's blood, not Mary's. Joseph was not Jesus' biological father, nor was Jesus' Father a son of Adam.

And yet Jesus was born subject to the law, which would have been the law of Moses. Jesus as covenantal head and mediator between God and humanity needed to be of the same biblical kind as those in the covenant, those for whom He would mediate. Jesus needed to be fully human in order to provide a typological model for human beings. And because human beings are under God's law, Jesus also needed to be under that law, and to be subject to its blessings and curses. Jesus needed to be under the law in order to fulfill it. It was necessary for the law to apply to Him—not necessary for God's sake, but for ours.

REDEMPTION

The purpose of Christ's redemption of humanity is to move people from one set, group, or category to another, from lost to saved, from the Old Covenant to the New, from death to life, etc. The rules or laws that determine set membership are determined by the definition, determination, or description of the set.[3] There are two ways to move members from one set to another: the definition or rules of the set can be changed, or the character of the members can be changed.

In the case at hand, the original set of humanity, whose bloodline originated from Adam, was under God's covenant of blessings and curses (Genesis 3, Deuteronomy 28). This one set was divided into two potential sets: the obedient and the disobedient, or the blessed and the cursed. The covenant included every member of humanity, and always will. The consequences or judgments of each subset result in eternal death for the cursed, and eternal life for the blessed. These con-

3   See footnote 1, p. 160.

sequences are eternally true, covenant breakers will always be cursed and covenant keepers will always be blessed. Eternal damnation then suggests that a particular *type* of individual (or behavior) will be always be cursed and a particular *type* of individual (or behavior) will always be blessed, not that particular individuals will exist forever.

The problem was that "none are righteous, no not one" (Romans 3:10, 3:23; Ecclesiastes 7:20; Psalm 14:3). The whole world had been under God's curse since Adam and Eve fell. So, the idea of blessings and curses was true enough, but no one could get out from under God's curse. Until Christ came.

The words *forever* and *eternal* in the Bible are not used in the sense of modern mathematical or cosmological precision, but in the common sense of ordinary life as it is experienced by human individuals. The proper meaning of the words requires proportion and scale, because nothing meaningful can be understood or said of the truly infinite. Meaning requires some frame of reference, human understanding requires a human frame of reference. This is why God began with history and manifested as a man. Because *eternal* is a measure of time, the lifespan of individuals provides an appropriate reference that dwarfs a human lifespan in comparison to eternity. Thus, *forever* and *eternal* in the Bible mean something like: as long as humanity exists as a species or kind. Individuals do not exist as individuals beyond this, and nothing meaningful can be said about time frames longer than the entire history of humanity. Beyond this we have no reliable witness.

Therefore, eternal damnation and eternal salvation apply to types and behaviors engaged in by individuals, such that obedience to God will result in blessings, and disobedience in curses within the lifespan of humanity. However, these results will not necessarily be immediately perceptible by the self-centered, coarse, shallow, limited, and sinful sensitivities of the individuals involved. In addition, the consequences of individuals accrue to societies, not just to the individuals themselves. And societies (populations), like crops and herds, increase and decrease over long, multi-generational, seasonal patterns. This is the frame of reference for the definitions of *forever* and *eternal* in Scripture.

Although biblical salvation and damnation are spoken of in eternal terms, the frame of reference pertains to the immediate life behaviors of individuals. Christ is presented as a kind of historical watershed in which individuals can immediately participate through union with Christ, which produces a change of direction with regard to individual futurity. Union with Christ brings individuals into harmonious flow with others toward salvation that is provided by the watershed of Christ.

Christ's redemption applies to *this* frame of reference because redemption is necessarily a group thing in that saved individuals are moved from one group to another, from being lost to being saved, from being cursed to being blessed, from disobedience in Adam to obedience in Christ. Prior to Christ, obedience was not even an option, though many Old Testament saints were saved by grace.

Thus, saved individuals are adopted as sons. Adoption is a legal term that applies to families, clans, or groups. An adoption is a legal proceeding that creates a parent-child relation between persons not related by blood, and the adopted child is then entitled to all privileges belonging to a natural child of the adoptive parents, including the right to inheritance. The adopted children do not initiate adoption proceedings. Initiation belongs to the potential parent, not the potential child. If the child is old enough, he or she may be asked to consent to the adoption. In the case before us Jesus Christ initiated the adoption and believers who are able, consent to it. Nonetheless, Jesus Christ has adopted humanity—the species, the kind, the seed. All humanity is still subject to God's eternal covenant—blessings and curses, but in Christ believers consent and conform to Christ and enjoy forgiveness and eternal salvation. That is, all who consent and conform to Christ will always be saved, forever and eternally, as long as humanity exists. This is the plain meaning of verse five.

REGENERATION

Precisely because Jesus Christ initiated and completed the adoption procedure by paying the price on the cross, "God has sent the Spirit of his Son into our hearts" (v. 6). The Spirit that motivates and animates Jesus Christ is the same Spirit that motivates and animates believers to consent to God's adoption and conform to Christ's desires for His people. This is nothing other than the fruit of regeneration.

The fact that Christ's Spirit is sent to our hearts and not our heads means that the Holy Spirit has been sent to affectively govern our hearts, our emotions, our desires, our love. Christ is the governor of love. He sets the rules; He sets the direction; He sets the context; and He sets the fire of passion. He lights the path; He lightens the load; He enlightens the mind; and He lights the fire of commitment. He is the object of love; He is the means of love; He is the essence of love; and He is the ardor of love.

The cry, "Abba, father!" (v. 6), is a cry of recognition. The child recognizes the Father as his own father. He recognizes himself as a child of his Father. It is not just the recognition that God is God, but that God is *my Father*. In a very real sense, it is the Spirit who has been sent to the heart who recognizes God the Father. Only the Spirit can recognize the Father because no one "has seen the Father except he who is from God" (John 6:46). The old adage, it takes one to know one, applies. The expression, the cry, is the proof of the existence of the cause in the heart of the believer.

Verse 7 then announces a change of category, the slave becomes a child by adoption. The irresponsible slave of sin becomes a responsible servant of Christ. The change from slave to servant is as important as any of the other changes. The slave does not become a self-centered master, but an other-centered steward. Slave and master are always in a symbiotic relationship. If there are no masters there cannot be any slaves. Both are caught up in a self-enclosed, mutually reciprocal bondage with one another. The definition of each one requires the existence of the other. Both are slaves to sin. The master is no more free than the slave. Christ's intent is not simply to abolish slavery, but to transform slavery into servant leadership. The former slave can become a better servant leader *because* he has learned to serve as a slave. Christians are slaves in willing and joyful service to Christ

Similarly, the transition from a slave economy to a service economy does not change what people do, it changes how people do it. The slave becomes a son, but the son does not forget or abandon what he has learned as a slave. As a slave he learned how to serve others, how to be attentive to the needs of others. But now he does not serve others because he has to, but because he wants to. He no longer sees it as a drudgery, but now sees it as an expression of love. Christians are not like former slaves who now despise serving others because they see such service as menial and below their new station in life. Rather, Christians serve others as an expression of their love for Jesus Christ, whom they now see in the lives of others.

> "For I was hungry and you gave me food, I was thirsty and you gave me drink, I was a stranger and you welcomed me, I was naked and you clothed me, I was sick and you visited me, I was in prison and you came to me.' Then the righteous will answer him, saying, 'Lord, when did we see you hungry and feed you, or thirsty and give you drink? And when did we see you a stranger and welcome you, or naked and clothe you? And when did we see you sick or in prison and visit you?' And the King will answer them, 'Truly, I say to you, as you did it to one of the least of these my brothers, you did it to me'" (Matthew 25:35-40).

By learning how to attend to others (which is another definition of δοῦλος), the slave-become-son is actually a better son because of that former training through service, through learning how to be a help to others. Consequently, the slave who has become a son does not disparage his experience as a slave, but is able to thank God for it, for the training and the lessons learned. This is not only true individually, but it serves as an analogy for Israel.

It is interesting and noteworthy that in the above quote the *righteous* are actively doing God's will, but don't realize it. While such a lack of awareness is not to be a norm, it does have significant implications. The behavior, serving the needs of the poor and infirm, is to be a norm. And those engaged in this service are being instructed that their service is also service to Christ. Ordinarily, knowing God and doing the will of God would go together, but when they don't, doing God's will trumps just knowing God, and especially if knowing God does not lead to some commensurate service.

The purpose of becoming a son is inheritance, and what is inherited from the Father are the Father's valuables, the Father's values in this case. The importance of inheriting the Father's characteristics is far more important than inheriting the Father's wealth because the Father's characteristics are what allowed Him to accumulate His wealth. To inherit God's characteristics does not mean that we become like God in His divine characteristics, it means that we inherit His human characteristics—but not His physically human characteristics, His spiritually human characteristics. We become like Jesus, able to grow, mature, and witness to our culture as Jesus did. We share His family values, His character—not perfectly, but progressively.

17. Return Not

Formerly, when you did not know God, you were enslaved to those that by nature are not gods. But now that you have come to know God, or rather to be known by God, how can you turn back again to the weak and worthless elementary principles of the world, whose slaves you want to be once more? You observe days and months and seasons and years! I am afraid I may have labored over you in vain.
—Galatians 4:8-11

This is not a new argument or idea. Rather, Paul was repeating himself in order to make the point clear that the Galatians were both exceedingly guilty and exceedingly stupid for their abandonment of the gospel that he had taught them—spiritually stupid. Genuine spiritual growth cannot return to some previous time or level, it presses forward. It may get stuck at times, but going backward is not an option. Anyone who actually does go backward was probably deceiving themselves about their growth in the first place. It's not that such people actually go backwards, but that they were never as far along as they thought they were.

Paul understood and taught that there is only one actual God, that all other so-called gods are figments of human imagination. This does not mean that the deception and damage done by such gods is not real—it is very real! The deception and damage, that is, not the gods. And that means that he was saying that they were slaves to imagination. They were slaves to their own thinking.

Before we come down too hard on them for such idiocy, we ought to examine ourselves for inasmuch as we, both individually and as a society, do not rely on God's Word in the Bible, Paul would accuse us of the same thing. We in the modern West are not unlike the Galatians because the roots of our civilization are decidedly Christian, yet in our contemporary situation we are in the process of abandoning our Christian rootage. Actually, this process has been going on for centuries and has accelerated its momentum over time, especially since the 1960s as the process has bled into the legal structures of society. Yet, the blame does not lie with the lawyers or the government, but with the people, and especially the people in the churches because the root is, above all, religious in nature.

To understand this we need to know how people came to know God, or rather to be known by God. The Galatian church was composed of both Jews and gentiles, which is important because it suggests that they both had similar experiences of both their former condition as slaves and as servants in Christ. Something common to both groups brought about common changes to both groups.

Paul was writing and preaching prior to the fall of Jerusalem and the Temple in A.D. 70. And because that event would have been the most significant event for the generations alive at that time we must consider the events that lead up it, which brings us to the life, ministry, and death of Jesus Christ. Paul was arguing that they had come to know God through Jesus Christ, or rather that God had come in the Person of Jesus Christ to know them, to get to know them through a personal relationship through the Person of the Holy Spirit.

Paul then said that these two groups, Jews and gentiles—the Romans in particular, had similar expectations about God. There was a common link between the lives and experience of Jews and that of the gentiles. And to see this we need to understand that Rome had much in common with the Temple regarding its understanding and use of law. Both were theocracies, in spite of their different theologies. The Temple was monotheistic and Rome was polytheistic, yet their similarities were many, in that they had similar beliefs that their God or gods demanded obedience to their laws. Both had substituted obedience to their laws for faithfulness to God or to their gods. Both were guilty of idolatry through the substitution of obedience to the laws of men for faithfulness to the laws of God.

This is more difficult to see in the case of the Temple, whereas in Rome the Emperor was understood to be god incarnate who was making law for Rome as she grew. In fact, Rome's growth through conquest and stability through military strength were understood to be blessings of the gods. Rome's successes were considered to be signs that the gods were pleased with Rome. Rome was renowned throughout the world for her religiosity and her tolerance of religion. Rome would tolerate any religion that was not claiming sovereignty over Rome. The Jewish establishment had a special relationship with Rome such that the Jewish establishment could say what they wanted to their people, as long as Rome could choose the High Priest. That choice gave Rome sovereignty over the Temple. Rome would have been satisfied with a Christianity that did something similar.

However, the God that Paul worshiped in Christ, the God that Paul had taught to the Galatians demanded sovereignty over Rome, just as the God of the Temple demanded sovereignty over the Temple. Rome's laws did not have sovereignty over Jesus Christ, nor did the Temple laws, Moses' laws, have sovereignty over the God of the Temple. And this issue stuck in the craw of both Rome and the Jewish establishment for exactly the same reasons.

The weak and worthless elementary principles Paul mentioned were the false ideas in both groups that encouraged and justified the sovereignty of the Roman system and/or the Jewish system over God in Christ. Elsewhere (Ephesians 6:12) Paul spoke of very real principalities and powers that prosecuted these false ideas. Both systems elevated their laws over Jesus Christ, thinking that Christ would exercise sovereignty just like they would, by lording it over their people. Neither realized that Jesus Christ is not opposed to law in itself, or that He could work with either group because He had come to redeem the people in both groups. He came to change the hearts and minds of people in both groups.

To be slaves to the principles of Rome and the Temple simply means two things: 1) living in slavish obedience to the law of Rome or the law of the Temple, Moses' law; and/or 2) doing what *you* think is right. God came in Christ in order to speak to His people, to clarify some of their misunderstandings, and to establish His church on the right foundation. Slavery is easy: follow orders. Freedom is difficult. Freedom takes preparation and responsibility.

The actual changes that Jesus Christ brought to the world are so drastic and far-ranging that it is easy to imagine that as people became more aware of the magnitude of those changes, they became fearful. To actually live as Christ calls us to live still changes lives beyond recognition. People are not who they think they are, they are who God made them to be. A change in basic identity, the essence of re-generation and conversion, is scary and difficult in any age. However, today we have centuries of testimony, support, and encouragement to help us with the transition. The Galatians did not have any such helps. All of which is to say that we should not be surprised that some of them changed their minds as they began to see what all was involved.

CALENDAR

Paul's allusion to "days and months and seasons and years" (v. 10) points to their return to the observance of religious holidays, which celebrate the religious system the Jews commemorated. So, it was not just about holidays, it was about returning to the religious values and structures that honor them. The days and events themselves were not the object of Paul's remonstrance.

This illustrates the problem of biblical literalism, the theological position that the contents of the Bible should be understood to be lit-erally true, as opposed to being interpreted as narrative, allegory, allusion, poetry, etc. The meaning of a passage or story is not in the words themselves, though it is dependent upon the words. Rather, meaning always issues out of perspective, interpretation, understand-ing, and acquisition. Meaning requires a marriage of proclamation and reclamation, of what is said and what is heard, of objectivity and sub-jectivity. However, it must also be understood that this marriage is not the calculation of an average or mean, but holds the marriage partners in an agreed unity that does not obscure, damage, or destroy their in-dividual uniqueness.

God's Trinitarian character guarantees the eternal value and main-tenance of personal individuality and uniqueness because each member of the Godhead eternally maintains its own individuality and unique-ness in the unity of the Godhead. Individuality means not divisible, and uniqueness is the quality of being one of a kind. Indeed, God is not divisible, and is the one and only of His kind—the Trinitarian God. Yet, He manifests in time as Father, Son, and Holy Spirit, each of which shares fully in His individuality and uniqueness. In fact, God's differentiation as Father, Son, and Holy Spirit make Him even more unique in His individuality than would be the case if the reality of the Trinity were not true.

And because Judaism has never acquiesced to the Trinity, and most certainly did not do so during Jesus' life on earth, the Galatian return to legalism expressed by Paul as the return to "days and months and seasons and years" (v. 10), their turning back, amounted to the rejection of the Trinitarian character of God in Christ. Or we could say that it amounted to the rejection of the divinity of Jesus Christ, who is divine because of His role in the Trinity—which, because of the unity of the Godhead, makes Him God Himself.

As Paul thought about the significance of all of this, he thought that he might have labored in vain among them. He thought that his teaching among them might have been in vain, that it might come to nothing. Perhaps his efforts with them never took root, if they could be so easily dissuaded from the truth he had taught them. He knew from his own experience that he could never return to Judaism, that he could never abandon Jesus Christ, even if it cost him his life! He knew that he was incapable of returning to some former time or belief. The arrow of time is irreversible.

It is important to notice that Paul doubted them, doubted their faith, and even doubted himself, his ability to effectively teach. But he never doubted God or Jesus Christ or the value and power of the Holy Spirit. This is a lesson well worth learning.

18. ALL TOGETHER NOW

*Brothers, I entreat you, become as I am, for I also have become as you
are. You did me no wrong. You know it was because of a bodily ailment that I preached the gospel to you at first, and though my condition was a trial to you, you did not scorn or despise me, but received
me as an angel of God, as Christ Jesus. What then has become of
your blessedness? For I testify to you that, if possible, you would
have gouged out your eyes and given them to me. Have I then become
your enemy by telling you the truth?*   —Galatians 4:12-16

There has been much speculation about these verses, about their
time reference, and about Paul's ailment. The word ἀσθενής
here refers to a weakness of the flesh, not a thorn (σκόλοψ, 2
Corinthians 12:7), so there is no reason to conflate them. Nor is there
any reason that Paul would wish anyone to be afflicted by either a
weakness of the flesh or a thorn in the flesh. Therefore, in keeping with
the larger theme of Galatians, that Paul was motivated by *The Backstory*
of the Old Testament, it makes sense to understand Paul to be referring
to the veil that had blinded the Jewish people for centuries, a veil that he
had known very personally and intimately, a veil that the Lord had also
removed from Paul. That veil was both a weakness and a thorn.

AILMENT
Paul had been like them, blinded by the veil. And he wanted them
to become like him—healed and whole in Christ, like he was after Christ
had removed the blindness of the veil from him. This understanding
would work better if the latter clause of v. 4 was rendered in the past
tense, which would then read: *become as I am, for I also have been as you
are.* This minor adjustment in the translation tense opens the verse up to

much greater depth and breadth of understanding, and dovetails nicely with the larger theme of Galatians.

Given the magnitude of Paul's concern in this letter so far, there is little reason to think that he would at this point mention some personal illness that has nothing to add to his argument of gospel and law. To do so would be very uncharacteristic of Paul, since he seems to have had very little regard for his own well-being or comfort. For instance,

> "I am talking like a madman—with far greater labors, far more imprisonments, with countless beatings, and often near death. Five times I received at the hands of the Jews the forty lashes less one. Three times I was beaten with rods. Once I was stoned. Three times I was shipwrecked; a night and a day I was adrift at sea; on frequent journeys, in danger from rivers, danger from robbers, danger from my own people, danger from Gentiles, danger in the city, danger in the wilderness, danger at sea, danger from false brothers; in toil and hardship, through many a sleepless night, in hunger and thirst, often without food, in cold and exposure. And, apart from other things, there is the daily pressure on me of my anxiety for all the churches" (2 Corinthians 11:23-28).

He was in the midst of making the most important argument in the history of the Bible—and he knew it! There is no place in the prosecution of this argument for tangential references to personal misfortunes. Yet, so many commentators continue to chase around petty concerns of still veiled truths because they are unaware or unwilling to accept *The Backstory* as the compelling context of Paul's insight.

Paul's illness or weakness of the flesh was the same illness of the flesh that humanity had suffered since the Fall—sin. As an active Jew and a Pharisee, he probably thought that his Temple participation had covered his sin, that prior to Jesus his sin was not a problem. But in fact, Paul's sin was the same sin that the Jews had fallen into since at least the preaching of Jeremiah and Isaiah, and probably even earlier. That sin set the context of *The Backstory*, and was the central sin that Christ had come to correct—to heal, to forgive, to overcome. Christ came to provide a new adaptation and application of God's ancient law for the new people who would transcend Adam and the world history that had developed in the image of Adam.

Beginning on the road to Damascus, the risen Christ had confronted Paul directly and personally, shining a light on and through him that was so bright that it blinded him. But in spite of his illness, his sin, and his blindness following his conversion, that light was also the source of his healing. And because of that healing he began preaching and shared Christ with everyone everywhere every chance he had.

The Christian community had taken Saul in, or at least Judas did (Acts 9:11). Ananias was then sent to Judas' house to heal Paul's blindness, after which Paul was baptized and began preaching. Paul, who had the authority to hound, arrest, and even kill Christians, began to preach Christ. Imagine how difficult that was for everyone involved. Paul confessed, "at first, and though my condition was a trial to you, you did not scorn or despise me" (vs. 13-14). The Christian community nursed Paul back to health from his crisis of conversion, which no doubt was dramatic and stark. Surely it took a psychological toll, as Paul readjusted himself to his new reality in Christ. He could not return to his former family and friends for help. For quite a while he probably couldn't show his face in public.

But as Paul began to piece together the message of Jesus Christ for himself, and as others listened to him, they received him as an angel or messenger of God. They heard God's message about Jesus Christ taking shape in Paul, and they received him "as an angel of God, as Christ Jesus" (v. 14). They received his message about Christ as if Christ Himself had been speaking through him because what he revealed about Christ could have come from nowhere else.

Paul's question about what had happened to their blessedness was about their former evaluation of his preaching, and their blessings upon him that had given him the right to preach among them. The Galilean Judaizers had turned their backs on what Paul had formerly taught them about *The Backstory* of Israel. It would have been quite easy to do because Israel had been blinded to it for eons—still is! *The Backstory* provided a perspective that seemed to turn history itself on its head as it shocked those who heard it into two groups: believers and unbelievers. And it was far easier to disbelieve than to believe because believing seemed so contrary to everything that they had understood and believed about reality as Jews. This made it fairly easy for the Judiaizers to turn the tables on Paul by claiming what the Jews had always believed, by returning to the comforting familiarity of the veil.

Paul's comment about gouging out their eyes must not be read literally, but metaphorically. And the metaphorical meaning of ὀφθαλμός (*eyes*) refers to the eyes of the mind, to the faculty of knowing. Paul's comment is not about physical eyes, but is about knowledge, about understanding something. And the understanding about Jesus Christ that Paul was communicating to them pertained to the role of Jesus Christ in the light of *The Backstory* of the Old Testament. Why would they want to pluck out their own eyes and give them to Paul? Because they did not like what Paul caused them to see, to understand. They did not want to see what Paul had shown them. Paul was suggesting that they could not simply reject what he had taught them because once you see the truth you cannot simply unsee it. Thus, they would have to remove their eyes in order not to see it because the truth was so plain and clear that it could not be denied unless one was completely blind.

"Have I then become your enemy by telling you the truth?" (v. 16).

The truth that Paul told them about Jesus Christ with regard to the law and the gospel has as much to do with correctly understanding the *The Backstory* of the Old Testament, which was the continuing and contemporary story for the Galatians, as it does with Jesus Christ Himself. In fact, it is only understanding Israel's failed mission[1] to the gentiles that makes any discussion of the gentiles relevant. Paul also said,

> "For I am not ashamed of the gospel, for it is the power of God for salvation to everyone who believes, to the Jew first and also to the Greek" (Romans 1:16).

Paul's message was directed to the Jews first in order to correct their understanding of their original mission and bring them back on board with God's primary mission to the whole world. Paul's allusion to the

---

1   Genesis 12:3 says that God's mission was for Israel to be a blessing to the whole world, but by the time of Paul in the Second Temple Israel had collapsed its concern to focus exclusively on her own nationality.

fullness of time that had come (Galatians 4:4) did not *only* mean that the world was now ready for the advent of Jesus Christ, it *also* meant that the history of Israel was full to the brim, that the path that Israel had been on since Moses could not continue. The story of Israel's denial could not continue, the truth could be ignored no longer. History was full, like a boil that had come to a head, like a pregnant woman about to give birth.

The birth of Jesus Christ lanced the boil of Israel's history, it cleared the way for Israel's healing and restitution in Christ. But to deny Jesus Christ amounted to the denial of His role and signaled the desire to return to the pestiferous history of Ancient Israel, which was for the Galatians, not ancient history but contemporary reality. Again, for the Galatians it would have been much easier to abandon Paul and Jesus than to abandon what they had up to that time considered to be their own history and culture. Imagine how difficult it would be to give up on America today, to renounce the proverbial American Dream as being nothing more than a delusional nightmare that brought suffering and difficulties to people everywhere.

19. Doubts

They make much of you, but for no good purpose. They want to shut
you out, that you may make much of them. It is always good to be
made much of for a good purpose, and not only when I am present
with you, my little children, for whom I am again in the anguish of
childbirth until Christ is formed in you! I wish I could be present
with you now and change my tone, for I am perplexed about you.
—Galatians 4:17-20

Verses 17-18 are about membership, about social inclusion and exclusion. No doubt the Judaizers were arguing that it was important that all Jews actively belong and participate in the Temple functions, that they not drop their membership in the Temple, however they understood it. The old argument that God's Temple mission could not be complete without all Israel actively involved was no doubt well-worn because it was effective. Paul was saying that the Judaizers had been wooing them back into the fold, but that there was no good reason for them to go back. Nothing good could come from it.

The other argument the Judaizers made was to threaten them with excommunication, exclusion from social inclusion. Such exclusion could affect their social standing and their work, their business, their occupation, their finances. The threat of exclusion was calculated to make them desire to be included, to want to maintain their position and standing in the community. It would be better for them to want to return to the fold than to be ordered to, or to return because they feared some threat. The best scenario for the Judaizers would be for the Galatians to beg forgiveness and reentry into good standing with the Temple.

Paul then acknowledged the value of making much of people, of wooing people to something, and especially if it is genuinely good. Being wooed into faithfulness is much better and much more effective than being chased from sin. Paul also wooed them, but for good reasons. Paul knew that the blessings of God in Christ were about to overwhelm the whole world. The details of God's time frame were unclear, but Paul was clear and certain that Jesus Christ was beginning a march through history that would change the world for the better by every measure imaginable.

Paul had been enjoining them to get aboard and stay aboard that train. He had done so when he had been with them previously, and wanted to do so again with them when he returned. But he wasn't sure that he would be able to. He knew that he had impregnated them with the gospel of Jesus Christ, that the Holy Spirit had used him to so impregnate them. But he was "again in the anguish of childbirth until Christ is formed in you!" (v. 19). It was unclear to Paul whether that birth would be live or still. The birth could not be properly celebrated until it occurred, because many complications could arise that could foul the birth of the Spirit in them. Nonetheless, whether the birth is live or still, the pain is excruciating. Birth is not a pretty process. It is painful, bloody, and messy—yet joyful!

He was hopeful that he could change his tone, that he could celebrate a live birth. But if a still birth resulted, the tone of his voice would most certainly be different than if it was a live birth. The celebration of a live birth is quite different from the anguish of a still birth. He was doing everything that he could to remain hopeful, but he was concerned, perplexed, baffled, and even in doubt about them.

They could not both remain in good standing with the Temple and worship Christ—not because Paul wouldn't allow it, nor because the Temple establishment wouldn't allow it, but because God Himself would not allow it. The Temple boil had broken open with the birth of Christ, and there could be no going back. Return was not even a remote possibility.

Paul knew that the whole world had already changed. But at the time the world didn't know that yet. Paul was an outlier, he was ahead of his time (1 Corinthians 15:8), and he was trying to help the Galatians see the truth of the history that was unfolding before them, the truth that the advent of Jesus Christ would result in the end of Second Temple Judaism. He thought that they were on board, but now in the light of various reports he had heard about them, about their turning back to days, months, and seasons, he was perplexed.

No, he was more than perplexed or concerned. He was flirting with active doubt about their salvation. Paul was usually eager to encourage people, to inspire people, and to exhort people to believe in Christ. But here he doubted. His doubt was rare, but the circumstances with the Galatians, and the character of their retrenchment in the face of the clarity with which he had taught them caused him to doubt. If they could be turned around with simple promises and threats about their membership in the Temple, then they had failed to understand what they had been taught about Christ being the real Temple. They could not be redeemed to the old Temple because the old Temple itself was irredeemable. Nor had the Judaizers been aware of any promises or programs for Temple redemption. They were fine with it as it was! They represented Temple business as usual.

20. Two Covenants

Tell me, you who desire to be under the law, do you not listen to the law? For it is written that Abraham had two sons, one by a slave woman and one by a free woman. But the son of the slave was born according to the flesh, while the son of the free woman was born through promise. Now this may be interpreted allegorically: these women are two covenants. One is from Mount Sinai, bearing children for slavery; she is Hagar. Now Hagar is Mount Sinai in Arabia; she corresponds to the present Jerusalem, for she is in slavery with her children. But the Jerusalem above is free, and she is our mother. For it is written, "Rejoice, O barren one who does not bear; break forth and cry aloud, you who are not in labor! For the children of the desolate one will be more than those of the one who has a husband."

—Galatians 4:21-27

Behind Paul's words is the accusation that the backsliding Galatians didn't really know what they were doing, that they didn't understand the law that they say they wanted to be under. And prior to Christ, understanding it was extremely difficult. Only a few prophets had a glimpse of what was coming because it is only by the light of Christ that our looking back on history can be faithfully illuminated. So, Paul was shinning that light back on Israel's history for them. Paul pointed to the history of Ishmael and Abraham, and saw in the light of Christ an allegorical interpretation.

We begin with what Paul assumed but didn't say, that God had promised that Abraham would become the father of many nations (Genesis 17:4). Abraham was seventy-five years old at the time, and he and Sarah had no children. Sarah was barren. This promise and the circumstances surrounding it were quite unusual. Nonetheless, Abraham and Sarah treasured God's promise and carried on as usual, but produced no children after a decade or so following God's promise.

Sarah, thinking that the fault was hers, turned to the law for a remedy. She concocted a plan to provide her handmaiden, Hagar, to Abraham to be a surrogate mother in order to give Abraham the son or lineage that God had promised. Apparently, law and custom allowed such a thing. Hagar would be able to help raise her son because she would also be nanny to the son of her lord and master, Abraham, and would be endeared for life to the family. The son would benefit by being a son of the master rather than a son of a handmaiden. And Sarah would also be the legal mother of Abraham's promised son. It was a win-win scenario. Everyone involved had something positive to gain. Ishmael was born to Hagar, and everyone was happy.

Many years earlier three strangers had visited Abraham, and were identified as angels or messengers. They prophesied that Sarah would have a son (Genesis 18:10). Sarah laughed at the prospect because both she and Abraham were very old, beyond childbearing age. Much later Sarah had a son, which changed everything. Those angels, by the way, then turned their attention toward Sodom, and Abraham tried to make a deal with a them not to destroy Sodom if he could find a number of righteous men. He couldn't. But that's another story.

Isaac was born to Sarah—her firstborn, which resulted in a rivalry about which son would receive the greater family inheritance, Ishmael, who by law was the elder son and therefore entitled by law, or Isaac, who was the natural son by the grace of an unexpected birth. Sarah, believing that she had caused the problem by giving Hagar to Abraham as a surrogate, dismissed Hagar and sent her and Ishmael away.

This story, said Paul, was a well-understood and well-accepted allegory about the history of Israel. It served to explain the history of the hostility between Israel and her neighbors. The allegory that Paul was pointing to suggested that just as Hagar and Ishmael represented the rightful heir by law, but was superseded by history—by the promise and grace of Sarah's son, Isaac. So, the birth of Jesus Christ was the fulfillment of an even greater promise of a Son, who both superseded and succeeded the lineage of Isaac as the legal heir of God's grace. Therefore, the inheritance that had been promised to Israel now belonged to Jesus Christ by the same argument.

In the same way that Isaac's birth trumped the law of inheritance away from Ishmael, so the birth of Jesus Christ trumped the law of inheritance away from Israel. So, if Israel acknowledged the validity of Isaac's inheritance, then she must also acknowledge the validity of Christ's, because both operated by the same principle, that the fulfillment of God's promise trumps existing law. To deny this argument would be to deny the validity of Israel herself as the people of God.

FLESH/PROMISE

Paul used a variety of ways to express his point: law/gospel, flesh/promise, slave/free, Hagar/Sarah, Ishmael/Isaac, Mt. Sinai/ Jerusalem, present Jerusalem/Jerusalem above. All point to the same contrast and illustrate the same point. Just as God's grace superseded Ishmael's inheritance, God's grace superseded Israel's.

These two historic stories about Ishmael and Isaac, and about Israel and Christ, point to changes of the law and the culture governing God's people. The first change, from the law and culture that governed Ishmael's right to inheritance would have been from the same law and culture that governed Abraham's father, Terah, which Terah had practiced on his journey. That was the law and culture that Abraham had inherited, which governed Ishmael's inheritance right as the eldest son by law or custom. Abraham was not governed by Mosaic Law because Moses was not yet born. The birth of Isaac initiated a change in the law and culture that Terah brought out of Ur and Abraham had inherited. The Old Testament is, among other things, the story of that change. Similarly, suggested Paul, the birth of Jesus Christ initiated change in *that* law and custom (from Abraham to Moses and the prophets), and the New Testament is the story of *that* change (from Moses to Christ).

Indeed the world changed very much with the advent of Jesus Christ, and the changes that Christ wrought are still in process. Because that change brought the gospel to the gentiles, to the whole world, and the world is very large. *That* change is still in process as the gospel continues to wreak its magic, its miracles. We are tempted to think that the changes that the gospel brought to the gentiles was pretty much worked out in earlier chapters of church history. But because the world is so large and has continued to change, and the changes have been so dramatic—especially with the development of science, technology, and the industrial revolutions—those changes are still in play as the world adapts to its changing situation in the light of Christ.

TWO COVENANTS

The two covenants are the covenant at Mt. Sinai with Moses, and the covenant at Jerusalem with Jesus Christ—the Old Covenant and the New Covenant. The giving of the Ten Commandments on Mt. Sinai was the high point of the change of law that began with the promise to Abraham and the birth of Isaac. The law of Moses was always a temporary covenant that would provide the conditions for the birth of Messiah, which was God's promise from of old. When Terah left Ur he was looking for something new. When Abraham left Haran he was looking for the promised land. But God was always looking for the promised people who would arise from the promised Son—Messiah.

God's promise of land was never simply about the land, it was always about the people. The promised land was simply a place for the incubation of God's grace to grow, not a place for the kingdom of Jewish blood to dominate. Of course, this insight was easier and more clearly seen in the light of Christ, which Paul was shinning back into history. Once this insight is seen it cannot be unseen, and that was Paul's problem with the Judaizing Galatians. Paul knew that history cannot flow backwards, that it must move forward in spite of all difficulties.

Paul's comment in verse 24 is curious: "One is from Mount Sinai, bearing children for slavery…." This refers to Moses' covenant and the giving of the Ten Commandments. The curious thing is that God freed Israel from slavery in Egypt to go into the desert to worship. There God gave them the Ten Commandments, which were to provide order in which their new freedom could flourish. So far, so good.

However, the Israelites were not ready for freedom. They were unable to interpret and adjudicate the Ten Commandments among themselves. When Moses came down from the mountain, the people had already gone astray under Aaron's leadership. In their ignorance, they went to Moses for interpretation and adjudication, but it became too much for Moses to handle. So, at the advice of Jethro, he recruited seventy elders to help, and in time they produced the Deuteronomic law, which ordered life around the Tabernacle during their forty years in the wilderness—all at the behest of the Lord, of course.

Following their wilderness excursion, Joshua led them to capture the promised land by force. Once in the promised land they became a settled people rather than a nomadic people, and the law and the Tabernacle that had served them well as nomads fell into disuse and disrepute during the period of the Judges. Law and order dissipated.

> "In those days there was no king in Israel. Everyone did what was right in his own eyes" (Judges 17:6).

At the fullness of that crisis the people called for a king so they could be "like all the nations" (1 Samuel 8:4). Don't miss the irony here. God freed Israel from slavery in Egypt, and after a time God's people rejected God as their king and asked to have a king like the nations, to be like the nations, like Egypt. They rejected the freedom that God had provided for them through Moses. Moses had given them the Deuteronomic law and the Tabernacle during their nomadic time in the wilderness. And they knew—or at least Moses knew—that their time in the wilderness was both punishment for their sin and sanctification for their character as a people. It was temporary. It had a forty year duration. But once they conquered the promised land and became settled, they could not or did not refresh their laws. Their judges warred incessantly, law and order broke down, and the Tabernacle languished.

Saul, the people's choice for king, proved to be a lousy king, but his kingship served as a platform to instruct David. God blessed David's kingship, though the kingship itself was anathema to God's will for His people. *David* created the model for Israel's kings, even though his kingship was *not* what God had in mind for His people. David, then, laid the plans for the Temple and renewed God's law in order to serve and support the Temple, much as Moses had done for the Tabernacle. Yet, David rejected the Tabernacle at Gibeon and planned to build his Temple in Jerusalem, his capital, where he had already built his palace. And God conceded to David's desires, knowing that Israel's kingship would not end well (1 Samuel 8:10-16).

Thus, Paul's comment in verse 24 about Moses' covenant on Mt. Sinai leading to slavery was an acknowledgment that the law of Moses led Israel into slavery to the Temple—idolatry. This idolatry proved to be so tenacious that repeated destructions of the Temple were not able to eradicate it. This does not mean that all of Israel suffered from this idolatry of the Temple, but it does mean that it has always been a significant issue. And Paul was saying that it was surfacing again among the Judaizing Galatians.

JERUSALEM ABOVE

Isaiah 54 is about the growth of the gentile church, its safety, deliverance from persecution, edification, and preservation. Isaiah 54 alludes to Sarah, who was barren but who by the promise of God gave birth to Isaac, the son of promise. So, Paul's quote of the first few verses of Isaiah 54 suggests the larger section pertaining to the church that would result from the advent of Messiah. These words pointing to Isaac, who came from Sarah's barren womb, also point toward Jesus, who came from the virgin womb of Mary as the ultimate fulfillment of God's promise.

Jerusalem, the place of Christ's crucifixion, represents God's covenant with Christ regarding the gentiles. Paul's reference to Jerusalem being *above* does not suggest some other worldly heaven, it suggests that the gentile church will be guided from above, as Christ Himself was, guided by God's will.

The will of God is always Other, not one's own will. We see this in the Trinitarian Godhead where each Person of the Trinity is guided by the will of all Three, not the domination of any One. God's will is always the agreement of all Three. No one Person of the Trinity operates in exclusion or domination of the Others. This Trinitarian relationship then provides a model for us, such that we, too, must not operate out of our own will, but always function in agreement with God's will through the Spirit, who has access to us through regeneration.

This is the Jerusalem above who is our mother and who gives birth to children, not by blood but by the Spirit (John 1:13). The Jerusalem above is populated by the regenerate who have died to the flesh in baptism and are born again in the Spirit with Christ. Here is the source of Christian unity, where differences in Christ are cele-brated, and uniformity of expression vanishes in the creativity of the Spirit to conform to the will of God through the diversity of the God-head in union with Christ Jesus.

21. ENMITY

Now you, brothers, like Isaac, are children of promise. But just as at that time he who was born according to the flesh persecuted him who was born according to the Spirit, so also it is now. But what does the Scripture say? "Cast out the slave woman and her son, for the son of the slave woman shall not inherit with the son of the free woman." So, brothers, we are not children of the slave but of the free woman.
—Galatians 4:28-31

Paul was not proclaiming unity with the Judaizers here, but he was addressing the Galatians, among whom were some Judaizers. But neither was he suggesting that it was okay to sympathize with the errant ideas and apostasy of the Judaizers. Rather, he was making a sharp distinction between flesh and promise, between law and gospel freedom. This reference takes us back to Sarah and Hagar, to Isaac and Ishmael, and the animosity between them that resulted from Sarah's various decisions.

Sarah grew frustrated while waiting on the Lord's promise. One of her primary functions as a woman and a wife was to bear children, but she was barren. No children had been produced after many decades of marriage to Abraham. So Sarah concocted the idea of providing a surrogate mother through Hagar (Genesis 16:2). But we soon learn that she had gotten ahead of the Lord with this idea, much as Eve had in the Garden. For after Ishmael had been born, the strangers who served as messengers from God promised that Sarah would soon have a son.

The implication here was that Abraham and Sarah were well beyond childbearing age, so, though not specifically stated, the son would be a miraculous conception regardless of how the ovum was fertilized.

The principle here is that miraculous supersedes the ordinary, and this principle guides Paul's argument.

When it became obvious that Hagar was pregnant with Ishmael Sarah "looked with contempt on her mistress" (Genesis 16:4). She was jealous and lamented her decision. Sarah then blamed Abraham and accused Hagar of looking with contempt on her (Genesis 16:5)! I suspect that both women had trouble dealing with the pregnancy, and the confusion of roles it provided. Abraham, then, failed to adjudicate the situation and told Sarah to deal with it. Sarah "dealt harshly" (Genesis 16:6) with Hagar, who then ran away.

ANOTHER PROMISE

The angel of the Lord then found Hagar in the wilderness and issued an important promise to her that He would

> "multiply your offspring so that they cannot be numbered for multitude…. 'you are pregnant and shall bear a son. You shall call his name Ishmael, because the LORD has listened to your affliction. He shall be a wild donkey of a man, his hand against everyone and everyone's hand against him, and he shall dwell over against all his kinsmen'" (Genesis 16:10).

This is a very odd promise in many ways. First, it was given to a woman, to a handmaiden. This would have made it suspect in a patriarchal society. It may have been edited and enhanced generations later as an explanation for the conflict between Israel and Edom, who were children of Ishmael. And eons later Mohammad would claim this promise on behalf of the people of Islam.[1] It is also odd because it characterized the offspring in a decidedly negative, coercive, and domineering manner. Their behavior is reminiscent of Lamech (Genesis 4:24).

Shortly after this desert promise, Hagar gave birth to Ishmael. Abraham was eighty-six years old, and Sarah was a decade younger. God gave Abraham the covenant of circumcision between the birth of

---

1 Because Islam grew initially through conquering huge amounts of territory in a relatively short time, Islam should not have been as concerned with blood lineage as Israel was. The initial converts to Islam were from a wide variety of families and nations. Yet, they appear to be obsessed with leadership through Muhammad's bloodline.

Ishmael and the birth of Isaac. Isaac was born immediately following this.

God's promise regarding Ishmael was given to Hagar in the wilderness, after she had been mistreated by Sarah, after she was pregnant, and before the covenant of circumcision had been given. That promise was that Ishmael would be a bully and a troublemaker, as would all of his progeny.

In contrast, God's promise concerning Isaac was given to Abraham before Sarah was pregnant. It was given during God's gift of the covenant of circumcision to Abraham, who initially thought that the promise was about Ishmael, but the Lord corrected him, saying that Sarah would conceive. Abraham laughed because he was ninety-nine years old at the time. God then promised to bless Ishmael and to make a great nation of his progeny. Isaac was then blessed with an everlasting covenant (Genesis 17:19). God also blessed Sarah and changed her name, promising to bring forth many nations from her, suggesting that she and Abraham shared this calling, this blessing. It was a blessing intended for the whole world.

Following this Abraham circumcised all the males in his household, including Ishmael. And after this the three messengers came to visit and told Abraham that Sarah would conceive, as a kind of confirmation of God's previous promise. The various details of this are then repeated in Genesis 21, which tells of Isaac's birth and Ishmael's expulsion. In spite of Ishmael's expulsion, God blessed him and repeated His promise to make him into a great nation (Genesis 21:18).

Sarah's two disastrous decisions were to give Hagar to Abraham as a surrogate mother, and to send Hagar and Ishmael away. Abraham's decisions were no better. First, he took Hagar. He didn't need to follow Sarah's advice. And second, he didn't work to alleviate the dispute between Sarah and Hagar that ended in Ishmael's expulsion. Could he have helped in this regard? Maybe, maybe not, but he didn't even try, according to the story.

THE POINT

This story tells the origin of Israel's blessing through Abraham, Isaac, and Jacob, who becomes Israel. But it also tells the origin of Israel's greatest conflict, its struggle with Ishmael who becomes Edom, and who is claimed as the ancestor of Mohammad. This conflict has run throughout history, and advanced with the birth of Islam. This conflict is very much alive and well in the world today, and is the cause of most of the world's suffering right now as the Islamic State drags the Middle East into the most significant war since World War I, which ended the Islamic Ottoman Empire.

Paul says that the situation with the birth of Isaac foreshadowed the birth of Christ. And in the same way that God took the birthright from Ishmael, He was now taking it from Israel. And that He did so for the same reason: their reliance on inherited *law*. Just as Ishmael's inheritance right was based on inherited laws and customs from Terah (Abraham's father), so Israel's inheritance right was based on the inherited law and customs from Moses. Paul was not arguing against law in general, but against law that opposes God's Holy Spirit, God's grace. The fact that God doesn't change doesn't mean that God cannot change His law when it devolves from its original purpose.

The argument here is that God is the ultimate law maker, and reserves the right to adjust His law to changing circumstances. But God doesn't make changes very often, we know of only two times in history that this has happened. First, when God called Abraham to the promised land, He provided new law for its inhabitants. That law came through Moses, first as the Ten Commandments, and then those commandments were interpreted and applied by Moses and his seventy elders to produce the Deuteronomic Law. The Deuteronomic law was always intended by God to be temporary. God knew what the Israelites would do with the law, and that Jesus would come to fulfill it when history was full of its abuse by the Temple establishment. The Old Testament is the story of the administration of that law, and the failure to bring necessary changes to that law as Israel's circumstances changed. The second change came through Jesus Christ.

Paul was saying that the story of the change of law from Moses to Christ mirrors the story of the change of inheritance rights from Ishmael to Isaac. The inheritance rights of Ishmael were based on the old law, which was trumped by the grace that birthed Isaac. The story of the Old Testament is the story of God's new law that came through Abraham, Isaac, Jacob (Israel), and Moses. And similarly, the inheritance rights of Israel, based on the laws of Moses, was trumped by the grace that birthed Jesus Christ. These changes took thousands of years to unfold. This story can be seen by loosely breaking history into five-hundred year chunks in order to see the arc of the story. The dates below are very roughly approximate:

- 2500 B.C. – Great Flood
- 2000 B.C. – Tower of Babel, Destruction of Sodom, Birth of Abraham
- 1500 B.C. – Exodus from Egypt, Moses' Laws
- 1000 B.C. – Building of David's Temple
- 586 B.C. – Destruction of the Temple, The Exile
- 0 – Birth Of Christ

The original expression of God's law came through Moses in the form of the Ten Commandments. Moses and the seventy elders put that law into practice in the Deuteronomic Law, which was fashioned to meet the needs of a willful, sinful, nomadic people. Those people could not enter the promised land because they could not live in obedience to the Ten Commandments, so God gave them the Deuteronomic Law in order to train them unto obedience.

But when God's people became landed or settled, they still rejected God's plan of obedience to the Ten Commandments, and asked for a worldly king. God warned them against it, but relented at Samuel's intercession. The people chose Saul to be their king, which ended badly. God then chose David to be king, and trained him in the shadow of Saul. But David was only the best option for a bad scenario. David then reissued/reformed the law to serve the Temple, with God's help and blessing. Nonetheless, Israel's venture into worldly kingship began as a bad idea and went downhill from there.

David's Temple was built out of the failure and rejection of Moses' Tabernacle, and was doomed to the same fate. Israel was then taken captive in Babylon, but failed to learn from her own failure. So, Israel rebuilt the Temple at the behest and funding of Cyrus, king of Persia. But this Second Temple was a mere shadow of the first, and was built amidst opposition and with foreign funding. The nation of Israel never knew national sovereignty again, as it was occupied by a variety of foreign powers, ending with Rome.

Jesus was born into this situation in order to redeem Israel from its own hard-headed stubbornness, and to recover the gospel to include the gentiles. The gospel that Jesus brought, the gospel that was built on the wreckage of Israel's failed Temple(s), remained centered in the Ten Commandments, but rejected much of Moses' laws. Jesus reformulated the Ten Commandments into the Two Great Commandments to love God and neighbors. These are *two* commandments, not one, though they are closely related. They cannot be merged, nor does doing one count as fulfilling the other. Both are necessary because one is subjective (love God) and one is objective (love neighbors); one is attitude, one is behavior; one is spiritual, one is practical. Both are necessary!

But Israel—the Temple establishment—rejected Jesus just as it had rejected God's prophets, and continued in its Temple idolatry. So, God swept the Second Temple from history in A.D. 70, destroying the nation of Israel in order to lift up the real Temple—the Risen Jesus Christ.

This brief overview shows the magnitude of Paul's comparison between the mothers of Ishmael and Isaac, and their progeny. Paul was talking about an historical event of mammoth proportion, larger and more important than any event that had occurred heretofore, or since. So, it should not be surprising that it has been so hard for people to grasp. We're still struggling with it more than two thousand years later!

DIDN'T SAY

This perspective is different enough from what most people understand about the Bible that it is important to say what it *doesn't* mean. It doesn't mean that the Bible is unreliable or untrustworthy. It doesn't mean that God did not author every word of the Bible. It doesn't mean that history trumps the Bible, or that philosophy trumps the Bible, or that the science of evolution trumps biblical truth. It doesn't mean that Old Testament law is not useful. It doesn't mean that the Old Testament can be ignored. It doesn't mean that the only important words in the New Testament are colored red (Jesus' words). It doesn't mean that everyone in the Old Testament was without salvation. It doesn't mean that everyone in the Old Testament was unfaithful. It doesn't mean that everyone is wrong except me. It doesn't mean that my perspective expressed here is infallible. The Bible is trustworthy, and this analysis and perspective rests squarely on the Bible.

It also doesn't mean that the Bible is the only source of trustworthy information, or that the Bible provides the only trustworthy information about God or Jesus or truth. The five *solas* from the Reformation still stand: s*ola scriptura* (by Scripture alone), s*ola fide* (by faith alone), s*ola gratia* (by grace alone), s*olus Christus* or *solo Christo* (Christ alone or through Christ alone), and s*oli Deo gloria* (glory to God alone) —all are necessary.[2] However, *sola* here does not mean *only* or *alone* in the sense of nothing else, but in the sense that these things have the final say. Each of these things—Scripture, faith, grace, Christ, and God's glory—have ultimate jurisdiction of the mind. It's not that they forbid reading and considering other things. This is what the Reformers intended them to mean, rather than the narrow-minded, reactionary, Fundamentalist understandings of the twentieth century that were inherited by the Evangelical Movement.

It also doesn't mean that I understand the Bible in the same way that the Reformers understood it. It would be foolish to ignore what has been learned about the Bible since the sixteenth century. And it would be foolish to ignore what various advances in math, science, biology, technology, physics, history, archeology, etc., have brought to the table either. Nor does it mean that everything that has come from modern and contemporary academia is useful or trustworthy. Much of it is not![3]

So, how can we sort the wheat from the chaff? By using the five *solas* in their intended way: to discern and adjudicate truth from falsehood. Such discernment has never been more needed! But given the amount of information that is available and must be sorted, it is a huge task. It is more difficult today than it has been in any previous era because there is so much information available and because of the quality of so many fantastic scientific and technological advances.

And yet, the discernment that is needed is no different than it has been in previous ages, in that it requires first and foremost the trust and mastery of Scripture, understanding the Bible *alone*—as a stand

---

2   See footnote 3, p. 161.
3   Mac Donald, Heather. *The Burden of Bad Ideas: How Modern Intellectuals Misshape Our Society,* Ivan R. Dee, 2001.

alone story, a living story that continues to speak to us today, to speak to the world and to the history of the world in a meaningful way. It is not necessary to master every area of academia or biblical studies, but to understand the central story of the Bible, and where the contemporary world is in the midst of that story. It is necessary to understand our place in God's history. Faith in Christ is necessary. But there is more to faith than believing in one's own salvation, believing that one is heaven bound. These things are necessary also, but are not sufficient. God's goal is not simply to take believers to heaven. God is also bringing heaven to believers, to this earth, "on earth as it is in heaven" (Matthew 6:10).

PRINCIPALITIES NOT PEOPLE

In verse 30 Paul reminds us of the Genesis story of Ishmael and his forfeiture of inheritance. However, the story does not teach a lesson about genetic purity because these brothers had the same father, and bloodline at that time followed the father's lineage. Nor is the story about Jacob and Esau about bloodlines. They were twins! These stories about Israel's concern for genetic purity and lineage do not teach a lesson to emulate, they teach a lesson to eschew because that concern was a product of sin. They yielded to the temptation to discount what God said, God's truth, thinking that they knew better than God—for us that means that they thought that they knew better than the Bible.

Sarah and Abraham sinned in their construing the birth of Ishmael, and then doubled down on that sin in their dismissal of him. Ishmael's birth was a consequence of their sin, and his banishment and loss of inheritance was a further consequence of their sin. But God used their sin to provide a larger lesson about His grace, and that lesson involved a major change of law and custom. God used their sin to provide the impetus to abandon the laws and customs of Terah, Abraham's father, and develop and institute the laws and customs that were finalized by Moses and the seventy elders.

When Paul reminded the Galatians what Scripture said (v. 30), he would have assumed their familiarity with the whole story, and with the following verses in particular:

> "So she said to Abraham, 'Cast out this slave woman with her son, for the son of this slave woman shall not be heir with my son Isaac.' And

the thing was very displeasing to Abraham on account of his son. But God said to Abraham, 'Be not displeased because of the boy and because of your slave woman. Whatever Sarah says to you, do as she tells you, for through Isaac shall your offspring be named. And I will make a nation of the son of the slave woman also, because he is your offspring'" (Genesis 21:10-13).

It was not that God told Abraham to cast Ishmael out. Those words belonged to Sarah, who was adding the sin of banishing Hagar and Ishmael to try to rectify the previous sin of not waiting upon the Lord—giving Hagar to Abraham for a surrogate mother in order to fulfill God's promise of an heir. The whole situation is a cascade of sin that ends in tragedy. Abraham was rightly troubled by Sarah's sin. He knew that banishment would be a sin toward Ishmael. But God counseled Abraham to go along with Sarah. God would use this situation pedagogically, as a teaching event. God would use Isaac as an illustration of His grace and mercy, and His right to establish laws and customs. And He would also take care of Ishmael and make a great nation of his offspring.

So, the takeaway lessons of this story do not include justification for genetic purity or racial bloodlines, nor do they justify the casting out of Hagar and Ishmael. Rather, God used the story of Ishmael to illustrate the consequences of sin—not of Ishmael's sin, but the sin of Sarah and Abraham. Ishmael should not have been born, but once he was born he should not have been banished. Sin banished him, but God redeemed him. God redeemed a bully (Ishmael) in order to demonstrate His grace and His sovereignty in history.

While the Genesis story is all about Abraham, Sarah, Hagar, Ishmael, and Issac, Paul's use of the story is not about the individuals involved. Rather, Paul was focusing on the larger story, the metastory, about the change of laws and customs from Terah to Moses as a model for the change of laws and customs from Moses to Christ. We so easily get caught up in the details that we fail to see the larger contours and implications. We so easily fail to see the forest for the trees. It is so easy to look at things individually, one at a time, and fail to realize that the individual trees comprise a larger reality—a forest. Paul was trying to step back and provide a little perspective, to help us see the larger picture.

Paul's concern was that in Christ the law was trumped by God's grace. But that doesn't mean that the world was suddenly free from law—not at all! Rather, Paul's point was that the laws and customs of Moses were being trumped by the laws and customs of Christ—yet those very laws and customs of Christ were not yet institutionalized. Paul was trying, not to institutionalize them, but to contrast the freedom in Christ to interpret and apply the Ten Commandments in Christ. Paul was demonstrating to the Galatians how to interpret and adjudicate the Ten Commandments for the new age. They had freedom from the inherited laws and customs of Moses and the errant Second Temple establishment—not the freedom to do whatever they wanted, but the freedom to do what God originally wanted humanity to do, not in the old model of Adam, but in the new model of Christ.

WE ARE FREE

Paul's message in verse 31 that we are free means that we—himself, the Galatians, and all who are in Christ—are the recipients of the inheritance rights of God's grace in the same way and by the same authority that Isaac was the recipient of the inheritance rights of God's grace. Just as Ishmael had lost them to Isaac, so Israel had lost them to Christ.

It's not just about the freedom of individuals, though individuals do have freedom in Christ. It's about a seismic shift in human history, from being dominated by the laws and customs of Moses that had degenerated into the laws and customs of the Second Temple establishment, to having the freedom in Christ to interpret and apply the Ten Commandments for a new world order. However, Christians were not being called to start over from scratch, but to learn from the history of the failure of Moses and the Temple. The Old Testament is a treasure trove of failures, ripe for the learning of many valuable lessons. I'm reminded of the Thomas Edison quote regarding his invention of the light bulb, "I have not failed. I've just found 10,000 ways that won't work." There is no real learning apart from failure.

22. I, Paul

For freedom Christ has set us free; stand firm therefore, and do not submit again to a yoke of slavery. Look: I, Paul, say to you that if you accept circumcision, Christ will be of no advantage to you. I testify again to every man who accepts circumcision that he is obligated to keep the whole law. You are severed from Christ, you who would be justified by the law; you have fallen away from grace. For through the Spirit, by faith, we ourselves eagerly wait for the hope of righteousness. For in Christ Jesus neither circumcision nor uncircumcision counts for anything, but only faith working through love.

—Galatians 5:1-6

There are always two sides of freedom: freedom *from* and freedom *to*. Freedom *from* involves escaping some sort of restraint, and freedom *to* involves the opportunity to do something. Paul will deal with both of these, but the first few verses above deal with freedom from the law of Moses, because the Second Temple understanding and administration of Moses' law had produced slavery to the past by undermining the development of the dynamism of the Holy Spirit in the lives of God's people. While Paul says several times that Christians are free from *the* law, he doesn't mean that we are free from *all* law. We know this because he said so several times.

> "To those outside the law I became as one outside the law (not being outside the law of God but under the law of Christ) that I might win those outside the law" (1 Corinthians 9:21).

> "Bear one another's burdens, and so fulfill the law of Christ" (Galatians 6:2)

Jesus also explicitly gave us two commands:

"And one of the scribes came up and heard them disputing with one
another, and seeing that he answered them well, asked him, 'Which
commandment is the most important of all?' Jesus answered, 'The
most important is, "Hear, O Israel: The Lord our God, the Lord is
one. And you shall love the Lord your God with all your heart and
with all your soul and with all your mind and with all your strength."
The second is this: "You shall love your neighbor as yourself." There
is no other commandment greater than these'" (Mark 12:28-31).

However, if Paul did *not* mean that Christians are *not* free from all
law, what exactly did he mean? The word he used (νόμος) simply
means law and suggests a norm, anything established, anything received by common usage, like a custom, law, or official command, a
traditional codified standard. Thus, Paul meant the Torah in its meaning at that time, and particularly the laws and customs associated with
the Second Temple.[1] But neither was he pushing for the laws and customs of the First Temple or of the Tabernacle because He was well
aware that Christ in His Risen form was/is the Temple Himself.

"So the Jews said to him, 'What sign do you show us for doing these
things?' Jesus answered them, 'Destroy this temple, and in three days
I will raise it up.' The Jews then said, 'It has taken forty-six years to
build this temple, and will you raise it up in three days?' But he was
speaking about the temple of his body" (John 2:18-21).

Jesus came to build a new Temple in the Risen form of His body
using "living stones" (1 Peter 2:5). His followers would be knit into an
indestructible Temple that would cover the entire earth. And this
Temple of the Risen Lord would follow the law of Christ, the two
Great Commandments: to love God and neighbor. Of course, these
two commandments only make sense in the context of the history of
the Old Testament. The freedom that Paul was talking about was the
freedom to abandon the Second Temple in order to build the Temple
of the Lord Jesus Christ (1 Corinthians 3:9, 16).

What he did *not* mean was that Christians are free to do whatever
they want, that Christians are free to sin at will, errantly thinking that
they can sin without consequence because of God's grace and forgiveness in Christ. It is easy to fall into this error by ignoring the first
Great Commandment to love God, and/or thinking that obedience to

1   *The Law*, p. 107 and *Torah*, p. 40.

the second Great Commandment to love one's neighbors satisfies both commandments. The danger here is to turn the gospel into social service on the one hand, and self-indulgence on the other. Of course, there is a social service element to the gospel, but there is also a radical command to love God with everything you have—heart, soul, mind, and body—to both witness and serve. And to love God means to want to know all about Him, which drives faithful Christians to Scripture to learn and understand as much as they can about God, about the one God of both testaments.

The "yoke of slavery" (v. 1) refers to the dispute that was brought to the Jerusalem Council.

> "Now, therefore, why are you putting God to the test by placing a yoke on the neck of the disciples that neither our fathers nor we have been able to bear?" (Acts 15:10).

Paul made the same argument there, and no doubt, some of the Galatians had been at that council. Paul's use of the term "yoke of slavery" issued out of his understanding of *The Backstory* of the gospel, which revealed the central thrust or meaning of that story. The Galatians knew *The Backstory* because Paul had discussed it in order to present to them the gospel as he understood it. And when the Judaizing Galatians rejected Paul and his gospel, it was his understanding of *The Backstory* that they rejected.

Many Christians today are confused about Paul's treatment of law and gospel in Galatians precisely because they don't know *The Backstory*, and without that knowledge, they begin speculating. But when the veracity of *The Backstory* is understood, when we understand the larger story of the Bible and how it all fits into a single narrative, the crux of which is Jesus Christ, Paul's deeper meaning becomes crystal clear.

LOOK

Paul used the word ἴδε, which means *behold, see here,* or *look,* as a way to present an example of how to make sense of his proposal. Abraham had instituted circumcision before Ishmael was born. Abraham is the father of Judaism because he received God's covenant that marked the transition between the law and customs of Terah, his father, and the new law that would manifest through Moses and the seventy elders—the laws and customs of the Tabernacle. So, Paul chose to make an example of circumcision, the rite associated with that covenant. To make an example of that rite would serve as a model and representative for the whole of the laws and customs of the Temple.

And in order to demonstrate how individuals in Christ are to live by grace rather than by law in the New Covenant with Christ, he specified that it was him personally, Paul, who was making this determination based on the grace that God had shown by sending Jesus Christ. What determination? "...if you accept circumcision, Christ will be of no advantage to you" (v. 2). *I, Paul, say this to you.* Abraham commanded that all faithful covenant men needed to be circumcised, but Paul said that Christ had fulfilled that covenant, so that command was of no effect anymore. But because it was of no effect, to return to it as if it were still in force represented a denial of the gospel, of history, and a denial of the logic that God had used to change the laws and customs from Terah to Abraham. Again, to deny Paul's logic would be to deny the validity of the change of law and custom that produced Judaism itself.

WHOLE

In verse 3 Paul argued for the wholeness of the law. If they accepted the validity of circumcision, the central rite of the covenant, they needed to accept the whole law, all of the Torah. And this is nothing more than classic, historical, traditional Judaic doctrine. The rite of circumcision represented acceptance of Tabernacle/Temple laws and customs. And the intent and purpose of those laws and customs was the creation of a uniquely Jewish culture, a culture different from all other cultures, a culture focused on the biblical conception of God. The definition of culture is necessarily holistic. Culture is central to the way we view, experience, and engage with all aspects of our lives and the world around us.

This argument harkens back to the Jerusalem Council, where

"some believers who belonged to the party of the Pharisees rose up and said, 'It is necessary to circumcise them and to order them to keep the law of Moses'" (Acts 15:5).

These Pharisees were the Judaizers that Paul was wrestling with at Galatia. It is interesting that at this point there was no doubt about the gospel going to some gentiles, that it had broken out of its Jewish bondage to the law. The question being considered at the Jerusalem Council was how the law applied to the gentiles as a whole. The Council did not decide that the gentiles were free to do whatever they wanted, rather, the Council adapted the inherited laws and customs of the Temple to accommodate the gentiles.

> "For it has seemed good to the Holy Spirit and to us to lay on you no greater burden than these requirements: that you abstain from what has been sacrificed to idols, and from blood, and from what has been strangled, and from sexual immorality. If you keep yourselves from these, you will do well. Farewell" (Acts 15:28-29).

The contributing elements in this decision are crucial. Luke named two of them—us and the Holy Spirit, and the unspoken participant is the inherited law—for them the Old Testament, for us both Testaments. Decisions about the interpretation and application of God's Word must involve all three of these contributors—living saints, the Holy Spirit, and the Bible.

The Council then gave them some requirements, but that did not end the controversy. It continued to rage at Galatia and elsewhere, which is why Paul wrote to the Galatians to address this issue again. Therefore, when Paul argued against the law and in favor of the gospel, the contrast that He made was not the whole law versus no law whatsoever. Rather, the contrast was the whole law of the Temple verses the wholeness of the law of Christ, also called the gospel.

The issue is the inherited laws and customs of the Temple versus the new laws and customs being interpreted by Jesus Christ and applied by the church—living saints, the Holy Spirit, and the Bible. Christ's laws and customs include loving God and neighbors, which will include the fruits of the spirit that Paul will soon delineate. Yet, Paul was not content with simply naming the fruits of the spirit that they were to practice (Galatians 5:22-23), he also named the desires of the flesh that they were to abandon (Galatians 5: 19-21).

NO EFFECT

The next argument that Paul brought to bear (v. 4) was that returning to the law, to circumcision, after what Paul had taught them about *The Backstory* and how God had used Jesus Christ to bring the story of the Old Testament to a conclusion that ended the old era and began a new era, would sever them from Christ because they were acting like Christ had no effect on them. The principle here is that truth is always compelling. People cannot help but be compelled by the truth.

> "For we are the aroma of Christ to God among those who are being saved and among those who are perishing, to one a fragrance from death to death, to the other a fragrance from life to life. Who is sufficient for these things?" (2 Corinthians 2:15-16).

God's people, people who love God and neighbor, grow in truth and represent truth. Such people are never neutral, they either smell like life or like death, which is a poetic way to say that others are either attracted to them or repelled from them. If there is no attraction or repulsion, there is no smell. And if there is no smell, there is no love of God. And if there is no love of God, they are not God's people.

RIGHTEOUSNESS

Righteousness is the one characteristic that is the most compelling for most people. It is impossible for people to come face to face with genuine righteousness and not be compelled, either attracted or repulsed. To understand this it is necessary to understand what righteousness is. The dictionary defines it as adhering to moral principles, which is true for us, but not for Christ. Jesus Christ, who is the incarnation of righteousness itself—God personified—does not adhere to principles. Rather, moral principles are defined by the character of God in Christ. God embodies righteousness in Christ, and from the story of Jesus Christ, which begins in Genesis 1, we derive Godly principles—patterns—of righteousness.

Paul's best descriptions of biblical righteousness, Christian righteousness, are found in 1 Corinthians 13, the great love chapter, and his delineation of the fruit of the spirit in Galatians 5:22-23. From the first we see that righteous people are loving, faithful, generous, patient, humble, not arrogant or boastful; they know God and are known by God, and are motivated by genuine love, understood as service and charity. And from the second we note that righteous people are loving, joyful, peaceful, patient, kind, good, and faithful. These are the characteristics of Christian morality, and where they are correctly exercised they are compelling. They either attract or repulse people. They are rarely met with apathy, indifference or acedia.

There are two versions of each of the corresponding reactions. The truly faithful will be attracted to truly faithful expressions of these characteristics, but the truly faithful will also be repulsed from hypocritical expressions of them. And conversely, the unfaithful will be repulsed from truly faithful expressions of Christian morality—thinking that such expressions are hypocritical because the unfaithful don't know genuine faithfulness. Those who feign faith for whatever reasons will also be attracted to hypocritical expressions of faith—mistaking them for the real thing because they don't know the real thing. Understanding this paragraph correctly requires knowing the difference between hypocrisy and faithfulness in the light of Christ.

The thing that is most repulsive about righteousness is the presumption that one has it. But such a presumption is actually the expression of pride, which contradicts Christian morality and is the foundation of hypocrisy. The curious thing about Christian morality is that the closer one gets to it, the better one gets to know it, to know Jesus Christ, who is the perfect expression of it, the more one realizes how far from it one actually is. The true Christians realizes that *the holier I get the more I realize how holy I am not!* And yet, this growth toward holiness amounts to genuine faithfulness because it generates the hope of righteousness (v. 5). True righteousness is always a hope and not a reality because true righteousness always remains a goal toward which Christians strive. Yet, while that hope is never fully manifest, it does manifest genuine joy as the fruits of the Spirit grow and ripen. To achieve it completely would put an end to striving for it, which must always remain a goal for the faithful as long as any sin remains, not just in one's self, but in the world. Of course, one day God will put an end to all sin, but we are currently in no position to speculate what that will be like. Our time is much better spent in the genuine practice of Christian faithfulness, which is founded upon humility rather than pride.

WHAT MATTERS

The conclusion of Paul's argument is that circumcision doesn't matter. It makes no difference in the light of Christ. And because circumcision serves as a kind of place holder and representative of Temple laws and customs, he means that none of those laws or customs matter. God doesn't care about them. This argument is not original with Paul, it goes way back in biblical history. But it was an argument that had been long forgotten in Israel, in spite of the fact that Israel's prophets repeated it ad nauseam. Here's a representative sample:

> "To do righteousness and justice is more acceptable to the LORD than sacrifice" (Proverbs 21:3).

> "The sacrifice of the wicked is an abomination; how much more when he brings it with evil intent" (Proverbs 21:27).

> "What to me is the multitude of your sacrifices? says the LORD; I have had enough of burnt offerings of rams and the fat of well-fed beasts; I do not delight in the blood of bulls, or of lambs, or of goats" (Isaiah 1:11).

> "For I desire steadfast love and not sacrifice, the knowledge of God rather than burnt offerings" (Hosea 6:6).

> "Oh that there were one among you who would shut the doors, that you might not kindle fire on my altar in vain! I have no pleasure in you, says the LORD of hosts, and I will not accept an offering from your hand" (Malachi 1:10).

Paul was simply bringing this argument to the Second Temple establishment in the name of Jesus Christ. The argument was not new. What was new was the advent of Jesus Christ and His great sacrifice once for all (Hebrews 7:27) as the crux that ended the old era and began the new era in Christ.

Rather, said Paul, in Christ the only thing that matters is faith working through love. Faith is a matter of trusting God in everything, and especially in the veracity of His Word in the Bible. Apart from trusting God, biblical understanding is not possible. No amount of study or preparation can substitute for faithfully trusting God. Too much biblical scholarship is faulty for precisely this reason: too many biblical scholars trust their scholarship more than they trust the veracity of Gods' Word—Scripture.

What matters to God is how we live. Our celebrations and ceremonies are less important. It's not that celebrations and ceremonies are unimportant, but if our lives are out of sorts with God, our celebrations and ceremonies can make no difference. Ideally, these things will reflect various aspects of God's truth and be pedagogical to those involved as a means of worship, witness, and service. We usually think of our celebrations and ceremonies as our worship, but biblical Christianity actually teaches that worship is what we do with our lives twenty-four-seven. Real liturgy is more about how we live our lives than about how we perform our ceremonies and celebrations.

Again, it's not that worship services are unimportant. Rather, they are like the tip of an iceberg, in that the bulk of the matter is what lies under the surface. So, if our worship services are not right or aren't what they should be, the problem lies under the surface, in our ordinary lives. And the needed correction cannot simply come from the tip of the iceberg, but must be permeated throughout its bulk.

If pressed too far this analogy breaks down because unlike icebergs human populations can be affected by worship services because, unlike icebergs, people are able to learn. So, corrections can be suggested through proper worship services, but only when those worship services genuinely reflect and teach the true character of God in Christ, and the people involved actually assimilate what they learn about God into their daily living.

23. Offensive

You were running well. Who hindered you from obeying the truth?
This persuasion is not from him who calls you. A little leaven leav-
ens the whole lump. I have confidence in the Lord that you will take
no other view, and the one who is troubling you will bear the penalty,
whoever he is. But if I, brothers, still preach circumcision, why am I
still being persecuted? In that case the offense of the cross has been re-
moved. I wish those who unsettle you would emasculate themselves!
—Galatians 5:7-12

Following Paul's previous visit, the Galatians seemed to have understood and had embarked under the guidance of the gospel, as Paul commended them. But something happened. His question about who it was that lead them away from the truth serves as an invitation for them to identify the persons involved for disciplinary purposes. But it also suggests the deeper issue, suggesting that Satan was the ultimate culprit. Who else consistently hinders people from following God's truth? Without a doubt Paul wanted them to identify the message that led them away from Christ as being Satanic. And yet such an identification would be difficult for the Galatians to make because it would also mean that the Temple itself had become a temple of Satan (Revelation 3:9). As harsh as this may sound, it was not beyond Paul to suggest it (2 Thessalonians 2:4). He had simply followed Jesus' lead.

The fact that Paul called this errant view a *persuasion* tells us how this view came to them. They were persuaded by it. One of the definitions of *persuade* is to twist someone's arm, which is another way of suggesting a threat to do worse if compliance is not forthwith. No doubt the Galatian believers had been threatened with various Temple sanctions, the disciplines against Temple apostasy—shunning, blackballing, casting out, etc. Such sanctions would seriously disrupt business and family relationships. Such sanctions are still effective and are still in use today by many different groups.

That persuasion, that arm twisting, that threat of sanctions was not from God, who had called them to faith in Christ. That persuasion which turned its back on Paul's teaching and left them in the grip of the status quo was not from God. It's easy for us to agree with Paul today because we have an abundance of history and resources that agree with him. But at that time, it would have been quite difficult to reject the status quo, regardless of how bad it was, and accept by faith what must have seemed to most people at the time as a wild and radical idea.

This is not to suggest that there was no significant content in the persuasion of the Judaizers. The Temple establishment had spent eons shaping and perfecting the arguments that supported their views by many of the most intelligent people in history. The reason that the Temple establishment could maintain control of Jewish society for so long and against the testimony of the prophets century after century was the quality of their arguments in support of their position. Arguing against their blindness in favor of *The Backstory* that Paul taught required (and still requires) courage and the leadership of the Holy Spirit in Christ. It succeeds because it is God's argument not man's.

We should not be too harsh on the Judaizers, but neither should we kowtow to their persuasion. We must learn to speak truth in love because our situation is not all that different from theirs. Too many Christians today are caught up in a status quo that doesn't serve the gospel. We, too, can be threatened by shunning, blackballing, casting out, etc. Though Paul addressed controversial issues in his various letters to the churches, many of the same controversies remain far from resolved in most churches today. And this issue of the law and the gospel continues to trouble Christians and churches today.

LEAVEN

Paul's reference to leaven is of the same kind as was his reference when he wrote to the Corinthians.

> "Your boasting is not good. Do you not know that a little leaven
> leavens the whole lump? Cleanse out the old leaven that you may be
> a new lump, as you really are unleavened." (1 Corinthians 5:6-7).

Paul was referring to the "leaven of the Pharisees and Sadducees" (Matthew 16:6, and 11-12), not the leaven of heaven (Matthew 13:33). The Judaizers were full of the pride that had kept Israel from seeing the truth of their situation for eons. It blinded them to the reality of *The Backstory*.

The leaven of the Pharisees and Sadducees referred to their various teachings that maintained the status quo of the Second Temple establishment. It taught that the Jews had received a special blessing from God, which was true. But they understood it in a self-centered way that caused them to be self-concerned, as if they had the obligation to keep God's truth and blessing to themselves. They understood it to apply to their own culture in a way that they had to protect the integrity of their culture through separation and self-containment, which was true during their Tabernacle period, when they were being purged from the leaven of Egypt.

Much of what they believed was true at one time, but not in the way that they thought during the Temple periods. God did—and still does—have a special mission for them, and that mission is to share the blessing of their example to the watching world. God set them apart, not because they were special, but in order to make an example of them that everyone, every culture, could relate to. However, it was not that they would become a good example of faithfulness, even though there remained a vein of faithful Jews from time immemorial, and they did faithfully record their aberrant history. Rather, the example they would set was an example of faithlessness in the face of God's enduring faithfulness. Their example demonstrated that, even with God's own help, they (as the best representatives of humanity) could not live in obedience to God's law. They could not of their own accord, and even with the help of God's law and cultural direction, live in faithfulness to God or sufficiently care for their own people. This was the testimony of their own prophets, their own history.

In this role the ancient Jews represented everyman, and their example stands as a testimony to human faithlessness apart from Christ, apart from regeneration in Christ, apart from the fullness of the dispensation of the Holy Spirit in the service of Jesus Christ. The failures and sins of the Jews provide no justification for anti-Semitism of any kind because no human culture could have done any better—and most would have done far worse! The world is deeply indebted to ancient Israel for her perseverance through the awful history she endured in the hope of faithful service to God. Israel's faithfulness and diligence in keeping records of their journey from slavery to freedom to their own self-imposed slavery is invaluable to humanity. The records they kept and the suffering they have endured throughout history provide a wealth of wisdom. Much of it involves the painful lessons of faithlessness, but the good news in Christ is that Christians don't have to repeat their errors. We can learn from their mistakes, from their hard-headed self-concern, how not to be, how not to hold onto God selfishly in the hope of special treatment.

CONFIDENCE

Paul's confidence that they would "take no other view" (v. 10) was more a confidence in Christ than in them. It was confidence that God would complete what He had begun (Philippians 1:6). Paul was so certain of the vision of *The Backstory* that Christ had given him that he was willing to stand completely alone in Christ, against the Temple establishment, against his fellow apostles, and against the leaders of the churches he wrote to. He had been given a glimpse of the unfolding of Israel's history such that he clearly saw the reality of *The Backstory* and its arc into the future, and saw equally clearly that Jesus Christ was the historical hinge of that story. It was not that Paul was brave enough to take such a stand, but that he could do nothing else. That vision had so caught him up in its historical momentum that he was swept down the stream of history driven by the gospel flood waters.

The confidence that he had was a kind of persuasion (πείθω). It was not that he was swept up against his will, but rather that the first thing that Christ captured was his will. This then increased his momentum as he added his own willingness to the undeniable will of God regarding his prosecution of Christ's case to everyone he could. It also enhanced Paul's ability to persuade others of Christ's cause and His position as the hinge of history, closing out one era and opening up another.

Yet Paul would be the first to argue that it was not his ability at all, but Christ's. It was the presence and power of the Holy Spirit working in and through Paul's regeneration that had begun on the road to Damascus. But it was also the presence and power of the Holy Spirit working through others to give them what Calvin called *election* or *irresistible grace*, what Wesley called *prevenient grace*. The Holy Spirit had been unleashed upon the world and was sweeping people into His wake as the language of the Spirit had broken out of its ancient Hebraic confines.[1]

Paul then pivoted to anathematize those who had caused trouble among the Galatians, those Judaizers who had stirred them up against Paul and his vision of Christ and Christ's cause. Whoever they were, regardless of their rank, position, titles, etc., God would bring judgment upon them. In essence, Paul was saying that they should not be swayed by the rank, position, title, etc., of the Judaizers because God was not a respecter of persons (Romans 2:11)—rank, position, title, etc. This was then proven by the destruction of Jerusalem and the Temple in A.D. 70, as God swept the Judaism of the Temple from the stage of history.

No Avail

Paul argued that circumcision no longer made any difference to God, but in v. 11 he said that he continued to preach circumcision. And he even circumcised Timothy in the midst of this argument (Acts 16:3). If it seems confusing that he argues against circumcision but doesn't stop preaching and doing it, it's because he was not actually arguing against it. Rather, he was arguing that God doesn't care about it, it has no spiritual value. Paul's argument was not that circumcision is a negative thing, but that it's a neutral thing to God because the covenant that it represented has been fulfilled by Christ. It's like getting a boarding pass for a trip that you had already taken and that has already concluded.

Yet Paul circumcised Timothy. He did that in order to remove the potential obstacle that the Jews might have toward Timothy, that might keep them from according Timothy sufficient honor to hear what he had to say. Paul had no problem arguing against circumcision and then circumcising Timothy because Paul's argument was not against circumcision, but was that circumcision had no religious value

---

1   Ross. Phillip A. *Arsy Varsy—Reclaiming The Gospel in First Corinthians*, Pilgrim Platform, 2008, p. 241.

in Christ. Except in the case of Timothy, who was sent to witness to the Jews, because Timothy would get a better reception if he was circumcised, and if the Jews knew that he had been circumcised by Paul. That would confuse the Jews enough to keep them from thinking that they already knew what Paul had to say, and encourage them to listen more carefully to Timothy.

This might seem to contradict Paul's previous statement:

> "Look: I, Paul, say to you that if you accept circumcision, Christ will be of no advantage to you" (Galatians 5:2).

But it doesn't, because the emphasis there was on the Galatians, not on Timothy. In their case, circumcision would mean renouncing what Paul had taught them. But in Timothy's case, it would not. The reason for Timothy's circumcision was very different from theirs. And because circumcision has no objective or religious value, whatever value it does have comes from the personal, subjective, contextual reason for doing it. To do it as a denial of Christ is one thing, but to do it as a means of evangelism for Christ is another.

OFFENSE

One of the reasons that the Judaizers opposed Paul was that they thought that he was preaching against circumcision. They misunderstood what he was saying. So, if they understood that he was not only not preaching against it, but was actively preaching about it, that might remove what seemed to offend them. At least that was Paul's hope.

Paul was well-aware that circumcision had never been anything other than a symbol of God's covenant with Abraham. It had no spiritual power in itself. It was simply a means of remembrance and social establishment. But over the centuries the Jews had built it up into something that it was never intended to be—a way to exclude others from the blessings of God. The Jews had turned it into a private genetic club marker, which was the opposite of what God had wanted it to be. The enemies of the Jews were their own brothers, not other races. Think of Cain and Abel, Ishmael and Issac, Esau and Jacob. The division of human beings by race or genetics is completely absurd! It makes no sense whatsoever. There is only one human race, and the sooner we get over this misanthropic deceit the better off we will be.

The real divisions in humanity are moral and cultural, not genetic or racial. This is not just true in the contemporary age, it has always been true from the day that Cain slew Abel. So, why did Cain slay Abel? Because God preferred Abel's sacrifice, and conforming to God's preferences puts people on the positive side of God's blessings. Was Abel a better person than Cain? Not at all! At least not at first. But Cain's slaying of Abel revealed a flaw in Cain's moral makeup. Cain would have argued that God made him do it because God had rejected him. But God didn't reject Cain, God simply preferred Abel's offering. Cain could have learned from that, but he didn't. He chose to act out his anger and frustration with God by killing his brother. God was not the primary actor in this murder. The guilt belonged solely to Cain.

Yet, God spared Cain! God did not reciprocate against Cain but provided a way for him to live in spite of his guilt. Even at this very early chapter in human history God revealed Himself to be full of grace and mercy, and not an avenging God. But that was not the way that Cain saw it. Cain harbored his wounded pride, and his spiritual progeny have nursed it into a maelstrom of envy, jealousy, hate, and violence that still threatens to engulf the world. Over time Cain's wounded pride morphed into competing adversities of envy, fear, pride, greed, anger, deceit, compulsion, and power among later populations.

Paul's hope that the offense of the gospel would be removed assumed that the cause of the removal would be preaching the gospel correctly, in his case clarifying his understanding of how the gospel affected the role and importance of circumcision.

Out With The Old

Paul wished that the trouble-making Judaizers would be cut off in every sense of the word. Yet, Paul was not simply being nasty by praying for the genital mutilation as a punishment for their orneriness. Sure, he was frustrated by their cantankerousness, but did not stoop to an adolescent slip of the tongue. Rather, his central point was that if they could not recant their remonstration against Paul's doctrine, they needed to be turned out from fellowship with the saints.

His wish was not so much that they "castrate themselves," as so many versions translate it, regardless of the accuracy of the literal translation. Rather, his wish was that the Galatians had cast out the Judaizers rather than listened to them. Paul was saying that he wished that those who had unsettled them would have been cast out by the Galatian faithful, that they would have had the wherewithal to excommunicate them rather than listen to them.

The allusion to castration was a poetic use of language that made a play on the idea of circumcision. But as accurate as it is to linguistically focus on the definition of ἀποκόπτω, which suggests the genital mutilation practiced by eunuchs, the point of the allusion was not the physical act of mutilation, but the result of infertility. Paul wished that the Judaizers would be infertile regarding their prosecution of circumcision as a necessity for the Galatians. Paul wished that the Judaizers would have been silenced rather than listened to.

The argument of the Judaizers for strict obedience to Moses' law was not new, but was the traditional argument that the Temple establishment had always used to quench the reforming spirit of the prophets. It was then and still is today an argument of substance and power because it rightly discerns but falsely appropriates many genuine characteristics of God, and of Scripture. For instance, it rightly acknowledges that God is unchanging and ever faithful to His promises. However, although God Himself is unchanging and His Word is steadfast from time immemorial, it is quite easy to neglect that fact that human language itself is not unchanging, that changes which accumulate in human experience, history, and language over time necessitate continual adaptation to the unchanging stability of God's Word. God Himself, being outside of time, is not subject to such changes. Yet, those changes are a necessary fact of *our* existence in time, and to neglect them distorts our understanding of God's Word. Not God's *words* but God's *Word*, who is described as the Person, Jesus Christ by John (John 1:1). In addition, such an argument wrongly understands God's promise to Abraham as being a function of genetics rather than grace, of blood rather than culture. While God doesn't change, we do. We change individually, socially, linguistically, and culturally. And our changes must be factored into our understanding of God's unchanging Word and character.

This factoring is the function of the Holy Spirit. It is not something that we can do individually or socially. It is not a function of human psychology or of history, but is the unique function of the Holy Spirit through regeneration, rightly understood. Biblical regeneration applies to both individuals and societies (or cultures) because of God's Trinitarian character. God is a divine community who exists both outside of time and within time, and yet functions as a unity of three individual Persons.

God transcends history in that He is present in history through His Holy Spirit. Thus, God is the same Person today He was before He created the world. But humanity is not the same human culture it was when, for instance, Adam and Eve walked in the Garden, nor when Moses wandered in the desert, nor when Solomon built the Temple, nor when Jesus and Paul walked in Jerusalem. Our contemporary languages are different, our cultures are different, our experiences of the world are different. So, for us to understand God in the same way that Adam, Eve, Moses, Solomon, Paul, and all the saints understood Him in His unchanging character, we must have access to a fresh presentation of His reality that speaks our language, relates to our culture, is accessible to our experience, and makes sense of our reality.

And yet, that fresh presentation cannot be other than the same essential presentation that God always makes to people of every historic epoch through the power and presence of His Holy Spirit through regeneration. The differences in presentation and representation must always reinforce God's unchanging character. Therefore, there must be continuity between the past and the present that is faithful to God's unchanging character. Maintaining such continuity is certainly beyond the abilities of any individual or the combined abilities of any culture. And this is why the function of historical continuity falls to God's Holy Spirit, who both transcends history and lives in history. The Holy Spirit is the link to the continuity of God's unchanging character.

This, however, is not an argument for a new gospel or a new interpretation of the Bible or a new Word from the Lord. Rather, it is a plea that the Lord make His original gospel, His original intent, speak to our world today. It is a plea that the Lord inhabit pastors, theologians, and scholars with the faithfulness of His Holy Spirit. And it is an acknowledgment that God, in fact, still speaks to His people today.

This is not an argument for anything *new*, but is a call to return to the "old paths" (Jeremiah 6:16), to the historical arc of God's trajectory through human history. It is not a call to retread some part of the path previously tread, but is a call to continue forward on the original path. It is a call for divine refreshment to renew a dying world.

24. Free To Serve

For you were called to freedom, brothers. Only do not use your freedom as an opportunity for the flesh, but through love serve one another. For the whole law is fulfilled in one word: "You shall love your neighbor as yourself." But if you bite and devour one another, watch out that you are not consumed by one another.

—Galatians 5:13-15

Not only is the freedom that Paul was talking about not free, because it came at a great price to Jesus Christ and to those who have followed Him, but Christian freedom doesn't mean what too many Christians today think it means. It is not license to do whatever you want, nor is it license to disobey the law—not even bad laws. Rather, it is the freedom from the laws and customs of the Temple in order to live in obedience to Jesus Christ. No verses of the Bible ever stand alone, but must always be understood in the context of the entire Bible, which includes *The Backstory*. Because *The Backstory* is the story of the Old Testament and the context of the New Testament, it governs our understanding of the story of the New Testament.

This is the freedom to which Christ calls all people, the Jews first and then the gentiles. It is a gift, completely free, unexpected, unearned, and undeserved. Yet it is a gift that must be taken and engaged. When your mother calls you for dinner, her call represents the fact that she had prepared it and set the table—and that it is for *you*, but you still must come and eat it. The call itself does not fill the stomach, nor does it recuse you from helping with the dishes.

Paul's theme is that Christ has paved the way from slavery to the Temple law to freedom to live in obedience to God in Christ. These verses serve *that* theme, not whatever theme we would like them to serve. In fact, gospel freedom is not ours at all. It belongs to Jesus Christ and can only be appropriated in Him or through Him. Christ is free to reinterpret and apply God's law, and we are free to follow that interpretation in Christ. Christ contains that freedom within the bounds of God's will. Human freedom always exists within bounds. Human beings are never absolutely free, but are always bound by desire, authority, ability, resources, time, reality, etc. In Christ we have been given the will power to want what He wants for us, to pursue Christ's path for us to witness and to serve.

They were not called to the freedom that the Libertines thought they knew about. Luke had mentioned the Libertines (Λιβερτῖνος) in Acts 6, who had argued against Stephen. Those freemen had formed special synagogues, which meant that they were still in service to the Temple establishment.

> "Then they secretly instigated men who said, 'We have heard him speak blasphemous words against Moses and God'" (Acts 6:11).

Stephen knew the freedom that Paul was talking about, and had preached it—and also found the opposition of the Libertines and Judaizers. It was very difficult for the Jews to hear the argument of Jesus Christ without understanding it to be in opposition to the Temple. But Jesus was not opposed to the Temple, rightly understood. He *is* the Temple! How could the Temple be opposed to itself? He was simply correcting a long-standing misunderstanding. Jesus then granted freedom to assimilate His correction, His reinterpretation and application.

The Judaizers misunderstood Jesus and Paul—and Stephen. They couldn't hear the true gospel. It was too painful for them. To hear the gospel rightly always means to respond to it. The failure to respond means that the gospel hasn't been heard rightly. I'm not saying that they did not—or that anyone else cannot—willfully refuse to hear it. People can—and do! Such a failure is always willful. Pride is always the central stumbling stone of the gospel of humility. And this is why it takes more than the correct preaching of the true gospel for people to hear it. It always takes the prevenient grace and/or movement of the Holy Spirit in people's lives to open them up to be able to hear and respond to the gospel.

OPPORTUNITY

To say that we should not use this "freedom as an opportunity for the flesh" (13) does not mean that we should neglect the needs of the body or of our health. Paul was not arguing for an other worldly, Gnostic gospel. He will go on to define the works of the flesh in verse 19, where we will pick up this thread.

Rather, we should use our freedom as witnesses to Christ's righteousness and in the service of others. Love is defined in Scripture as concern for and care of others, and not as a romantic interlude. But we are so blinded by our addiction to the culture of romance that we fail to hear Christ's call to freedom through service. Like the ancient Libertines we believe ourselves to have been emancipated from all forms of slavery, and are offended by any suggestion that we should engage in any form of service whatsoever. In spite of the fact that all of the servants on the PBS show, *Downton Abbey*, are white Anglo-saxons who occupy well-respected jobs, we associate all such service with slavery. Our own service-sector jobs are considered to be at the bottom of the pile. And we engage in volunteer service only to salve our inflated egos by making us feel better about ourselves, which makes it more self-concern than concern for others. It's no wonder that love has fallen on hard times in our contemporary culture.

WHOLE LAW

As I write, Liberal scholars and others are making the argument that the Golden Rule (Luke 6:31) provides justification for same sex marriage. They are happy to do unto others as they would have others do unto them. One such scholar has suggested that Jesus' two Great Commandments, to love God and neighbor, can be fulfilled by engaging the second Great Command to love one's neighbor as one's self.[1] The argument is that loving one's neighbors is the same as or counts as loving God, which is the classic argument of the Social Gospel Movement of the early twentieth century and a foundational pillar of Liberal Christianity.[2]

1   Wood, Michael, *Paul On Homosexuality*, Tubi Publishing, LLC, 2011.
2   See Machen, J. Gresham. *Christianity and Liberalism*, 1923. Machen, a pivotal figure in American Christianity, argues that Liberalism is a different religion than Christianity. That argument may be overly broad, but today there are elements in Christianity, both liberal and conservative, that are not Christian.

Much of the weight of this argument rests on Galatians 5:14:

"For the whole law is fulfilled in one word: 'You shall love your neighbor as yourself.'"

Where Jesus boiled the Ten Commandments down to two—love God and neighbor, Paul *seems* to have boiled Jesus' two Great Commandments down to one—love your neighbor as yourself. But did he? It only appears to be the case if the verse is taken out of its context.

The immediate context of the verse directs it to the Judaizers, the Jews who were following the teachings of the Second Temple establishment. Paul had been one of them for most of his life. He knew them well, and he did not doubt their love for God or for Scripture. It was their love of God that had driven them to honor the Temple establishment as they did. They were very faithful to the Temple, to Temple worship, to tithing, and to teaching the basics of Jewish culture, which was founded on circumcision and Abraham's covenant. Their love of God caused them to search the Scriptures, to study them and to live in obedience to their understanding of them.

But *their* love of God, *their* understanding of Abraham's covenant as a blood or genetic covenant with the Jewish people who had a special relationship with God, was the source of their failure to include the gentiles in God's covenant. And that was part of the problem that Jesus Christ had come to correct by providing a renewed adaptation and application of God's law. Thus, Paul assumed that they loved God, but where *they* had gone astray was that they had not included the gentiles—their neighbors—in the family of God. What *they* needed to hear and to do was the second Great Commandment. They needed to include the loving of their neighbors into their spiritual practice. So, Paul put all of his emphasis there when writing to them.

Paul was not suggesting a general practice for all Christians to neglect the love of God or to assume that love of neighbors fulfilled both of the Great Commandments. Christians who do or teach the conflation of Jesus' two Great Commandments into one commit a *huge* error. Loving one's neighbor cannot be done apart from loving God because God is the source of all love, and God teaches us how to love. Denying the source, power, and model of love *in the name of love* is foolishness of the highest order.

The Social Gospel enthusiasts of the early 1900s made the same error. They focused all of their effort on service, and neglected Jesus' First Commandment to love God first and foremost. The love of God then produces what we call *witnessing*, expressing our love for God. The Social Gospel focused on service in the hope that people would see their love—and that's not a bad thing. But we are also called to witness our love for God in Christ, verbally as well. Both are necessary.

Atheists and others will argue that they *can* love others without loving God, that they naturally know how to love without the instruction of the Bible. However, regenerate Christians counter that the world in which we currently live has been undeniably infused and affected by the God of the Bible through the power and presence of the Holy Spirit working both evidently and preveniently. God's presence and efficaciousness is so plain as to be glaring, and can only be denied through great effort and stubbornness. Christianity permeates our language, our institutions, our habits, our history, and our culture so thoroughly that it can only be denied by the ignorant and those for whom God has not lifted the veil of self-importance.

Of course, it is possible to be ignorant of all of this, just as it is possible to breathe air without knowing what air is or where it comes from. But ignorance of air does nothing to shield one from its benefits. One of the reasons that many people deny this reality is that there has been an intentional and sustained effort to alter, reduce, and/or undermine our Western Christian heritage and history over the past fifty to a hundred or so years. Part of that effort has come through pastors, professors, seminaries and churches.

It would be convenient to call that effort Godless and chalk it up to communism or some other intriguing conspiracy—and there most certainly are communists and others who are actively engaged in changing the American system. However, the truth is more robust because God is involved. Yes, God is involved in a sustained effort to alter, reduce, and/or undermine our Western Christian heritage, but not all of it. Just the parts that He doesn't like, the parts that are not quite true, the parts that don't provide an accurate portrayal of His character with the integrity of its fullness.

God is involved in correcting errors in Western Christianity just as He was involved in correcting errors of the ancient Jewish Temple establishment. God's methods use organic growth, He grows His culture by refining a new one from within the old one. New life grows from the inside out, both individually and socially. And God's timeframe is humungous. He always uses His original idea as the basis for renewal.

TEMPLE OF CHRIST

His original idea, issuing out of His covenant with Abraham, was to replace the old religion of performance and vengeance, the roots of which go back into Ur, with a religion of grace and forgiveness, the fruit of which manifested in Jesus Christ, the New Man for a new world. Just as the Temple was the fruit of Moses' Ten Commandments, Christ's church is the fruit of Christ's two Great Commandments. But whereas the Temple of the Jews was a Jewish product, the Temple of Christ is an international (or intercultural) product that is still in process of construction.

God is plowing under unfaithfulness in order to prune the tree to stimulate new growth and more fruit. However, we must not think that God is blessing successful churches and Christians, or abandoning the unsuccessful. God's definition of success is different from the world's definition. God has never been a fan of popularity, but has always preferred the narrow way of genuine righteousness fueled by genuine love and service. Righteousness has never been popular with people because it produces guilt and envy apart from Christ.

Christianity in all of its various manifestations is full of both blessings and curses. God wants people to comport with reality, and no one knows more about human reality than God. He created it. The depiction of Jesus Christ in the Bible provides the best contact with reality when seen and understood in the power and presence of the Holy Spirit through regeneration. The historical aggregation of Christianity provides both improved models of ship design for sailing on spiritual seas, and an abundance of barnacles that impede the ship. The positive aspects of Christianity belong to the former, the negative aspects to the barnacles.

THE ERROR

The thing that God doesn't like is the failure to acknowledge His holiness, His wholeness—not blind obedience to Moses' law, but faith-

ful obedience to the wholeness of Christ. The failure to see the wholeness of a thing is the failure to see its essential character because it is its
wholeness that defines it as the thing that it is. The failure to understand God's holiness amounts to a failure to stand under His
wholeness. People do this when they engage in compartmentalization,
the unconscious psychological defense mechanism used to avoid the
mental discomfort and anxiety caused by having conflicting values,
knowledge, emotions, beliefs, etc. within themselves. That experience
is also called *cognitive dissonance*, or a lack of personal integrity. Cognitive dissonance occurs when one's expectations (beliefs, hopes, dreams,
etc.) conflict with reality. It is quite common.

The most obvious example of compartmentalization is found in
the homosexual justification that Christianity has nothing to do with
same sex marriage, that one's faith and marriage are unrelated. This argument is heard often among supporters of same sex marriage. In an
Oregon case a baker refused to make a cake for a same sex marriage
because he believes that participation in a religious ceremony that celebrates a sin is not pleasing to God. He believes that part of his
Christian faith involves honoring God in all things and especially in
worship, and that the celebration of homosexuality does not honor
God and dishonors the worship involved in a wedding service. He is
being sued by a same sex couple for discrimination of them on the basis of their sexual preference, which is forbidden by law.

The baker argues that his choice to honor his conscience is foundational to his Christian faith, that he should be allowed that
expression as a First Amendment right, and that no harm is done to the
couple because other bakers are willing to work with them. The couple argues that the baker is discriminating illegally against them on the
basis of their sexual preference, and that their right to equal treatment
in the public square violates their constitutional rights and existing
law. They argue that the practice of Christianity has nothing to do
with the baker baking them a cake—and this is the error that demonstrates their failure to understand Christianity and the denial of God's
wholeness, His holiness.

This errant view issues from the failure to understand Christian
worship, and is quite common, even among Christians. The common
understanding is that worship is what happens at church on Sunday

mornings. This in itself is not wrong, worship includes Sunday morning services. But it is woefully inadequate to the fullness of the
meaning of worship that we are called to in Christ Jesus.

The worship service is structured to model how we are to live as
Christians, how we are to honor Christ, and relate to Him through
prayer, praise, witness, service, and fellowship. It is pedagogical. The
worship service is more like training in Christian living than the actual
practice of living in Christ. On Sunday mornings we learn how we are
to live in Christ, and our worship, the worship of the laity, the liturgy
or work of the people happens during the ordinary living of their lives
—at home, at school, at work, at play, wherever they are, twenty-four
seven.

Thus, the baker who professes to be a Christian on Sunday mornings is expected to act like a Christian at work. So, His Christian faith
does impact how he behaves at work. The admonition to avoid sin applies very much to his working life. The holiness of God in Christ
demands the wholeness of Christian faithfulness at all times and in all
places.

This error begins in the churches, and is very common among
Christians of all sorts. The common belief is that Christian worship is
limited to Sunday mornings and is fulfilled by attending worship services. Pastors and churches have encouraged this belief for eons as a
way to establish Christianity in society, and to ensure the continuity of
the church as a social institution. Their jobs depend on it. But it is a
kind of compartmentalization, a cognitive dissonance that keeps faithfulness from impacting our whole lives, the wholeness of our living.

And it is *not* biblical! God views it as a kind of faithlessness, and
that kind of faithlessness among Christians has allowed the scourge of
increasing sin in society—sins of every sort. Sin is not a thing, it's an
activity. Sin is a team sport. It has many members who work in many
different ways to advance its flag, its cause. Thus, sins cluster. Where
one is found, others also lurk. This error is as old as sin itself, and is the
central sin that the prophets railed against. It is the central sin that Jesus
came to correct by providing a new adaptation and application of
God's law. Segmented faithfulness is not a minor issue, overcoming it
is central to the faithful practice of biblical Christianity.

However, much confusion exists about segmented faithfulness because so many Christians and churches fail to understand it, or inadequately understand and teach against it. So, Christians themselves in large numbers don't understand or practice genuine holistic faithfulness in Christ, which means that the watching world—those who are not Christians—learn about Christianity from an errant model. The world then thinks that this errant model—segmented faithfulness—is Christianity, and rejects it. And rightly so! That model needs to be rejected by everyone!

The wholeness of real Christianity reflects the holiness of God. Just as holiness is central to God's character, wholeness is central to Christianity. And wholeness means that life in Christ impacts everything that Christians think, say, and do—everything. The holiness of Christianity impacts everything, no aspect of life is excluded, and especially not one's work.

HYPERCRITICAL

> "But if you bite and devour one another, watch out that you are not consumed by one another" (v. 15).

As a philosophy major in college I learned the value of critical thinking. According to a definition by Kompf & Bond (2001), critical thinking involves problem solving, decision making, metacognition, rationality, rational thinking, reasoning, knowledge, intelligence, and also a moral component such as reflective thinking. Having been so armed I then entered the world where I quickly learned that the world does *not* value critical thinking, and the better people are at it the worse the reception they get. Another way to say the same thing is that everyone thinks that they are able to think critically, mostly without any training or study whatsoever. It's called opinion, and everyone not only has at least one, but everyone thinks that they have the right one, the only one that makes sense.

In fact, human sanity requires that people think that they are able to think rightly, correctly, that what they think, their opinion, is true. To think otherwise is the very definition of insanity. It is important for our observations, evaluations, and opinions to accord with reality. Our very lives depend upon such correspondence. Whether we began as hunter gatherers or farmers, our thoughts needed to correspond to reality if we were to be successful. In today's world, our science needs to correspond to reality in order for it to be successful. So, the correct correspondence between thinking and reality is still very important.

Given the importance of critical thinking to human life, it is *not* likely that Paul was saying that we should *not* be critical thinkers. Paul himself applied critical thinking to the Bible in order to learn and prove the gospel that he taught about Jesus Christ. If Paul did *not* mean that we should *not* be critical of our own and of one another's thinking —beliefs, ideas, habits, etc.—what did he mean? If we do not avoid criticism, defined as serious examination and evaluation, how do we avoid the biting, devouring, and consuming of one another that he warned us about?

There are two aspects of such avoidance. The first aspect Paul calls "speaking the truth in love" (Ephesians 4:15). Love must be the context in which truth is spoken. Our communication of truth must be saturated in love, where love is understood as genuine care and concern, and not just the lip service of concern. Truth will be better received in an environment of love and trust. While it takes time to establish such an environment, that *doesn't* mean that truth should be withheld until that love and trust can be developed. Such an approach will fail because one who practices it will not be seen as a truth teller. To be considered to be a truthful person one must always be truthful, which brings us to the second aspect.

While the first aspect involves what we say, the second involves what we hear. Conversation flows in two directions: from us, and to us. So, we must attend both directions of the flow. While we cannot control what others say, we can control what we say. And while we cannot control what others hear us say, we can control what we hear others say. We can control *our* speaking and *our* listening, and we must do both.

There are also two aspects of the biting, devouring, and consuming of one another that Paul warned us about: giving offense and taking offense. We must be careful not to offend others unnecessarily. In order to do this, our thoughts and ideas need to be about thoughts and ideas, not people. Paul called attention to this when he said:

> "For we do not wrestle against flesh and blood, but against the rulers, against the authorities, against the cosmic powers over this present

darkness, against the spiritual forces of evil in the heavenly places"
(Ephesians 6:12).

When we argue with others we must not argue against them personally, but against their ideas and plans. When we argue against
cosmic powers and spiritual forces, we must not argue against the people they manipulate, but against their ideas, authority, and right to do
what they do. In all cases, we must frame our arguments, our critical
thinking, as being in opposition to ideas and authorities, and not in
opposition to the people who hold them. This is one way to reduce
biting, devouring, and consuming of one another that Pul warned us
about.

But there is another way, an even more important way for believers to practice. We must not *take* offense when others are critical of
our thoughts, beliefs, and ideas. We must *not* take offense, as a way of
teaching others how to follow suit by modeling how to listen to and
discuss our own thoughts and ideas critically without being offended.
This is by far the more important and more difficult aspect of watching out that we are not consumed by one another (v. 15). We keep
ourselves from being consumed by not consuming others.

The best way to understand what this word *consume* (ἀναλίσκω)
means is to see it in another context:

> "And when his disciples James and John saw it, they said, "Lord, do
> you want us to tell fire to come down from heaven and *consume*
> them?" (Luke 9:54).

We can avoid being destroyed ourselves by not destroying others. Our
destructive responses to others originate in our understanding of what
they have said to us. Our response begins with our hearing. And even
if we determine that we are confronted by an enemy, we are commanded to love them, to respond to them in love, defined as genuine
care and concern. For the most part, people will reflect back to us the
attitude that we show toward them.

25. Adverse

But I say, walk by the Spirit, and you will not gratify the desires of the flesh. For the desires of the flesh are against the Spirit, and the desires of the Spirit are against the flesh, for these are opposed to each other, to keep you from doing the things you want to do. But if you are led by the Spirit, you are not under the law.

—Galatians 5:16-18

Providing another example of how to make sense of the freedom in Christ that he proposes, he again calls attention to the fact that what he is saying is *his idea*. He was showing us how living in Christ can trump living in the flesh. By saying that *he* was saying this he meant that he was able in Christ to circumvent his own fleshly desires, that he was not a slave to them. He was able to escape the habituation of his old habits, that he was not locked into his own personal established beliefs and behaviors. It was a kind of testimony.

The flesh is about coarse desires and distractions that appeal to our baser selves, where the Spirit is about the more refined ideals and principles that appeal to our higher selves. Living in Christ does not negate the desires of the flesh, or the law, it supersedes both desire and law. Conformity to the Spirit provides deeper satisfaction, more long-lasting results, and avoids entanglement with the law, because the law only comes into effect when it is violated. Putting our attention on the flesh increases our attention to the desires of the flesh. So, putting our attention on the Spirit decreases our attention to the desires of the flesh. It is often the desires of the flesh that lead into lawlessness. Thus, dimming those desires reduces the grip that the law has on us, so that we can be led by the Spirit.

If you don't violate the law, the law does not take effect for you. If you don't violate the law, you don't have to worry about the legal consequences of violating it. To live by the concerns of the Spirit will produce a life that does not violate the intent of the law, which is the essential purpose of the Ten Commandments.

Paul was arguing that the role of Christians is first and foremost the interpretation and application of law to their own lives. And the essential question or issue here is what Paul meant by the word *law* (νόμος). Though he used only one word, he used it in two senses: one suggests God's law in a positive light, and one suggests it in a negative light. The positive understanding of God's law refers to the central or essential meaning and intention of the Ten Commandments. And the negative understanding refers to the Torah, which includes the first five books of the Old Testament, *Torah Shebichtav* (Torah that is written), and *Torah Shebe'al Peh* (Torah that is spoken).[1] Paul considered the Torah to be not in force any more. Jesus had fulfilled it by adding the final chapter.

Issuing from Paul's understanding of *The Backstory*, he believed that Israel had been enslaved to a wooden understanding of the law, understood as Torah in a negative sense that kept them locked into old solutions to new problems. They needed to be freed from that wooden, negative understanding of the law in order to practice a dynamic understanding of the law in the positive sense that freed them to maintain the intent of God's Ten Commandments to meet current problems with creative yet faithful solutions. We see this in his application of the Tenth Commandment to himself in Romans 7. And the catalyst for that change was the death and resurrection of Jesus Christ, who had fulfilled or completed the story of the Old Testament longing for and predictions about Messiah.

However, given the difficulties that Israel had as a result of codifying the law of Moses in the Old Testament, Paul was aware that any similar codification would likely produce similar results. They would become obsolete over time. Thus, his emphasis against law-based religion. Every application of the intent of God's Ten Commandments would calcify over time, just as the law of Moses did. And that calcification (or lack of dynamic, fresh application to new problems) would

1   *Torah*, p. 40.

pose a similar problem later in history. Thus, Paul's reliance on the Spirit rather than the law.

He didn't mean that Christians should avoid God's law altogether, but rather that individuals are best served by applying God's law, God's original intention regarding the Ten Commandments, to themselves— without neglecting Christ's command to be in unity and of like mind with Him. In order to do that we need to know the Ten Commandments, and then we need to see how Israel interpreted and applied them throughout her history, so we can learn from her mistakes. Then we need to know the story of Jesus and His refinement of them in the two Great Commandments, and how Christians have applied them throughout their history, and learn from their mistakes. Then we need to know Jesus personally, and apply what we have learned to ourselves. This is why Christians understand the law as a tutor, a teacher. In reality, this is a tall order and no one will master it during their lifetime, but all who seriously apply themselves can live in adequate compliance from quite a young age. God is gracious, merciful, and is very patient with those who seriously engage Him.

26. NOT THIS

Now the works of the flesh are evident: sexual immorality, impurity, sensuality, idolatry, sorcery, enmity, strife, jealousy, fits of anger, rivalries, dissensions, divisions, envy, drunkenness, orgies, and things like these. I warn you, as I warned you before, that those who do such things will not inherit the kingdom of God. —Galatians 5:19-21

Paul just said that the flesh lusts against the spirit (Galatians 5:17), and now refers to that lust as work. We are aware of his contrast between works and grace, that which we earn on our own and that which we are given as pure gift. He employs the contrast between these verses and Galatians 5:22-23 as the works of the flesh versus the fruits of the spirit. The fact that these works are evident means that they are commonly recognized by everyone because they are commonly engaged.

The fact that these things are associated with the body helps to focus the contrast even more because they also have a spiritual aspect. A spirit is involved, and it is the spirit of Adam, who opposes Christ. We can also identify them as the spirit of Satan, who opposes God, or the spirit of evil, which is opposed to the spirit of good. All of these things set up the same contrast. And because they do have a spiritual aspect to them, we are invited to see the contrast as between the spirit of Adam and the Spirit of Christ, the Holy Spirit.

The items on Paul's list are neither arbitrary nor capricious. Each points to a particular class or category of sin.

ADULTERY

We don't use this word much in our contemporary world, probably because it is so common. Common sin produces an interesting social phenomenon: the more a particular sin is practiced, the more the biblical words that define it as a sin drop from the common vocabulary. People don't like to be offended or to offend others, and using the biblical term offends sinners—it's supposed to. This elimination of words over time can be more clearly seen with the ancient word *acedia*. If my own case is typical, people will not know its definition. The dictionary defines it as apathy and inactivity in the practice of virtue, personified as one of the deadly sins. While the word is unknown, the sin is widely practiced. As the practice has grown, the word has disappeared.

The first work of the flesh Paul lists is μοιχεία, which means adultery or extramarital sex, any sex outside of marriage. Both Jews and gentiles are indicated because of the universality of marriage. Of course, marriage practices and customs differ widely, but the commonality of couples formally paring for child bearing and rearing was unquestionably universal.

The reason that this is so serious is that the marriage covenant is modeled after God's covenant with us, and dishonoring any one covenant weakens all covenants. If we can't keep a promise to a spouse, we are more likely to abandon other promises. Dishonoring the marriage covenant is an attack on the structure of covenant keeping, and weakens all covenants.

It is curious that so many modern translations render the word *sexual immorality*. Perhaps because *adultery* is not in the current vernacular. But sexual morality can mean almost anything. People often judge morality by comparing themselves with other people, which allows them to justify their behavior with the "I'm not as bad as such and such" defense. A common argument is that others are worse than me, so I'm not so bad.

Paul teaches that we are not to compare ourselves with one another, but we are to use Christ as the model. When Christ sets the moral markers we get a very different result.

FORNICATION

If *adultery* is an unpopular word in contemporary society, *fornication* trumps it by a factor of ten. This word is so out of style that most people won't know what it means. Though we seldom hear it, the dictionary nails it: voluntary sexual intercourse between persons not married to each other. This might be the most practiced form of sex today. Most modern translations call it impurity, where Strong's calls it illicit sexual intercourse. Without question, *impurity* simply obscures its true meaning. Again, the clear meaning is all sex outside of traditional marriage regardless of consent, status, age, preference, etc.

PROFLIGACY

The Greek word ἀκαθαρσία is defined as the impurity of lustful, luxurious, extravagant living. Our modern Bibles provide a variety of translations of this word: *sensuality, promiscuity,* and *depravity*. Again, the idea of living a luxurious, unrestrained, extravagant life is understood in today's world as the proverbial holy grail of success. Profligate living is widely encouraged and lionized across the age and class spectrums. To suggest that there is anything wrong with such living is met with derision and ridicule, particularly in the media.

It seems that we want our corporations to be responsible, ecologically sensitive, sexually moral, and economically efficient. But we encourage people—our media stars and role models—to be irresponsible, wasteful, sexually immoral, and economically extravagant. The media, which pushes both sides of this contradiction, appears to be completely blind to the conflict or their complicity in it—probably because the consumers of media are equally fascinated by both positions. And interestingly, both idolize—encourage, support, and further—consumerism.

IDOLATRY

Idolatry (εἰδωλολατρεία) is the worship of false gods, but since false gods are not actually real, it might be called false worship, the worship of the wrong things, or worship in the wrong ways. Idolatry has a long history in the Bible, and is probably the most common sin. The Greek word is composed of two words that mean service rendered to an image. And since humanity was created in the image or likeness of God (Genesis 1:27), idolatry is a misunderstanding and/or misappropriation of our identity as creatures of God. Idolatry issues from not knowing who we are in Christ. And the fix is not just knowing, but being who we are in Christ, being the person and the people that God created us to be.

One of the major themes in all of Scripture is that of God's Trinitarian character, and of His creating humanity in *that* image because His Trinitarian character is that which makes Him most unique and most personal.[1] We share in God's Trinitarian character through the power and presence of the Holy Spirit through regeneration. The Holy Spirit, who is God Himself in the Triune Godhead, comes to inhabit His people, who live in Christ, who is also God Himself in the Godhead. While no one manifests the Holy Spirit perfectly—other than Jesus Christ, all who are in Christ manifest Him sufficiently. All who refuse or deny such manifestation practice idolatry, defined as the failure to identify, manifest, and/or understand God in Christ.

SORCERY

Paul lands me in trouble with this one because φαρμακεία (*pharmakeia*) is defined as the use or the administering of drugs. The *Authorized Version* calls it *witchcraft* because witches were associated with herbs and potions. Actually, the historical roots of modern medicine (pharmacology) go back to herbs and potions.

My understanding of Paul's admonition here is that the problem is not just herbs and potions, but the deceptions and seductions of sorcery and the magical arts, often found in connection with them, which are fostered by idolatry. God has no problem with herbs and potions—He created them, and made them useful for us. The problem is the falsity of magic that takes credit for healing, and creates false images about the nature of reality and who we are as human beings. Magic always involves deception and gives the wrong impression about the magician. It makes him/her to appear to be godlike in a way that diminishes God's glory. Dispensing drugs can also make people dependent upon the drug dispensers in a way that steals and also diminishes God's glory.

The question for us to wrestle with is how this prohibition relates to modern medicine and pharmacology. Does God, Paul, and/or the Bible have anything to say about our modern medical industry? What would God, Paul, or Jesus think of our medical industry? Does the Bible have any application to modern medicine?

1   Natan, Yoel. *The Jewish Trinity: When Rabbis Believed In The Father, Son And Holy Spirit*, Createspace, 2003. Also, most of my books explore what I call *presuppositional trinitarianism*.

A strong case can be made in the affirmative. Medicine, or more properly called *healing*, is a function of Christ's church, evidenced by the many healings that the prophets and Jesus performed during their time on earth. In addition, there are various biblical terms that are directly related to health and healing—*salvation* (the root of which is *salve*), *holiness* (has the same root as wholeness), *shalom* (meaning peace, completeness, prosperity, and welfare), and others.

Paul's admonition against sorcery is best understood as an admonition against idolatrous medicine, which comes in two forms: attributing healing to false gods, and the failure to attribute healing to the only real God—which is the very definition of secular medicine. Another problem that the Bible brings to light involves the business of modern medicine, or the way that modern medicine practices healing for profit. Again, it is unlikely that Paul, Jesus, or God would have any problem with paying doctors and clinicians a living wage, but the degree of both profit and waste involved in modern medicine would likely bring about some over turning of tables.

ENMITY

Various translations render the word ἔχθρα differently: *hostilities, hatred, strife*. The point is that Christians are at war against principalities and powers—ideas—not people. We are to love our enemies, to be charitable, understanding, tolerant toward one another. We are not to judge one another, but we are to judge one another's ideas and behaviors—a distinction mostly unrecognized. If Christians are to be moral, and we are, then that means making judgments about ideas, behaviors, and actions, but not about the inherent worth and value of persons. Doing so involves controlling what we say to others and what we hear others say to us. We can control what we say and how we interpret what we hear.

I am not what I do, and you are not what you do. We must learn to separate our identity from our behavior, and we must separate the identity of others from their behavior. However, this has proven to be quite difficult in a self-absorbed culture. The exception to this rule is found in the function of law where we are held accountable for our behavior. This is exactly the purpose of law. Laws are rules against certain behaviors, i.e., speeding, jaywalking, stealing, murder, tax evasion, etc. Law *does* judge on the basis of behavior. Those who are guilty of speeding are judged—punished—as speeders. Those who jaywalk are understood to be jaywalkers. Those who steal are understood to be thieves, etc.

This is the way that law works because laws are designed to address behaviors, to encourage law abiding behavior and discourage law breaking behavior. It cannot be otherwise. But in this regard systems of law are also systems of self-fulfilling prophecies. Because legal systems keep records, they keep track of infractions. And a person's record is kept because the individual is likely to repeat the errant behavior, and increased punishments are mandated for repeat offenders. People who work in law tend to make this assumption because they see it day in and day out. Consequently, this assumption is also shared by many people generally. People convicted of stealing are expected to be thieves. Those convicted of speeding are expected to be speeders, etc. The gospel of Jesus Christ counsels against this practice, but the gospel is mostly not believed. Inasmuch as we judge people on the basis of their actions and behaviors, we are basing those judgments on law rather than on gospel.

Of course, it is also true that the second crime people commit is easier to commit than the first, and the third is easier than the second. We are creatures of habit and the more a behavior is repeated, the more habitual it becomes. And when the expectation of other people is paired with the temptation of the individual, the pattern of behavior is doubly reinforced. Thus, the self-fulfilling prophecy gains ground. This whole damnable process is the natural outcome of legality. It's just the way that legal systems function in a fallen world.

And that was part of Paul's message. As long as people function on the basis of legality, this self-fulfilling prophecy of criminalization will continue. No system of law can ever change this process. And that is why Christ came to put an end to the law as a governing principle, an end to living on the basis of legalities. The spirit of grace opposes the law, which exacts retribution and exacerbates the practice of character assassination. Grace and mercy, on the other hand, separate identity and behavior such that a new identity or a deeper identity can extricate people from bad behaviors by asserting an expectation of change rather than an expectation of repetition. If I understand myself to be a thief, that understanding justifies my behavior of stealing. But if I understand myself to be a sinful child of God and forgiven, that forgiveness then justifies a change of behavior.

If I understand that God's grace and mercy have come because of the action of Jesus Christ on the cross, and that puts me *in debt* to Jesus, that's okay. Even if I'm not really in debt to Jesus because Jesus operates out of a system of grace, not law. Debt is a function of law, so in a system of grace and mercy debt has no function. But such a belief in debt is okay because the right motivation for the wrong reason is better than the wrong motivation for the wrong reason. God understands that we will grow out of the coarseness of law-based behavior into the sensitivity of grace-based behavior, and that it takes time for such growth to mature.

It is better to live in thankfulness to Jesus Christ, than to live in debt to Him. Debt is a function of law, but thankfulness is a product of grace. We can pay a debt begrudgingly, but we cannot be thankful and resentful at the same time. Thankfulness trumps debt, just as grace trumps law, and love trumps rancor.

WRANGLING

People need to learn to argue righteously. Yet, we live in a world torn asunder by arguments of every kind. But the problem is not arguing, defined as expressing differences. Differences make life interesting. Differences are not the problem. The problem is fighting about our differences, rather than learning from them. We need to learn how to express our differences without becoming defensive, without becoming angry at those who disagree with us. And more importantly, we need to learn how to hear someone disagree with us without feeling personally attacked. We need to dissociate our own being with our ideas.

We need to become deeper people, to understand ourselves and others more deeply. If we can find deep commonalities with others, we won't be so passionate about superficial differences. When we live superficial lives we are more argumentative about superficial differences because we aren't aware of our deeper commonalities. Shallow living develops shallow roots, and shallow roots are easily threatened by superficial conditions.

Again the Greek word ἔρις is translated in various ways: *strife, rivalry, variance.* We are to strive, but not against one another. We must strive for righteousness, but not for self-righteousness. All self-righteousness is counter to the gospel of Jesus Christ and Christian morality. We are to live in variance to the system of the world, but not in variance to Jesus Christ. We are free to differ in our opinions about a variety of things, but we are not free to attack or undermine the image of God in others. Rather, we should do what we can to support and encourage it.

Some people argue from principle, some argue from conviction, others argue from experience. Some use logic, some use passion, and some use authority. All of these things are important, and no one can corner the market on all of them. Our differences are important. We are each unique, but our uniqueness does not diminish our commonality in Christ. Rather, Christ enhances our uniquenesses, which accentuates our differences—without disturbing our union in Christ.

ZEAL

We tend to like zeal when we agree with the cause it supports, and we find it objectionable when we disagree with the cause. It is important to be enthusiastic about the right things. That kind of enthusiasm can accomplish much. When the cause is right, much good gets accomplished. But when the cause is wrong much damage can also be done by enthusiasm for the wrong things. Did Paul mean to discourage all kinds of zeal (ζῆλος)? Of course not.

He was aiming at indignation, anger that is aroused by some perceived offense or injustice. He was aiming at the zeal that takes offense, that is easily offended. Shallow people are easily offended because they cannot keep an even keel. More important than not judging others, we are not to take offense. We must not allow ourselves to be offended by the opinions of others because taking offense engenders becoming defensive. Once we become defensive, justification sets in and we escalate to the position that offense is the best defense. So, we protect ourselves by becoming offensive.

We must learn that other people do not and cannot offend us. Rather, it is we who *take* offense. It is something that *we* do, not something that *others* do to us. Taking offense is like becoming defensive in that offensiveness and defensiveness feed on each other. My offense encourages your defense, which encourages your offensiveness as the best defense. It sets up a tit for tat scenario of retribution and revenge.

The *English Standard Bible* translates the word as *fits of anger,* other version use *outbursts of anger* and *emulations.* The idea of emulation puts a slightly different spin on it, suggesting the ambition to equal or excel others in some regard, which really describes zeal. Zeal can seem like anger to others, particularly those close to it. But it is the defense of self-righteousness that often uses offensive tactics as the best defense. The problem is not the emotion or enthusiasm associated with zeal, but the self-righteousness that it defends.

RIVALRY

These terms all have very close meanings, which is sad because it means that we have a lot of different ways to engage this sin. The root of rivalry (θυμός) means to immolate, to sacrifice (die or kill) for religious purposes. Clearly, people were not practicing human sacrifice. Paul used the word symbolically or analogously to suggest a kind of ritualistic character assassination.

Today we can clearly understand this word through our experience of the Internet, where the verb *flame* means a hostile and insulting interaction between Internet users, often involving the use of profanity. Flaming is a mode of interaction or conversation where the flamer ceases to listen and simply dumps his or her most incendiary comments on the other person in the effort to destroy the opponent. Of course, this mode of communication was not invented on the Internet, and has been in use since the beginning of time. But our modern proclivities tended toward politeness prior to the Internet. Forty years ago people were generally more polite than they are today. Interaction on the Internet also tends to be and to feel more remote, more distant, more anonymous, which has increased the use of flaming.

Just as every sacrifice must have a sacrificial victim, rivalry also involves victims by way of scapegoating. Scapegoating involves attributing sins that don't belong to the sacrificial "goat" with the expectation that the immolation of the goat will atone for our sins. We tend to blame and accuse others of our own sins in order to justify their sacrifice, our immolation of them. It is both a way of denying our own sin and issues out of our denial of our own culpability that was very much part of Second Temple Judaism, and is still part of our culture today.

The ritualistic aspect of flaming suggests a rehearsed and practiced pattern or script that becomes increasingly habitual the more it is used. Like religious ritual, it becomes rote, almost automatic. And Paul disparages the practice because it destroys trust, love, fellowship, conversation, and communion between people.

ELECTIONEERING

Also translated as *strife, dissensions, conflicts*, ἐριθεία is defined by Strong's as electioneering or intriguing for office, as putting one's self forward. It's a kind of calculated, scheming selfishness that works to advance one's self over others.

There is a difference between doing one's best and doing everything you can to win some favor or position. We are all called to be the best person we are able to be, to excel to the best of our abilities, and to use our abilities and successes in the service of Jesus Christ. But the kind of strife indicated by this word suggests clawing our way to the top by any means possible in order to put ourselves in a position of power, authority, or superiority.

DIVISIONS

Another term with political overtones, διχοστασία simply means divisions, but it carries the sense of insurrection and political strife. Of course, it is not limited to politics but pertains to what we might call the body politic of a community. It involves a spirit of divisiveness and disagreement that leads to dissension. Divisions begin with a spirit of criticism where one always finds fault in others. Such criticism is often thought to be a sign of intelligence by those who engage it. But it issues from a sense of inferiority that works actively to compensate by working to make one appear to be superior to others.

ENVY

φθόνος points to the Tenth Commandment against coveting. The root of envy is the desire to have what belongs to someone else. It involves a discontent with what one has, with one's own gifts, talents, possessions, or lot in life. Only when Paul discovered that he was guilty of violating the Tenth Commandment, which uncovered his own sin and guilt, did he come to understand the relationship between law and gospel.

> "What then shall we say? That the law is sin? By no means! Yet if it had not been for the law, I would not have known sin. For I would not have known what it is to covet if the law had not said, 'You shall not covet'" (Romans 7:7).

As a Pharisee, Paul had been aware of this commandment all of his life. He had studied it, preached it, lived with it, prayed about it, etc. But at some point, beginning on the road to Damascus, the Holy Spirit brought conviction to him as he realized his own complicity in sin and felt his own guilt, in spite of his learning, his preaching and prayer as a Pharisee, a religious leader. He was surprised by his guilt because he had been taught that his participation in Temple sacrifices and services would alleviate it. But it didn't! No doubt, during Paul's early years as a Christian he felt a powerful envy of the peace and wisdom of the humble Christians he came to know. No doubt, he wanted to have what they had—the Spirit of Jesus Christ that passes all understanding (Philippians 4:7).

And yet, it was the spirit of envy and coveting that distorted his understanding and compelled him to search in all the wrong places, to look for the spirit of hope and love, which he witnessed among Christians, in his traditions of law. However, it could not be found there because it wasn't there. Only by accepting the gift of Christ's love, which he could not earn, did his envy subside.

MURDER

This term is absent from some manuscripts, but is present in the majority of them. But whether it is included or excluded here, clearly murder is both well-understood and prohibited.

INTOXICATION

Drunkenness is to be avoided, but not the consumption of alcohol. We know this because Paul recommended that Timothy drink a little wine to settle his stomach, or possibly his nerves since nervousness is often felt in the stomach (1 Timothy 5:23).

Drunkenness diminishes our inhibitions and self-control, which means that the avoidance of drunkenness would maintain our inhibitions and self-control, our self-discipline. To inhibit involves the conscious exclusion of unacceptable thoughts or desires. It involves the maintenance of social boundaries and norms of behavior. Drunkenness leads to moral decrepitude.

This does not mean that we are never to challenge norms, boundaries, or patterns of behavior. It means that Christ has set the norms, boundaries, and patterns of behavior that are to characterize His people. We are to champion these fruits of the Spirit, but challenge all norms, boundaries, and behaviors that fall outside of Christ's definitions.

REVELRY

Strong's defines κῶμος as

> "a nocturnal and riotous procession of half drunken and frolicsome fellows who after supper parade through the streets with torches and music in honor of Bacchus or some other deity, and sing and play before houses of male and female friends; hence used generally of feasts and drinking parties that are protracted till late at night and indulge in revelry."

The old adage applies: early to bed, early to rise, makes a man healthy, wealthy, and wise. The problem with revelry is not the merrymaking, but the lack of restraint that fans the flames of sin.

Paul ended his list with "and things like these" (v. 21), suggesting that he could go on, but was satisfied that this list, while not comprehensive, was adequate. The list was important because "those who do such things will not inherit the kingdom of God" (v. 21). Will such behaviors really keep people out of the kingdom, out of heaven? No. To the Corinthians Paul wrote:

> "Or do you not know that the unrighteous will not inherit the kingdom of God? Do not be deceived: neither the sexually immoral, nor idolaters, nor adulterers, nor men who practice homosexuality, nor thieves, nor the greedy, nor drunkards, nor revilers, nor swindlers will inherit the kingdom of God. *And such were some of you.* But you were washed, you were sanctified, you were justified in the name of

the Lord Jesus Christ and by the Spirit of our God" (1 Corinthians 6:9-11).

And such were some of you! The operative word here is *were*. They used to do such things, but no longer. What changed? They became washed, sanctified, and justified by the character of Jesus Christ who inhabited them through the power and presence of the Holy Spirit through regeneration.

The unrighteous will not inherit the kingdom, but the righteous will. The purpose of Christianity is the establishment of the righteousness of God in Christ through regeneration in humanity. Unrighteous people are to become increasingly righteous in Christ. Only those who are growing in the character of Jesus Christ will inherit the kingdom. It's not that Christians are to be sinless, but we are to sin less over time.

27. Righteousness

But the fruit of the Spirit is love, joy, peace, patience, kindness, good-ness, faithfulness, gentleness, self-control; against such things there is no law. And those who belong to Christ Jesus have crucified the flesh with its passions and desires. If we live by the Spirit, let us also keep in step with the Spirit. Let us not become conceited, provoking one another, envying one another. —Galatians 5:22-26

In contrast and opposition to all of the previous two verses, Paul described in a few words the fruit of the Spirit as the objective for Christian living. All of the fruits he mentioned are aspects or traits of character. It is important to see this because it means that Christian fruit is not about what we call churches or evangelism. It is about our own individual character development—our own, not some other's. This does not mean that Christianity is *not* about churches or evangelism, but that the planting of the fruit of the Spirit precedes both church member-ship and evangelism—not that the fruits are to be fully ripe before mem-bership is granted, but that they have begun growing.[1] Christianity and evangelism are about the fruit orchard, not the fruit that grows on the individual trees. It's like the difference between sociology and psychol-ogy, one is group oriented and one is individual oriented.

The purpose of the fruit is to feed the seed. The fruit is food. The fruit of the Spirit will feed the growth of the Spirit, and without fruit the Spirit will languish. Where the Spirit is strong and growing, there will be much fruit. And where it is not, there will be little fruit. From this we learn that the way or method of growing the Spirit—discipleship—first and foremost involves the growth of fruit in the lives of believers.

---

1 Ross, Phillip A. *Informal Christianity—Refining Christ's Church*, Pilgrim Platform, Mari-etta, Ohio, 2007.

Discipleship is not simply telling others about Jesus, or witnessing about our own conversion to unbelievers. These things are important, but they must be introduced in the right way and nurtured, just as to grow a plant involves nutrients that must be introduced into the soil in the right way, in the right soil, at the time, and nurtured in the right ways if it is to produce its maximum crop of fruit. The primary thing that individual Christians are to do is to produce fruit in *their own lives*, through the development and maturation of the fruit of the Spirit in their own character. Interestingly, this is done mostly through service to others.

It is both interesting and important that the fruits that Paul listed cannot be grown alone, in isolation. While they involve individual character qualities, they can only be practiced socially. They involve both the individual and social aspects of human identity. The fruit that each Christian is to produce in their own lives can only be practiced and matured in community with others. It is not necessary that the community be composed of only Christians, nor even of any Christians. While it is helpful to see what mature fruit looks like, we must not model our spiritual growth on others. Rather, Jesus must remain our model at all times. It is safe to imitate the best character traits of the best Christians, but it is better to imitate the character traits of the apostles, and best to imitate those of Christ Himself.

Love

The Greek word is agape (ἀγάπη), which has been transliterated into English. It is defined as the love of God or Christ for mankind; selfless love of one person for another without sexual implications, especially love that is spiritual in nature. It is also defined as a religious meal shared as a sign of love and fellowship. Our modern understanding of love has been dominated by the idea of sexual expression so much that it is difficult for us to conceive of love apart from sex. So, for us the use of the word *love* tends to communicate the wrong things in a Christian context.

It might be better for us to return to the *Authorized Version's* translation as *charity*, or even *benevolence*, the intention or showing kindness, consideration, and sympathy. The idea is to serve the well-being of others as much as or more than we serve our own well-being. It is the practice of putting others first.

JOY

Joy (χαρά) is not a mere feeling, but is a commitment to being thankful regardless of one's circumstances. Thankfulness produces delight and contentment that tends to wash away worry. We see this in Paul's second letter to the Corinthians:

> "In all our affliction, I am overflowing with joy" (2 Corinthians 7:4).

In spite of struggle, pain, and difficulty, Paul was full of joy. Joy celebrates the love, grace, and mercy of God in spite of our circumstances. It is not a response to our circumstances, but transcends or overcomes them. And for this reason joy is undefeatable. It refuses to recognize defeat because it will not let go of the hope of God's promise of redemption.

PEACE

εἰρήνη is not something to hope for in the future. Peace is not something or some condition of being that we should seek, it is something that we give, that we demonstrate. We shouldn't look for it as coming from others, we should give it to others. Peace is not a prize that we win, it is a responsibility that we exercise. The Greek word is transliterated in the English word *eirenic* (*irenic*), which is the character attribute of peacefulness, of promoting peacefulness.

Rather than simply seeking the absence of conflict, the peaceful person will actively work to eliminate the causes of conflict, which usually involve injustice of some sort. Peace is usually disturbed by injustice or the perception of injustice. And in the same way, justice is not something to seek for, it is something to give. We give justice to others by living righteously ourselves. We make our world just, not by going to court for reparations, but by actually being righteous in our own lives and dealings with others. The only way to cure injustice is to live justly, righteously. Thus, justice is an important part of the commitment to peace. The best way to eliminate injustice is to exceed the expectations of fairness by treating others, not with the minimum standards of equity, but with the extravagance of love understood as benevolence and charity.

LONGSUFFERING

Another way to actively promote peace and justice is to patiently bear continual wrongs or trouble one's self, to not take offense at the sins of others but to bear injustice patiently. My lack of righteousness only makes the injustices perpetrated by others worse. If I disparage those who disparage me, I'm only increasing the world's dissonance. Longsuffering (μακροθυμία) actively works to reduce dissonance by not contributing to it. It requires patience, endurance, constancy, steadfastness, and perseverance in the face of difficulty, struggle, injustice, offense, and sin.

That's what God does for us, that's what Jesus modeled in His life and death, and what He expects us to do for others. Longsuffering is an expression of love, grace, and mercy. The best way to create a society of grace, mercy, and forgiveness is to give these very things to others, to lead with them, to take responsibility for promoting them. We cannot be responsible for the behavior of others, but we can be and must be responsible for our own behavior, including our response to others. The old adage applies: Want a friend? Be a friend.

MORAL GOODNESS

To say *moral* goodness is redundant because all goodness is necessarily moral. Nonetheless, morality is such an unpopular term today that it needs to be emphasized. Morality is concerned with principles of right and wrong, conforming to standards of behavior and character based on those principles.

Christian morality is based on the character of Jesus Christ, who modeled the principles we are to emulate. But we must not neglect the fact that Jesus Christ is also God Himself because of God's Trinitarian character. And that means that Christians must also factor in the character of God in both testaments of the Bible, and that factoring must also be done in the light of Christ. God's character must be understood in the light of Christ.

We are to interpret the Old Testament through the lens of Jesus Christ, which means that we are to believe about the Old Testament what Jesus believed about it, not what Moses believed. We are to see it and understand it as Jesus saw it and understands it. We are *not* to see it and understand it as the Old Testament Temple establishment did—

nor could we if we wanted to! Many of the lessons of the Old Testament that were for Old Testament Jews are not the lessons that Christians are to learn. Many of those lessons are not for us. More importantly, we are to learn what the Old Testament taught Jesus and Paul and the Apostles. Granted that there is much overlap, but there are also many very important things about the Old Testament that Jesus has revealed, things that were veiled—hidden—from the Old Testament Jews.

Thus, to fail to see and understand the character of God in the Old Testament apart from the light of Christ produces a gross misrepresentation of God today. The character of God as the Old Testament Jews saw and understood it, without the light of Christ, produces a sadly deficient view of God for Christians. Yes, Jews and Christians worship the same God, but they have very different views and understandings of that God. God Himself has not changed. But Christ has come! He came to reveal, fulfill, and correct Old Testament law for Christians by providing a new adaptation and application of God's law. That is what Paul was telling the Galatians. Paul's call for righteousness, for goodness, for moral goodness, is at the heart of the gospel of grace that Jesus brought to complete our understanding of God's justice. God's justice is not found in the Old Testament or the New Testament. Rather, it is established by living in the righteousness of God in Christ. We don't *find* God's justice, we *found* it in our own lives—or rather, Christ founds it in us. Justice is not something we get, it's something we give.

FAITH

Faith is not a noun, not a thing. It's a verb, an action, an activity, a behavior, a way of life. Faith is both the conviction of the truth of a thing and the commitment to stake one's own life on that truth. In this case, we are talking about the truth of the gospel of Jesus Christ found in the New Testament, which is grounded on the Old Testament.

Faith also refers to a character quality of one who can be relied on. It is the character quality of fidelity, trustworthiness, and loyalty. Faith is a persuasion in that it implies a position or conclusion of a thought process. Faith is like knowledge, but where knowledge follows a process of proof, faith precedes proof.

And yet the object of faith makes a huge difference. The correct object of faith is God, truth, God's truth in Christ Jesus. Faith in something false is quite different than faith in something true. Jesus Christ is truth itself, but Jesus Christ is also the way, the truth and the life (John 14:6). This means that faith in Christ is not a static thing, but a living thing, a dynamic thing. Faith is the way of truth, the way that leads to truth, the way that issues out from truth. It is a path that leads to a permanent, fixed endpoint in the future. So, as long as faith conforms to that path, it will lead to that permanent, fixed endpoint—even if the path is not a straight line. Conformity to the path guarantees that the endpoint will be reached. That's faith.

MEEKNESS

The root definition of πραότης is humility, gentleness, not timidity or faintheartedness. It requires an accurate self-assessment, seeing one's self as God sees you, being honest about your own strengths and weaknesses. It involves a willing submission to God's authority and direction. The fact that the submission is *willing* is extremely important.

When willing submission is not present, the Holy Spirit recedes from awareness as reliance on His authority and direction fades from one's intention. This results in classic acedia, defined as apathy and inactivity in the practice of virtue. Acedia, described as the noontime demon, has been the bane of the practitioners of ascetic spiritually throughout the ages, who often become withdrawn and depressed rather than meek and humble. Religious sloth engages and facilitates the chain of deadly sins that ends in damnation.

It is also important to note that willing submission must be given to the Holy Spirit and not to some substitute. Missing this will land you in idolatry as you submit to something other than God Himself. It is particularly important to discern the difference between submission to the power and presence of God's Holy Spirit through regeneration versus submission to a guru, pastor, bishop, spiritual director, or government representative (a king, or the principalities and powers of godlessness), etc. While it is important to recognize and respect various social authorities, a distinction must always be maintained between social conformity and submission to God. The development and maturity of meekness strengthens the ability to make such discernment.

TEMPERANCE

This is the opposite of having a temper, getting angry easily. When a thing is temperate it doesn't fluctuate. Tempered steel gets stronger. To be temperate is to have an even keel, to be moderate, steady, solid, consistent. Many versions translate ἐγκράτεια as *self-control*. The word root means strong and robust. Control of one's self means control of one's desires and habits, versus surrender to addiction or idolatry. Temperance is the discipline of self-restraint.

Self-control makes it seem like the source of the control is the self, but it's not. Christians are submitted to God through the Holy Spirit to God's Word in Scripture. So, the control comes from submission to God's Word, which means that God is the source of the control, not one's self. Though it also means that the person does not need someone else to direct him or her, so it looks like self-control from the outside. But it can also look like submission to another when the other person is also submitted to the Spirit and provides genuine Godly counsel. When God's counsel comes through others it can look like submission to the counselor, but it's not. Knowing the difference requires knowledge of God's true counsel.

NO LAW

Paul summed up the list by saying, "against such things there is no law" (v. 23). There is no law against the fruit of the Spirit because the development and exercise of these character qualities is above or outside of the law. The law does not deal with these things because the law deals with infractions and offenses against God and other people. And these things, these spiritual fruits, not only don't harm others, these things are good for other people. The development and exercise of these characteristics, the fruits of the spirit, will benefit others, as well as one's self. The law is about prohibitions, not benefits, about correcting poor performance and bad behaviors, and not about godly goals that lead to right future outcomes.

The things on this list are concerns of the Spirit not the law. So, where these qualities reign, the law has no use, no purpose, no jurisdiction. So, the Galatian Judaizers who were calling people back to the law were actually calling people to abandon their concern for the things of the Spirit. It is good to live in a community where people don't break the law, but it is far better to live in a community where people are filled with the fruit of the Spirit, and go out of their way to be a benefit to others. A return to being concerned about law would be a step in the wrong direction.

To be concerned about the passions and desires of the flesh is self-concern, and self-concern is opposed to concern for others. My passions and desires of the flesh are all about *me*. Love is concerned about others. The Second Great Command, to "love your neighbor as yourself" (Matthew 22:39), is often twisted far beyond its simple intent. It is not a command for self-love, but simply recognizes the reality that people naturally take care of themselves.

There are two ways that this commandment can be stretched beyond its intent. It can be seen to command an increase of self-concern by thinking that we can increase our love for others by increasing our love for ourselves. So, our resources become self-directed rather than other-directed. This understanding errs by keeping the focus on ourselves. On the other hand, it can be seen as a command to neglect ourselves by loving and serving others to the point of self-detriment. But this understanding errs because if we neglect ourselves, we reduce the effectiveness of our love and service to others. For instance, if I give away all I own to others, I become unable to help others escape poverty and become a statistic of poverty myself, and then require the help of someone else.

If we keep Jesus' two Great Commandments, to love God and neighbors, we will not be in violation of Moses' Ten Commandments. Nonetheless, the Ten Commandments as standards of moral behavior continue to provide guidance and instruction about proper conformity to God's will. Even though our lives or obedience will be within the bounds of the Ten Commandments, we can improve our conformity to God's will for us by hearing the subtleties of instruction that the Ten Commandments provide, and reflect on the history of their use and abuse. But the fact that we are not in gross violation of them ourselves in no way changes or reduces the jurisdiction of the Ten Commandments. They are still in effect, and our lack of perfect conformity will remain an issue all our lives "until we all attain to the unity of the faith and of the knowledge of the Son of God, to mature manhood, to the measure of the stature of the fullness of Christ" (Ephesians 4:13).

The crucified flesh is dead, and is no longer commanding, demanding, or directing our attention and behavior. Because Christians belong to Jesus, His crucifixion is our crucifixion. Paul uses this language to encourage us to relate to Jesus, to identify ourselves with Him, to link our plight with His. His crucifixion was both real (fleshly) and spiritual. His resurrection was also both real (fleshly) and spiritual. He died to the flesh in order to live again in both body and Spirit. When we die spiritually through baptism He is able to live spiritually through our flesh.

IN STEP

We are to dance with the Holy Spirit. While Paul didn't use the language of dance, he certainly wouldn't object to it. Dancing requires keeping in step, which requires knowing the steps, practicing the steps, mastering the steps, and then actually dancing with a partner, with the Spirit.

No one learns to dance alone because dancing is necessarily social. Even performance dance needs an appreciative audience. No one walks in the Spirit alone. Dancing with the Spirit is never simply about one's self, one's own maturity in Christ, it's a community event.

The walking in the Spirit that Paul was talking about is actually more like marching. The Greek word he used was στοιχέω, which means to proceed in a row as the marching of soldiers, to go in order. Here we see that it is not just me and the Spirit, but involves a company of people who are marching together in the Spirit. It is necessary to have a personal relationship with God in order to do this, but it is also necessary to have a personal relationship with the others in your marching company. No one can march in a company alone, it involves actual practice with actual people.

28. CHRIST'S LAW

Brothers, if anyone is caught in any transgression, you who are spiritual should restore him in a spirit of gentleness. Keep watch on yourself, lest you too be tempted. Bear one another's burdens, and so fulfill the law of Christ. For if anyone thinks he is something, when he is nothing, he deceives himself. But let each one test his own work, and then his reason to boast will be in himself alone and not in his neighbor. For each will have to bear his own load. —Galatians 6:1-5

No one is perfect. Everyone makes mistakes. Christians are no better than anyone else, but they should be better tomorrow than they are today. Those who are immature raze other people for their screwups. The shallow keep score and gossip when they discover others in transgression. Liars exaggerate the sins of others. The hateful spew anger at those who cross them. The jealous scheme and plot to take advantage of the misfortunes of others. Quarrelers argue with the fallen. No doubt, Paul was privy to much of this in Galatia.

So, he counseled them to rise above such petty concerns by helping one another toward restoration. Those who are caught up in error don't need their errors pointed out to them, they need help overcoming them. Paul not only provided help and direction for the Galatians who were caught up in the retrograde spirituality of the Judaizers, he modeled how to provide it.

The spirit needed for restoration is πραότης, meekness. Correct self-assessment will produce the humility that knows that *'er for the grace of God go I*. Humility doesn't reach down from above to offer a helping hand, it shares the liferaft that it clings to by offering a sin-stained hand that has been drenched in the muck of life. Humility says, "I know. Me, too. This helps." It doesn't chide or laugh or look down its nose.

Of course we need to help others, but we don't need to police fellow believers. That's not the way we are to function with one another. Help them, yes. Police them, no. Policing is a function of law, not grace. God is perfectly able to police His people through the power and presence of the Holy Spirit through regeneration. We are, however, called to witness, to lift up the moral model of Jesus Christ, and to testify, to reveal the evidence of our own lives that are being increasingly conformed to Christ, to the fruits of the spirit. But it is not our responsibility to change the hearts and minds of others, only the Holy Spirit can do that.

Correction best helps when it is sought, not when it is imposed. The regenerate are sensitive to the leading of the Spirit, but the unregenerate will refuse instruction and rebel against every effort to help them, until they find themselves under the influence of the Spirit. The help that sin needs is the help of the Holy Spirit, and sinners will rail against all other attempted aid. Only when the Spirit in the sinner reaches out to the Spirit in Christ can the help of Christ take effect.

This means that transgressors need to be reached by the Spirit of Christ, not by the spirit of helpfulness. More than anything else, the transgressor needs to see the Spirit of Christ in me (for instance) before s/he will accept any help from me. God's help travels along the bonds of spiritual fellowship, or relationship, which means that it won't connect until such bonds exist. No one accepts genuine spiritual help from strangers, or from people they don't trust and respect. Bodily help, yes! Band aids, blankets, bread, beds, and volunteered time are readily received.

But genuine spiritual help is a different matter. Those doors are only opened with humility, genuine meekness. Those doors only open from the inside, which is why even Christ stands and knocks. It's not that Christ is too weak to enter on His own, or that we have the power to keep Him out. It's that He is waiting for His Holy Spirit to open the door from the inside. That's what makes it a real opening. The answer to a question must wait for the question to be asked. It's useless to provide an answer to a question that has not been asked.

SELF-CONTROL

The policing that needs to be done is self-policing. This is the most effective and consistent policing because you always take yourself with you. You are in a unique position to observe and critique your every action. But Paul asked for more. He asks us to observe and critique our temptations as well as our actions, to evaluate our actions before we do them. And before policing begins we need to inspect our equipment, to make sure that it is functioning as it should.

> "You hypocrite, first take the log out of your own eye, and then you will see clearly to take the speck out of your brother's eye" (Matthew 7:5).

Jesus calls people who fail to inspect their own equipment *hypocrites*. We distinguish between those who are hypocritical and those who are hypercritical, but Jesus doesn't. Hypocrites say one thing and do another. They judge themselves with a different standard than they judge others. The hypercrites, on the other hand, nitpick. Hypercrites are super critical about everything. They cannot be pleased—*will* not be pleased.

> "Now receive the one who is weak in the faith, and do not have disputes over differing opinions" (Romans 14:1, *New English Translation*).

In order to watch ourselves and keep ourselves from temptation, we need to know the standard of behavior that we are to keep. If we don't know the standard, we can't possibly keep it. So, the first step of this self-watching is to learn the standard, which of course is found in the moral truth of Scripture, particularly in the life of Jesus. We are to emulate Him, to imitate His character qualities in ourselves.

Paul spelled them out in his list of the fruits of the Spirit, and he also mentioned the things we are to guard against in his list of the works of the flesh. Those two lists should be committed to memory and consulted regularly. These show us what to do and what not to do, how to be and how not to be, how to live and how not to live.

BEARING

To bear a thing is to put up with it. To bear a weight is to carry it. To bear a child is to give birth. To bear with one another is to put up with each other, to carry one another through tough times, and to share in the birth of the Holy Spirit in one another's lives. We are called to bear with others because its hard to do.

Paul said that bearing with one another fulfills the law of Christ. This means that there is a law (νόμος) of Christ in the same sense that there is a law of Moses. The law of Moses was for the administration of Moses, and the law of Christ is for the administration of Christ. We are not currently in the administration of Moses, but we are in Christ's administration. So, the law of Christ takes precedence over the law of Moses. The administration of Christ has supplanted the administration of Moses. In fact, even the administration of king David supplanted the administration of Moses, but no one knew it at the time, except a few prophets. But no one believed them.

All of God's covenants are eternal because God is eternal, and because God is perfect He doesn't make mistakes. However, the fact that God's covenants are eternal does not mean that they are eternally at the forefront of our growth and maturity in the same ways. The Bible teaches that there has been a succession of covenants with God, and that each covenant inherits the essential truth(s) of the previous one. Thus, each of these covenants is eternally valuable and useful. The lessons we learn in our childhood do not become invalid when we become adults, but our relationship to them changes. Those lessons don't become untrue when we become adults. Once we learn those lessons we move on to new lessons, harder lessons. We can always review the earlier ones, and they will still be true for the situation that they addressed, but they may not always be useful in our current situation. God's covenants are eternal, yet also seasonal, in that they don't all produce fruit equally in every season of humanity.

The fact that Paul mentioned the law of Christ is extremely important because it shows us that some sort of law is still in force. Jesus Christ does have expected standards of human behavior. In fact, Christ's standards, to love God and love neighbors, is actually higher than the Old Testament standards, the Ten Commandments. Or another way to say the same thing is that Jesus' interpretation of the Ten Commandments, to love God and neighbors, is higher than Moses' interpretation, the Deuteronomic Law.

However, the fact that Christ's interpretation has supplanted Moses's interpretation does not mean that Moses's interpretation has no value or use for Christians. Moses' law has a pedagogical function, it teaches us about ourselves, about God, and provides a backdrop to highlight some important elements of Christ's teaching (Romans 3:20). There is truth to every aspect of Moses' law that helps us understand ourselves and God better, but Moses' law must always be subjected to the light of Christ in order to illuminate the moral truth of Christ. To fail to see Moses' law in the light of Christ is a failure of catastrophic consequence because it points to the failure to assimilate the teaching of Jesus Christ.

STONING

For example, take the stoning of the disobedient son:

"If a man has a stubborn and rebellious son who will not obey the voice of his father or the voice of his mother, and, though they discipline him, will not listen to them, then his father and his mother shall take hold of him and bring him out to the elders of his city at the gate of the place where he lives, and they shall say to the elders of his city, 'This our son is stubborn and rebellious; he will not obey our voice; he is a glutton and a drunkard.' Then all the men of the city shall stone him to death with stones. So you shall purge the evil from your midst, and all Israel shall hear, and fear" (Deuteronomy 21:18-21).

The first thing we must say about these verses is that they are very clear. The accusation made by his parents, which is very important to this story, was that he was stubborn and rebellious. But we must also understand that God accused the Israelites of this same behavior time and time again (Deuteronomy 9:6-7, etc.). Stubborn rebellion was not something unique to this son, but would have been a common problem. Their second accusation was that he would not obey their voice, and thirdly they accused him of being a drunkard and a glutton.

The Fifth Commandment is to honor our father and mother, which is usually interpreted as to obey them. The Ten Commandments do not provide punishments for disobedience, though the Fifth Commandment does add a reason for obedience, "that your days may be long upon the land which the Lord your God is giving you" (Exodus 20:12). Notice that the commandment itself is directed to individuals, but the reason for obedience is directed to the community.

The punishment of stoning was added to the Ten Commandments by Moses' and the seventy under God's direction. The question is whether God *introduced* this punishment, or whether He *allowed* it. Notice that I'm not challenging that this is the Word of God, I'm inquiring about the purpose of the punishment. If God intended it to be strictly enforced, there would not have been a man left standing because they were all stubborn and rebellious.

Furthermore, when we ask about whose voice they, including the son, were to listen to we find that they were all to listen to *God's* voice. Parental instruction is a temporary substitute because parents are to teach their children how to hear *God's* voice, to resonate with biblical moral truth in the light of Christ. So, when the parents are dead and gone their now grown children can continue to hear God's voice, and teach *their* children. This particular son was a drunkard and a glutton, which means that he was of age, an adult. He should have been listening to God's voice, but the parents accused him of not listening to *their* voice. Would the voice of the parents have been in harmony with God's voice at that point? Probably not, because the son was an adult and had not learned to hear/obey God's voice from his parents. The parents had failed to teach the son to hear/obey God's voice.

There are two infractions here: the son's failure to heed his parents, and the parent's failure to teach their son to hear/obey *God's* voice. The punishment of stoning, then, would be the responsibility of the parents in two ways. First, the accusation needed to come from them, and second, the accuser(s) were to cast the first stone(s). The administration of such a punishment would, then, be possible only by the coldest of cold-hearted, sociopathic parents.

Would God introduce such a punishment with the intention that it be carried out to the letter? Or would God allow such a law to be on the books as a way to teach children the importance of obeying their parents, and teach parents the importance of teaching their children to hear/obey the voice of God? Anyone who knows God personally will dismiss the first question because it is absurd and offends the character of the God they know. I imagine that this was true even for the Old

Testament saints who preceded Christ, but it is even more true for Christians who have seen God in the face of Jesus Christ.

Are these verses in Deuteronomy the Word of God? Absolutely! The real issue is what they mean, what they teach, and how we are to understand them. I don't for a minute believe that God intended most people to blindly or literally carry them out, though no doubt some did. Through the execution of this law its poignancy would become even more clear. I suspect that the purpose of this law was not its execution, but its careful consideration, that it has always had a pedagogical function.

So, as we look back at this law in the light of Christ we must apply the grace and mercy of Christ, and conclude two things: 1) that a guilty son would receive mercy, and 2) that parents who were guilty of the failure to properly teach their children to hear/obey God's voice would also receive mercy. The son would understand the depth of his guilt and the seriousness of disobedience, but he would also understand that the grace and mercy of Jesus Christ is greater than his guilt and failure. The parents would come to understand their own guilt and the seriousness of their failure, but would also come to understand that the grace and mercy of Jesus Christ is greater than their guilt and failure, too.

This, then, provides an example of how we are to understand and use the Old Testament in the light of Christ, how we are to apply the light of Christ to the Old Testament. Those who are offended by the Old Testament laws have yet to make this application, so they dismiss the Old Testament because they think that it offends the character of God, which then makes such an application impossible. The fact that the Bible comes in two testaments begs us to make this application. It is a testimony to our own dullness and faithlessness as Christians that we have done as little with this project of bringing the light of Christ to Old Testament law as we have, even after two thousand years of Christian history.

The world desperately needs, not just the proclamation of the grace and mercy of Jesus Christ, but the application of the grace and mercy of Jesus Christ to the Old Testament, because the Old Testament is the primary context of the New! We should only apply God's Old Testament law after we understand it in the light of Christ, for then the application becomes quite different from what might otherwise be expected. This is an example of how the light of Christ is to be applied to the law of Moses that Paul was teaching the Galatians.

EXAMINATION

The purpose of God's grace and mercy has always been to get people involved with His Holy Spirit. Christ came to replace retributive justice with restorative justice. After twenty-five hundred years of history (Moses to Christ), God's plan to replace the religion of vengeance with the religion of forgiveness had clearly demonstrated man's inability to accede to God's law. God had established the Jewish people as a case study, and given them every external, cultural help possible. He gave them the Ten Commandments and the prophets to interpret them. In addition, He helped them to develop the Deuteronomic Law, the Tabernacle, the Temple and the Kingdom.

At the end of that twenty-five hundred years, they had made a wreck of it all. Moses had led them out of captivity in Egypt and through the wilderness, only to have them end in captivity, not just to Syria, Babylon, Persia, and Rome, but to their own stubborn, rebellious, self-centeredness. And to make it all the worse, they now justified their self-centeredness with the very things that were supposed to free them—the Temple, the culture of circumcision, and their Scripture.

This does not mean that the Temple, the culture, and Scripture have no value, or that God had not been intimately involved in all of it. God was involved, and there was much value in the Temple, the culture, and Scripture. There are many positive, useful stories and lessons that have come out of that history that must not be neglected. Nor does this mean that none of the Old Testament saints were ungodly. God allowed sufficient slack (grace and mercy) in the Old Testament times and teachings to save and nurture His people.

But His primary purpose of establishing that Old Testament history was to provide a backdrop for the ministry of His Son, Jesus Christ. He didn't do this because He could do nothing else, He did it because *we needed it*. The ministry of Jesus Christ makes little sense apart from *The Backstory* of the Old Testament. This should be quite clear today as the gospel of Jesus Christ has been broadcast, especially

since the Great Awakenings of the eighteenth and nineteenth centuries, to people who are increasingly deficient of that context.
Communication fails for the lack of proper context.

When Jesus said that His mission was to the Jews first, He meant
that His mission was to reveal their own history, *The Backstory*, to
them, because too many of them had spent most of their history denying it. I'm not saying that God wasn't with them, or that God didn't
use them, or that God deceived them. God was with them, God did
use them, and God allowed them to deceive themselves for a while.
The veil that blinded them to the truth of their own situation was necessary in order for the fullness of that blindness to manifest in history,
in order to establish God's truth in the wider world through Jesus
Christ.

God is still not through with them, or with us! Too much of this
world still runs on vengeance rather than forgiveness, on retribution
rather than restoration. God's mission now is the application of the
light of Christ to the Old Testament in order to teach the world about
the necessity of hearing/obeying the voice of God through the power
and presence of the Holy Spirit through regeneration. It is precisely
the application of the light of Christ to the Old Testament that requires the discernment of God's voice to sort out what is true from
what is false, what is good from what is evil. This—the establishment,
maturity, and application of moral truth in human culture—has been
God's project on earth since He put Adam in the Garden. The deception that Paul mentioned in v. 3 is the same deception that deceived
Adam and Eve in the Garden.

PROOF!

The only way to know if God is real is to live as is described in the
New Testament, to live according to Galatians 5, to avoid the works
of the flesh and practice the gifts of the Spirit. God rewards all who
genuinely engage Him in conversation/prayer. Prayer is a form of
conversation with God. God graces us with His presence, in order that
we may prove His reality, not to others, but to ourselves.

Paul said that we must test or prove our own work, our own efforts. Proving the existence of God, as the idea is popularly
understood, has never been a matter of providing logically argued pa-

per proofs, as if God were some sort of geometry puzzle. The proof of the existence of God utilizes a different definition of *prove*—as an act of validating. *Proof* is a verb not a noun. To prove a thing is to test it, to see if it holds up.

Because God is a Person, because we can know Him personally as well as abstractly, the proof of God or proof of the veracity of His Word is also a personal thing. So, my proof is not your proof, nor is yours mine. Rather, we each must prove Him to our own satisfaction. We must each practice prayer and the fruits of the spirit ourselves until we are satisfied that He is real and His way of life is in fact what Christ said it is. This means that the proof of God is available only to the faithful because it is subjective. The refusal to personally prove the reality of God involves the failure to engage the connection provided by the Holy Spirit through regeneration, through grace. There is certainly more to God than our experience of Him, but our experience with Him is our connection to Him. So, no personal experience means no connection, and *visa versa*.

This is not to say what that experience is or is supposed to be. We miss the importance of the creativity of God's diversity in the world when we insist that others must experience God as we do. God is far more sensitive and responsive than that. Even so, the question remains about what constitutes personal experience with God. It begins with exposure, and it comes in a gazillion ways. It comes from any reference of any kind to God, but for it to have any significance it must catch our attention and spark our curiosity. God is such a common term in every society that multiple references to God are available to every person alive. I venture to add that all people are naturally curious about God, and because God is truth the only thing that can dissuade people away from God is bad information and false ideas.

By proving the reality and efficacy of God to ourselves by engaging God through prayer, study, contemplation, service, and character emulation we can then boast (καύχημα) in ourselves and not simply refer to the reality of God in the lives of others. Many versions translate the Greek as *boast*, the *Authorized Version* uses *rejoice*, and the *New English Translation* reads, "he can take pride in himself." Of these choices *rejoice* is the best because pride, the root of boasting, is a sin. The idea is to have confidence. But the nagging concern of conscience challenges our confidence. Are we to have confidence in ourselves? No. Our confidence is in God, and that confidence gets a huge boost when we find the proof of the reality and efficacy of God in our own lives.

RESPONSIBILITY

In this way each individual can take personal responsibility for proving the reality and efficacy of God for him- or herself. This issue of law versus grace is usually misunderstood in one of two possible ways: 1) overemphasis of the role of law, which leads to legalism, and 2) overemphasis of the role of grace, which leads to antinomianism (legal abandonment). The Second Temple establishment was overwhelmingly legalistic, so Paul pressed hard to provide the counterbalance of grace. That was the context of this letter to the Galatians. However, he did not intend to abandon the role of law, which can be seen in his reference to the "law of Christ" (v. 2). The law will always have a role to play. Paul's point was not the abandonment of that role in Christ, but that Christ brought a significant change in the nature and function of that role.

Today we regularly engage in both misunderstandings. To compare our contemporary society with that of ancient Israel, which was a theocracy, we need to look at both church and state today. The contemporary state is awash in legalities that make modern society the most legalistic society in the history of the world. And the church tends to be the most antinomian, in that their understanding of the gospel is that grace has completely replaced law. And the more popular the church, the more likely this is to be true.

Contemporary culture errs in both directions, which means that both ends of the spectrum are involved in the problem and both need to be fixed. The fix(es) is not a one-size-fits-all kind of thing that can be broadly slathered throughout society. Rather, the fix involves living in Christ, personally and socially. And in order to learn how to live in Christ we need to apply the light of Christ to the Old Testament, especially to Old Testament law, in order to see how the light of Christ effects each aspect of the Old Testament. When we are able to see exactly how the light of Christ effects the Old Testament, then we may better understand how the light of Christ should effect us today, how

it should effect our churches, our civil government, and our political,
economic, and social systems. There remains much work to do toward
this end—and this is a good thing because God's people are workers,
and workers need a job, a task.

29. Doing Good

Let the one who is taught the word share all good things with the one
who teaches. Do not be deceived: God is not mocked, for whatever
one sows, that will he also reap. For the one who sows to his own
flesh will from the flesh reap corruption, but the one who sows to the
Spirit will from the Spirit reap eternal life. And let us not grow
weary of doing good, for in due season we will reap, if we do not give
up. So then, as we have opportunity, let us do good to everyone, and
especially to those who are of the household of faith.

—Galatians 6:6-10

The Godly teachers in Galatia were probably being sidelined and pastoral support was going to the popular teachers. The Judaizers had gained prominence in Galatia, which was the reason that Paul wrote this letter. Calvin wrote of this verse:

"...it is, and always has been, the disposition of the world, freely to be-
stow on the ministers of Satan every luxury, and hardly to supply
godly pastors with necessary food."[1]

Fiction is always much more exciting than truth, and the truth about human beings is downright depressing apart from Christ. Christians are called to love one another, which means faithful commitment to the ordinary things of life. God's time frame is so large that personal growth, maturity, and improvement require great patience and steadiness. And these things tend not to be attractive or interesting to the Godless. But like the race between the tortoise and the hare, the hare rushes ahead in the excitement of the world, while the tortoise plods along honoring the things of God, and finds that the slow, steady mastery of Godly disci-

---

1   Calvin, John. *Calvin's Commentaries,* Galatians 6:6, public domain.

pline produces a much more interesting and meaningful life in the long run.

Faithful support of those who teach truth is like saving for retirement in that it's not very sexy. In comparison, support of false teachers is much more like investing in a stock bubble that is rising rapidly in value. That kind of thing is much more exciting in the short run, but downright dangerous in the long run.

SOWING & REAPING

Paul began this section with a warning about being led astray by those who mock God. We are tempted to think of this warning to be counsel against treating God with contempt, and while Paul would agree that we should not do that, that's not really what he was saying here. Mocking is a kind of imitation, and we are to imitate God by imitating Christ's characteristics. We are even called to imitate Paul and the apostles in their imitation of Christ.

All mocking is not necessarily contemptuous, but all mocking does fail in its imitation. It falls short of faithful expression of the character of that which it imitates. It misses the mark, and that was Paul's point. He warned people to not be deceived by those who teach about God, but who don't really understand Him. And in this case he had in mind the Judaizers, who rejected *The Backstory* of the gospel, and called the Galatians to return to Second Temple Judaism in the name of Jesus Christ.

Paul knew well the bankruptcy of the Temple establishment, and that no one could go back. In fact, Judaism itself as it exists today stands as a testimony to the truth of Paul's teaching. Judaism itself did not return to its ancient Temple practices. And any such return in the future would constitute a complete travesty against God and man. History does not and cannot flow backwards. The future lies ahead not behind us.

The Bible is full of verses that teach the relationship between sowing and reaping. And quite honestly, there are two sides to the relationship. The first teaches that we get what we give (Luke 6:38). This is much like the Eastern teaching of *karma*, a kind of reverse Golden Rule that teaches that life will return to us what we give to it, usually featured in the negative sense. Bad things happen to us because we do bad things to others. But karma also teaches the good side, that good things will happened to us as we do good things to others. Karma seems to function like a law of reciprocity. We tend to get what we give, so do unto others as you would have them do unto you.

But the doctrine of grace stands this law on its head.

> "Those who sow in tears shall reap with shouts of joy! He who goes out weeping, bearing the seed for sowing, shall come home with shouts of joy, bringing his sheaves with him" (Psalm 126:5-6).

> "Blessed are the poor in spirit, for theirs is the kingdom of heaven. Blessed are those who mourn, for they shall be comforted. Blessed are the meek, for they shall inherit the earth. Blessed are those who hunger and thirst for righteousness, for they shall be satisfied. Blessed are the merciful, for they shall receive mercy. Blessed are the pure in heart, for they shall see God. Blessed are the peacemakers, for they shall be called sons of God. Blessed are those who are persecuted for righteousness' sake, for theirs is the kingdom of heaven. Blessed are you when others revile you and persecute you and utter all kinds of evil against you falsely on my account (Matthew 5:3-11).

The gospel teaches that in Christ we don't get what we deserve, what we have given to others. Rather, we were conceived in sin and live lives of sin, but God has saved us while we were yet sinners. Christ lived a life of obedience and died for our sins, and we who have lived lives of disobedience are to live in the reward for Christ's faithfulness.

Nonetheless, Paul was teaching that the seeds that you plant grow into whatever they are. If you plant corn, you get corn. This is so obvious that it hardly merits saying, except that it is the obvious things that are the easiest to overlook. Paul's point was simple: if you plant worldly seeds you get worldly rewards, and if you plant spiritual seeds you get spiritual rewards.

Of course, the world is not interested in spiritual things. So, worldly people are happy to sow worldly seeds. But Christians know that the world does not satisfy and that those worldly seeds will one day reap a harvest of worldly frustration and disappointment. We are to imitate Paul who was imitating Christ by sowing spiritual seed. And like the farmers in Psalm 126, we find that sowing spiritual seed is difficult, painful, frustrating, and time consuming. But when it takes root and produces a harvest, the hope, joy, and blessings of that harvest far outweigh the difficulty we had planting it.

SPIRITUAL SOWING

The word *sowing* (σπείρω) is better understood as introducing something into an environment. Even the Greek has a metaphorical sense, and that is the intended sense. Fruit is food for the seed, and to sow spiritual life, we need to feed the seed, to introduce the fruits of the spirit into whatever environment we find ourselves in—home, work, play, government, shopping, whatever. We are to sow seeds of love, joy, peace, patience, kindness, goodness, faithfulness, gentleness, and self-control. And we sow them by practicing them. The world would be a much better place if we could grow a large crop of these things.

The kingdom of God is like a farm that produces a harvest of these things, "some a hundredfold, some sixty, some thirty" (Matthew 13:8) fold. The kingdom of God is like a mustard seed that has grown into a large bush (Matthew 13:31) that provides much shelter for all kinds of creatures. The Lord's farm is a multi-generational venture that grows populations of Godly people. For thousands of years the population of the earth has been growing, and for most of it people hardly noticed. Today the population of the earth will double in about thirty-seven years. I suspect that God has known about this issue forever, and that it is a central element of God's plan. God said to Abram when He called him out of Ur,

> "'Look toward heaven, and number the stars, if you are able to number them.' Then he said to him, 'So shall your offspring be'" (Genesis 15:5).

Clearly this was a prediction of massive population growth.

The *World Factbook* gives the population of 2013 as just over seven billion, and the distribution of religions as Christian 31.50 percent, Muslim 23.20 percent, Hindu 13.8 percent, Buddhist 6.77 percent, which leaves about 25 percent, of which various other religions are about 10 percent, non-religious almost the same, and atheists are about 2 percent. The Jewish faith is about a third of a percent, and Baha'i is about a tenth of a percent. So, 57.4 percent of the world's population has issued from Abraham. These facts sound like a very old prophecy on course to fulfillment.

Of the three biblical religions that trace their heritage to Abraham —Judaism, Christianity, and Islam, Judaism has not been the recipient of this blessing. For 99.7 percent of Western history (since Christ) the Jews had no nation. Clearly, God's blessing of Abraham did not manifest on the Jews. And yet the Jewish impact on Western history has far exceeded their population. The world has been blessed by Jewish creativity—and even by their stubbornness because of the lessons they have provided in the light of Christ!

Of course, the predominance of one religion over another does not necessarily constitute spiritual fruit. Recalling what Isaiah said about worship in ancient Israel, that God could not endure their iniquity and solemn assemblies (Isaiah 1:11-17), we must conclude that all worship is not genuinely spiritual. So, the mere prevalence of self-defined religious adherence is not a necessary indication of a similar prevalence of spiritual fruit as Paul defined it. Jesus had the same evaluation of the Pharisees and the whole Temple establishment.

God is not impressed by religious affiliation. It's not that religious affiliation means nothing, but that *apart* from genuine spiritual fruit it is worse than nothing. Without the manifestation of genuine spiritual fruit, religious affiliation becomes an indictment against one's self and one's society, a testimony of greater faithlessness, guilt, and responsibility than those who profess no religious affiliation.

The practice of spiritual fruit cannot be measured by polls or surveys. Rather, it is measured primarily in one's own life by those with whom one relates. All other measures are unnecessary. Nor is one's own spiritual fruit a self-measurement. Our fruit is measured first by God, then by others, by how we practice the fruit of the spirit in their company. No other measure is needed.

SOW WHERE?

Paul said that we are not to sow in the flesh (σάρξ) but in the Spirit (v. 8). In spite of the literal meaning of σάρξ the *International Standard Version* provides a better translation:

"The person who sows through human means will harvest decay
from human means, but the person who sows in the Spirit will harvest eternal life from the Spirit" (v. 8).

The idea is that human values and ideals decay, but God's values and
ideals are eternal, sustainable in all generations. This also refers to
Paul's lists of the works of the flesh (Galatians 5:19-21) and the fruit of
the Spirit (Galatians 5:22-23).

We are to sow God's fruit in our own lives, which includes our
bodies. So, our flesh is involved. Paul was not waxing Gnostic here by
suggesting that this spiritual practice is something merely abstract,
some kind of mere belief. No, it involves real flesh and blood. However, spiritual fruit does not originate in ourselves, or in our ideas or
values. It originates from God through the Spirit in Christ. Nor can
we sustain it with our own strength or commitment. It is sustained by
the Holy Spirit through regeneration.

To say that those who engage such beneficial practices will reap
life everlasting or eternal life does not simply point to heaven, as if
performance on this planet provides a ticket to life somewhere else.
God's purpose is to bring heaven to earth, so that things on earth will
be done as they are done in heaven. Heaven is not a particular place,
its a way of life, an administration—a way to manage the affairs of
people, a dispensation—a way that God relates to human beings. Eternal life is sustainable life, to put it into current vernacular. And because
eternal life begins with our regeneration unto salvation, it begins here,
on this planet. In the short run, we are to pursue sustainable living here
through the practice of spiritual fruit. Real sustainable life is not about
electric cars, it's about electrified hearts. It's not about tank-less water
heaters, it's about the living water that flows from Christ.

MORE THAN GRACE

God's grace provides a ticket to the game, and it provides all of
the benefits of the game, even the strength and skill to win the game.
But the players must still actually play the game, not just watch. Too
many Christians are like the young boy who said, "I asked God for a
bike, but I know that it doesn't work that way. So I stole a bike, and
asked for forgiveness!" It's true that it doesn't work that way. And it's
true that God can and will forgive stealing. He'll even forgive our mis-

understandings of Him. But in spite of all of God's gracious forgiveness, there is something horribly wrong with the young boy's action.

It was presumptive. It's not that the boy takes God for granted. We are supposed to take God for granted, to trust in God's loving kindness and forgiveness, to assume it, to rely on it. We are to assume that God is gracious, and we are to do so without doubt—but *not* without question or examination. We must ask all of our questions, even the hard ones. But at the same time we are not to doubt God's love, integrity, grace, mercy, etc. We are to trust in the character of God revealed in Jesus Christ as we explore the troubling and difficult verses and stories in the Old Testament—but not abandon the character of God in Christ, or the veracity of Scripture.

The young boy has seriously misunderstood something important about God's grace and our behavior, about gospel and law. And such misunderstanding is quite common today. Clearly articulating the problem is not easy because it involves holding fast to the commitment that God's character is best revealed in Jesus Christ, and the veracity of all of Scripture—New Testament and Old. These two commitments can seem to come into conflict at times, and the reconciliation of that conflict forces us to reevaluate everything we think we know about Jesus and about the Bible.

Such reconciliation is the project of this book. The effort to reconcile these issues—the character of God in Christ and the veracity of Scripture—is the source of the presentation of *The Backstory* that fueled Paul's understanding of law and gospel that he presented to the Galatians. Understanding the Bible, and the wholeness of the Bible, is a huge task. It's a large book that covers some twenty-five hundred years of very old, complex history—and does so without loosing its relevance to today's world. It's not just that it takes a lot of time, but that we must continually adjust our own beliefs, ideas, and values that originate from Scripture because intellectual calcification is an enemy of clear thinking, emotional hardening is an enemy of love, and spiritual adulteration is an enemy of faithfulness. Remaining intellectually flexible, emotionally sensitive, and spiritually child-like is the challenge that commitment to both the character of God in Christ and to the veracity of all of Scripture provides—in spades! It constantly challenges everything we believe, love, and work to accomplish because we have to continually readjust our thinking based on newly discovered information—which is often experienced as being personally threatening and can look flaky to others.

It is easy to "grow weary of doing good" (v. 9), of holding on to both the goodness of God and the veracity of Scripture. It is easy to lose sight of the harvest season because of God's long, inter-generation timetable. Nonetheless, God's promise is that "in due season we will reap, if we do not give up" (v. 9).

DO-GOODERS

Christians are called to be do-gooders, but not to be pharisaical. We are called to work out our faith in fear and trembling, but not to try to work up brownie points with God. Discernment, discretion, and discrimination are required to know the difference. It's not that faith eliminates works, but that faith enables faithful works. Nor does grace eliminate law. Rather, law originates in grace. The giving of the law was an act of grace.

Nor are we to simply go about doing good works whenever we stumble on an opportunity to do so. Rather, we are to hold fast to the commitment to do good in every circumstance, in every situation. It's not that we wait for opportunities to come along, but that we are to create opportunities for doing good to others everywhere we go.

It is curious that Paul singled out the family of faith, as if we might ignore the people closest to us in our passion for do-goodery. Wouldn't churches naturally become bastions of doing good for others? How could an army of do-gooders not do some good in their own ranks? Yet, Paul must have singled out the church because he saw a problem there.

Imagine a fully functioning church, flush with tithes of every sort, overflowing with resources and talent eagerly looking to get engaged in some good doing. We'll have to imagine such a thing, because no such thing actually exists. Nonetheless, we persevere in our creative thinking. Imagine an institution with virtually no limit on its resources—money, materiel, people, resources, money, talent. Did I mention money? The closest thing imaginable is the federal government. Of course, it doesn't have unlimited resources, but close enough for our purpose here.

Imagine every state in the nation sending faithful do-gooders to Washington D.C., year after year, decade after decade, century after century. Imagine the horde of good from which great causes could be launched for the benefit of …. Well, the good would be done to whoever could receive it. And that line begins in the lobby of the white house on the other side of the barricades. What could go wrong!

Washington is filled to the brim with do-gooders out to impose their idea of good on the world, for the benefit of … well, everyone, of course. Everyone wants to fix the problem(s) that binds us, but it seems that no one in Washington knows exactly what the real problem actually is. This scenario was probably not what Paul imagined.

Paul imagined doing good with the resources immediately at our disposal, not with those that would be collected into the Temple. Paul knew what happened at the Temple—the corruption, the greed, the self-interest—*The Backstory*, and Paul understood Jesus' teaching that Jesus Himself was to be the new Temple. Yes, Paul supervised a collection for Jerusalem, but it wasn't for the Temple. It was for the needy, Christians and non-Christians.

Paul knew how the passion for religious service can blind people to the obvious needs closest to them. Pastors too often experience such a thing today. David and Solomon certainly did! Their families were filled with sin and intrigue. The old adage is that the carpenter's children go without shoes. So, Paul put a fix in place—"especially to those who are of the household of faith" (v. 10). Especially *them*, start there. The idea was that everyone should help to take care of the needs of those who are closest to them.

Such practice wouldn't eliminate poverty, but it would help. A lot. We begin with our own families, but we don't stop there. We move from there to the church, the local gathering of neighbors who are doing likewise. Paul wanted us to focus our efforts there because by doing that people would be encourage to be involved in the church—and would be taught to do likewise by the church. It was a way to multiply the effectiveness of doing real good where it is most needed.

30. Big Idea

See with what large letters I am writing to you with my own hand. It is those who want to make a good showing in the flesh who would force you to be circumcised, and only in order that they may not be persecuted for the cross of Christ. For even those who are circumcised do not themselves keep the law, but they desire to have you circumcised that they may boast in your flesh. —Galatians 6:11-13

Large letters? I suppose that there is a sense in which this translation is true because the words can literally mean that. But Paul was not talking about his penmanship or the font size that his secretary had chosen to use. A better translation would be *great writings*, but neither was he talking about the quality of his prose. Rather, he was talking about the major thrust of his message—*The Backstory* of the gospel.

He was talking about the fact that the idea he was trying to convey was a very large idea in that it incorporated twenty-five hundred years of history, and that the true understanding of that history had been veiled to the Jews and was only now being brought to light by the advent of Jesus Christ. He was telling them that it was a very big deal, not that he was a great writer or a superior calligraphist, nor that it tired him to have to write his own letters. He was talking about the content of his central communication pertaining to rightly understanding law and gospel. He understood the significance of his insight.

He also understood that he was working in his "own hand (εμη χειρι, v. 11). According to Strong, χειρι had a more complex meaning that alluded to helping, as in *to lend a hand*. So, he was suggesting by this phrase that the work he had done in uncovering *The Backstory* was his own. He had not pirated it from someone else, so whatever responsibility that might accrue to it belonged to him. Of course, he was not without the help of the Holy Spirit, either. He taught and modeled that in regeneration the Holy Spirit was dispatched to be of help to God's people. That is a central message in all of Paul's letters.

So, neither was he discounting the help of the Spirit in the formulation of *The Backstory*. But he was also saying that *The Backstory* was a very human story, that it was about the failure of the Jews (really of humanity) to accommodate God on their/our own. So, it was not a story that was simply dictated directly by God, like the Ten Commandments had been. Nor was it like the work of Moses and the seventy as they interpreted the Ten Commandments for the people in Deuteronomy. It was not the work of a committee or group. Rather, it was an example of what could be done in cooperation with the Holy Spirit.

We know this because verse 12 is about circumcision, which served in this letter to represent the larger issue of how law and gospel are related. The Judaizers who wanted Christians to return to the law, to Second Temple Judaism, so that they could honor Christ without being persecuted by the Jews. It was a noble effort in the sense that they did not want to wholeheartedly abandon Christ, but wanted to bring Him into line with Second Temple Judaism. And no doubt, they talked about the flexibility and magnanimity of Second Temple Judaism to receive the teachings of Jesus Christ—if only they were understood to be in line with Second Temple establishment teaching.

But Paul understood that the gospel of Jesus Christ could not conform to that version of their history without being gutted of its central importance. He could not compromise with the Judaizers without forfeiting the gospel. But the issue was not the generic relationship between law and grace, as is so commonly understood. The issue was the corruption that had been developed and even treasured by the Temple establishment in order to prop up the ancient Deuteronomic Law and hide the fact that it was an interpretation of God's Ten Commandments for a different time, for an era that was long past. The establishment had gained position and prominence that would be lost if *The Backstory* was true. Jesus turned over the tables and chased out the money changers from the Temple because the corruption evidenced by *The Backstory* had become full to overflowing.

So much of religion is understood to be an effort to preserve the past in the hope of modeling the consistency of God. So much church theology is stuck in the nineteenth, or the sixteenth, or the seventeenth, or the fourth, or the first century, depending on your preferred tradition. Faithfulness is often associated with maintaining the theology of the past, which when properly understood is not a bad thing. But we cannot look only to the past for guidance into the future, as if the ideal is to make the future like the past. Every moment, every historical era is unique in the history of the world. Every era faces unique problems and must find unique solutions to those problems. Historical continuity is also important and necessary. Yet, the uniqueness of each era does not dissolve the similarities. Navigating a dynamic path that honors both the uniquenesses and the similarities of each historical era requires sensitivity to both concerns. This is why the historical consistency of Christianity is described as a trajectory rather than a straight line. We cannot simply reproduce past solutions for current problems, nor can we simply invent new solutions out of whole cloth. Thus, the consistency of the living God, biblical consistency, must be understood exponentially rather than linearly, dynamically rather than statically. God is not a principle, formula, or algorithm. God is a Person.

Too many Christian theologians have failed to understand this point because they have failed to see *The Backstory*, to understand Paul from his perspective, rather than the perspective of Second Temple Judaism. Important scholars have saddled Paul with the views of Second Temple Judaism because that was the common understanding and historical context in which Paul wrote. And, while there is no disagreement that this is true, it misses the point that Paul argued against the common understanding and context of his peers.

On the one hand, it is surprising that so many otherwise good scholars fail to see this. But on the other hand, it is not surprising because they are just following in the long tradition of Jewish history and scholarship that couldn't see that the ancient prophets had argued the same thing, less Jesus Christ, of course. Too many modern scholars are similarly saddled with the baggage of maintaining positions of prominence and power that have accrued to the churches over millennia of cultural dominance, in similar ways enjoyed by the ancient

Temple establishment. The ancient prophets had argued against the corruption of the Temple establishment that had put the Deuteronomic Law on life support in order to prop up and justify the Temple, to justify themselves and their positions of power and wealth in God's name.

The error that the ancient Temple establishment made was the glorification of formal worship ceremonies that substituted for the life of the Spirit. This is not a denial that worship is very important, or that the neglect of worship is a serious sin that leads to a cascade of other sins and errors. However, the issue is not worship *per se*, but *right* worship. Only right worship works. Only right worship is received by God. Only right worship in Christ brings about the changes in human character that were distorted by the Fall.

Right worship is not about getting the ceremonial liturgy right, though God appreciates right ceremonial worship and is disturbed when it is wrong—and it can be wrong in so many different ways. Right worship discerns the difference between the sign and the thing signified, between the symbol and the reality, between the ceremony and the real liturgy—work to be done in the lives of people. Right worship is about the emulation of the characteristics of God in Christ. Much Temple theology is quite helpful with the various symbols involved in Tabernacle worship.

However, the purpose of Tabernacle worship was not to transfer those symbols into Temple worship, but to transfer the symbolized reality of God's character into the lives of worshipers. King David wrote about right relationship with God with great truth and eloquence, but writing is not necessarily doing. It would be an error to find fault with the writing of King David. Yet, he was a wreck himself and he made a wreck of his family, though he was far better than his peers as he matured spiritually. The writing and the history of King David make clear the difference between the sign and the thing signified, between idea and reality in his life, And it is a crucial lesson to learn.

Solomon fared no better. He learned from his father, to his own detriment. Solomon was the wisest of the wise, and was able to build the great Temple his father had envisioned. And as David planned, the Temple was the center of ancient Jewish society. It was everything—the center of worship, the center of government, of banking, of health, etc. Solomon was a great writer of wisdom, and like David, was able to exercise some of that wisdom in his administration. But Solomon's love life and family, like David's, were disastrous. In spite of their wisdom, their position, their power, their efforts to be faithful, and their many blessings from God, they failed to manifest sufficient Godly characteristics in their own lives to effect their families or their kingdoms. In spite of all of their efforts, their kingdoms descended into civil war and chaos while each side believed that they were being faithful the God of their forefathers. This should be no surprise because the biblical record shows that the Temple kingdom was established on and by warfare, like the pagan kingdoms.

The building of the Temple was, like the building of church buildings and great cathedrals, not wrong. But it shifted the concerns of those most responsible to the maintenance and use of the building rather than the maintenance and exercise of God's character in the lives of individuals and institutions. There's nothing necessarily wrong with buildings or corporate worship or worship ceremonies, as long as they don't detract from the main purpose of worship, which is the establishment of God's character in human individuals and societies.

FLESH

Paul used the term *circumcision* to represent the Temple establishment. It represented what the Jews thought to be their most fundamental covenant with God and the primary symbol of their uniqueness in human history. It represented everything that separated the Jews from the gentiles, and therefore was the primary symbol that Paul understood Christ to have come to destroy—or perhaps *change* would be a better word. Paul understood that Jesus had come to restore God's ancient plan to open the gospel to the gentiles, to reconcile the whole world with Him and with one another, and to supplant the Second Temple.

The Jews had turned inward and tried to keep God for themselves, and circumcision was the central symbol of this effort. They thought that that was what God wanted, that God's plan was to save *them*, and that contact with other people would destroy the purity that God had given to them. So, they built courtyards—walls, walls around the Temple, walls around Jerusalem, walls that kept them from mixing with others. They understood the covenant of circumcision to be fleshly, to be about them as a unique people, as a sign of their genetic superiority. So, they built cultural walls that protected their uniqueness by differentiating between themselves and others, between us and them. These were the walls that Jesus had come to destroy, and by destroying these walls of division, to take God to the gentiles.

God's larger purpose for establishing circumcision among the Jews was pedagogical. It was to provide a lesson. The Jews understood that lesson to be about the necessity of maintaining cultural purity as a way to honor God, who was Himself pure. But if that was the lesson that God intended, it failed because the history of the Temple, of the Jews, was filled with sin—bloodshed, intrigue, civil war, corruption, and disregard for their own poor. We see this in the writings of the prophets who called Israel, the Temple establishment, to abandon the sins that led to these things. The prophets accused the Temple establishment— and the people who followed their lead—of faithlessness, and called them to return to the God they claimed to love and honor. If maintaining Godly purity was the lesson, then God's Jewish experiment in the desert had failed miserably according to the light of Christ which now illuminated the dark recesses of ancient Jewish history.

In reality, the gospel of Jesus Christ provided a different lesson, a larger lesson, a more inclusive lesson. The lesson of Jesus Christ brought the period of Jewish errors to a close with the destruction of Jerusalem and the Temple in A.D. 70. But that was not the end of the story! It was the beginning, not of a different story, but of the old story of the mission of the God of Genesis. Not a new story, but a renewed story, a new start, a new chapter.

REGENERATION

And with that new start, the lesson about the Jews was seen, not to be about their special place in the kingdom of God, but about how pride destroys community. The pride of the Jews was religiously motivated. They thought that their special relationship with God made them different, which of course it did—and does. But they thought that they honored God's purity by separating themselves from other people. What God had planted in human culture, in the Jews, was quarantined by the Jews in order to protect it from corruption. It was a noble effort—and we must not be too hard on the Jews because no one would have done any better. Nonetheless, in the light of Christ it turned out to be a gross failure.

That failure did not surprise God, or cause Him to suddenly turn to Plan B—not at all. Rather, the lesson that God intended was that God does not belong to any particular nation or ethos because God's concern has always been to replace the religion of vengeance with the religion of forgiveness, to end the national and ethnic feuds that have fueled war, selfishness, envy, greed, and pride that go back farther than we can remember, farther than written history. God's purpose is to bring His own character manifested in Jesus Christ into the lives of human beings in order to put an end to the most destructive force in the world—humanity, our guilt and lack of forgiveness.

God's purpose is not to destroy the world, nor to cull the population. God's purpose is to put an end to sin, to reduce the destructiveness of sin, one person at a time.[1] God's purpose is the regeneration of humanity, and the establishment of *shalom* by creating a great harvest of the fruits of the Spirit (Galatians 5:22-23), and eliminating or seriously reducing the works of the flesh (Galatians 5:19-21). And the success of this grand plan requires planting Christ's seed—the grace of Jesus Christ—in every culture, in every individual.

Paul accused the Jews of not obeying the law themselves, which would have been quite an affront to the establishment. They thought that they had kept the law, particularly the Pharisees and the Temple establishment. They thought that they were hated by the world *because* they kept the law. They were unable to see the many prophetic accusations that preceded Paul. They failed to hear Isaiah's accusation of them:

> "...this people draw near with their mouth and honor me with their lips, while their hearts are far from me" (Isaiah 29:13).

Or Jesus' repetition of it in Matthew 15:8. The veil that had blinded them from time immemorial was still in place. Paul himself had been blinded by it during his years as a Pharisee. He knew it well. So, when the Lord removed it from him, and he was able to see the larger lesson

---

1   For more on this see: Ross, Phillip A. *Peter's Vision of Christ's Purpose in First Peter*, 2011, and *Peter's Vision of The End in Second Peter*, 2012, Pilgrim Platform.

that Christ brought to light, it changed everything. He would never be the same. The world would never be the same!

Paul had previously shared this vision with the Galatians, and it rocked their world, too. The changes that had come to him had begun to manifest in them. We must not be too harsh on them for reneging. It is hard for us to see the severity of the implications of Paul's vision for the lives of those who would follow him in this at that time. They were bucking thousands of years of well-established Temple history that had denied and declawed the teachings of the prophets, and brought them to heel to the twisted theology of the Temple that denied God in the name of God.

Paul accused the Judaizers of trying to bring the Galatians back into the established teaching of the Temple establishment so that they could pay lip service to Jesus, by interpreting Jesus' mission and ministry to be compatible with established Temple theology. They were trying to bring the Galatians back to their senses, back to reality, back to the reality of the Second Temple establishment, which completely dominated Jewish society. Doing so would be a win for them in which they could glory.

But doing that would utterly distort the meaning, message, and ministry of Jesus Christ. It would deny the central purpose of Christ's mission, and of Israel's purpose in history revealed in the light of Christ. It would hold the ancient veil in place and hide God's mission and purpose from the very people He had chosen to use to reveal that purpose—the Jews. It was completely inimical to everything that Paul believed and taught. And this was what Paul was trying to say to the Galatians.

31. This Rule

But far be it from me to boast except in the cross of our Lord Jesus Christ, by which the world has been crucified to me, and I to the world. For neither circumcision counts for anything, nor uncircumcision, but a new creation. And as for all who walk by this rule, peace and mercy be upon them, and upon the Israel of God. From now on let no one cause me trouble, for I bear on my body the marks of Jesus. The grace of our Lord Jesus Christ be with your spirit, brothers. Amen.   —Galatians 6:14-18

First Paul told them that they were to test or prove themselves, their own faith in Christ, and then they wouldn't need to boast in other people. They wouldn't need to point to other people who had faith because they could point to themselves, to their own experience and know personally what faith in Christ is like. And here he told them that he could boast in nothing but the cross of Christ. He boasted or pointed to the cross as an example of what faithfulness looks like. So, he wasn't boasting in himself. Or was he?

He looked to the cross as the ultimate test or proof of God and of faithfulness as a way of highlighting the faith of Jesus Christ. Christ's faith would not deny God even if it meant His own death. That's extreme faithfulness. But here he also said that the Spirit of Christ had crucified the world to him and him to the world. That meant that he was dead to the world and the world was dead to him, which means that the world neither tempted him nor motivated him. He did not respond or react to the things of the world.

He was not afraid of the various threats that the Temple establishment made against him, even though there was a contract out for his life, and he had been chased from town to town by Temple authorities.[1] He wasn't afraid of being blackballed by the Jews. He wasn't afraid of losing his tent making business, partly because he was probably opening up new shops outside of Jerusalem among new converts to Christianity who needed work.

He saw that the crucifixion of Christ applied to him. He took Jesus' admonition to take up our cross and follow Him (Matthew 16:24, Mark 8:34, Luke 9:23). Today Christians view the cross as a cherished symbol of atonement, forgiveness, grace, and love. But in Jesus' day, the cross represented social degradation and a torturous death. The Romans forced convicted criminals to carry their own crosses to the place of crucifixion. Bearing a cross meant carrying their own execution device and being ridiculed along the way.

But Paul saw that it also means being willing to die in order to follow Jesus. Sometimes we call it *dying to one's self*. It's a call to surrender, to live as Jesus would have us live.

> "For whoever would save his life will lose it, but whoever loses his
> life for my sake will find it. For what will it profit a man if he gains
> the whole world and forfeits his soul? Or what shall a man give in re-
> turn for his soul?" (Matthew 16:25-26).

NOTHING

When Paul said that circumcision means nothing he was still using the term to represent the whole of Second Temple Judaism. It meant that the Temple means nothing, that Temple sacrifices mean nothing, etc. Circumcision was the rite by which membership in the Jewish community was reckoned. So, Paul also meant that membership in the Jewish community meant nothing. He was not eschewing all community involvement, but was pointing to the end of the Temple administration. Everything associated with the Temple no longer bound him, nor should it bind anyone.

As a student of Scripture and history Paul knew about changing administrations, about the various covenant administrations that had changed over the centuries. As the administration changed, loyalties and practices changed. Things were different under Noah, and differ-

---

1   Ross, Phillip A. *Acts Of Faith—Kingdom Advancement*, Pilgrim Platform, Marietta,
     Ohio, 2007.

ent again under Moses, and again under David, etc. Yes, there were consistencies and commonalities, but there were also differences. And the change that Jesus ushered in provided the most significant change since Moses, even since Adam.

However, Paul's denial of circumcision and the Temple establishment was not an abandonment of a covenant relationship with the God of Israel. Paul was careful not to throw out the baby with the bathwater, the baby being Jesus Christ and the veracity of Scripture— but not the whole of the Torah, understood in its extra-biblical sense. Nor did he say that God meant nothing. He was not teaching what we know as libertarianism, or the abandonment of law and government. Jesus did not introduce libertinism (Acts 6:9), nor is Christianity like libertinism, libertarianism, or some forms of liberalism.[2] Of course, it is not like conservatism, either.[3] Jesus was conservative in some things and liberal in others. Both ends of the left/right political divide are inadequate, and they are in a symbiotic relationship such that each side of the divide needs the other to exist. Jesus would put an end to both. What we think of as left/right politics mean nothing to Jesus.

New Creation

Paul abandoned circumcision and all that was related to it, not for nothing, but for the new creation in Christ. How new (καινός)? The Greek word suggests a new kind, something unprecedented, novel, uncommon, unheard of, and therefore unexpected. A new what? A new creature, a new creation (κτίσις). Translations differ, but in Greek it's not a noun, but a verb, an act of founding, establishing, building something. It's a new building of something.

Paul understood Christ to replace Adam as the central type or norm for being human. Christ fixed what Adam wrecked. He removed the consequence or curse for the sin of Adam. Paul understood Christ to have founded nothing less than a new humanity, a new way to be human. The old way was inextricably caught up in sin, shame, curse, and revenge. God had cursed Adam, Eve, and the serpent, and the curse extended to everything that humanity touched. The history

2   See footnote 2, p. 229.
3   Greeley, Andrew M. and Hout, Michael. *The Truth about Conservative Christians: What They Think and What They Believe,* Hardcover, University Of Chicago Press, 2006.

of the Old Testament proved that humanity in Adam was a lost cause. It validated the fact of God's curse by documenting and recording the consequences.

The mission of Jesus Christ is, therefore, no less traumatic than the original creation or the Great Flood. The Flood spared Noah and his family because they were the best that could be salvaged. But the Bible again shows us that the scourge of sin continued to dog Noah and his family. The Flood failed to cleanse the world of sin—which would mandate the elimination of humanity—because of God's grace and mercy through His acts in human history. He spared Noah and his family to confirm that sin could not so easily be eradicated. Biblical history testifies to the fact that it wasn't. Noah had the same sinful heart that Adam had. Nonetheless, God promised never to bring a flood like that again. Why would He? It didn't work.

Ezekiel prophesied that God would have to give humanity a new heart, by which he meant a new psyche, a new way of being, a new set of values, new desires (Ezekiel 11:19, 18:31, 36:26). Jeremiah said the same thing:

> "For this is the covenant that I will make with the house of Israel after those days, declares the Lord: I will put my law within them, and I will write it on their hearts. And I will be their God, and they shall be my people" (Jeremiah 31:33).

The prophets are full of this kind of idea, which is why Paul believed that Jesus was the long-expected Messiah who would establish this central promise of God.

Given all of this, Paul could not go back to the Temple, and neither could any of the Jews—nor have they ever over the past two millennia. But they didn't know that yet. *We* have access to all of the theology and history since Jesus Christ, but they didn't. Today when someone asks about Jesus Christ we have a lot to point to. They didn't! It took great faith and strength of character to do what Paul did. Then again, he wasn't operating under his own influence. Christ had grabbed him by the nape of the neck and was hauling him into the future.

The Temple had acted like a great spiritual dam that had kept the waters of life from flowing freely through humanity for thousands of years. And like a great dam, it held back a great reservoir. This was what Paul meant when he said that "when the fullness of time had come, God sent forth his Son" (Galatians 4:4). The crucifixion of Jesus Christ cracked the dam, and it finally and catastrophically broke beyond repair in A.D. 70 when the waters of life began to pour out into the gentiles.

Paul saw the crack, and was preparing a channel for the waters of life to flow into. He was also preparing people and showing them two things: 1) how not to be destroyed by the ensuing flood, and 2) how to make use of it. When the dam finally broke, the world was forever changed. There could be no going back—ever. This was Paul's argument with the Judaizers—they were rearranging deck furniture on the Titanic.

Paul knew that the cataclysm that was unfolding in history would change everything, and it did. Many Christians today argue that people haven't changed, so the whole Bible is just as applicable to day as it was when it was first written. The argument has had a long and honorable history. It is the argument of the Old Testament, the argument of first Temple establishment, and of the Second Temple establishment. It is the Temple argument because the theology and practices of the Temple always looked back to the Tabernacle, to Moses and the Deuteronomic Law as the way to satisfy or appease God, to live as God wanted people to live.

Remember that King David, who reset the laws for the Tabernacle to work in the Temple, was the very embodiment of what God warned Israel against when they asked for a king. God said that a kingdom like those of the world wouldn't work, but David showed the people how to make it work. He fused the Temple to the palace. What could go wrong! He set out to create a perfect society, and that society crashed and burned several times until it finally crashed and burned for the last time in A.D. 70. Not even the Jews tried to resurrect it.

It would be nice to be able to report that in a few years, decades, or centuries after Paul's death that the new humanity in Christ was finally working together splendidly. But no such report will be forthcoming. The new humanity was born into the midst of the old, and because of God's promise not to bring a new flood—that is, not to kill everyone and start over, the old humanity needs to be washed in the waters of life through baptism in order to establish the new humanity in Christ. It's a never ending struggle because people continue to be born, and history continues to carry its vengeful momentum forward. So, cultures continue to apply their old baggage that they inherited from Adam to individuals. Individuals continue to be contaminated by the sinful cultures and influences into which they are born.

Nonetheless, progress has been made as the influence of ancient cultures lose their impetus and influence. Humanity today is not the same as humanity was during previous eras. To argue that there has been no improvement in human culture is to argue for the failure of God's mission in Christ. The establishment of Christian culture is a central feature of Christ's mission. That process is gradual, and does not mean that the history of Christian culture is without sin. The history of Christianity is filled with its own sin, much of it no better than what preceded it. And yet, progress has been made.

But this is not an endorsement of every new thing that comes down the so-called Christian pike. Many aspects of what seems to be new in Christian history are nothing more than warmed over sin dressed in different garb. An ancient tactic of the enemy, Satan, is to dress sin in the robes of faithfulness, of authority and respectability. That's what the Temple establishment did. We see this tendency as Christianity embraced formalized worship and cathedral building, and again as it embraced capitalism[4] as a way of baptizing greed in order to make it more socially acceptable, even successful. This is not an argument against Christian worship or capitalism, it is an argument against wrong worship and greed.

We see similar errors as people embrace the importance of news media as a way to shine the light of truth into the darkness of sin, but too often confuse news with gossip. And we see it in the contemporary activities of the homosexual movement to reframe the biblical values of tolerance and love to include legally mandated tolerance and love of what God calls sin.

4   This is not an argument against capitalism *per se*, but against what capitalism has become in the modern world—a system of debt-based monetization. "Like the proverbial fish who doesn't know what water is, we swim in an economy built on money that few of us comprehend" (Greco, Thomas H. *The End of Money and the Future of Civilization*, Chelsa Green, 2009).

In each case, the sin that is embraced does not advance the progressive revelation of Jesus Christ in history. Reversion to ancient sins like false worship, idolatry, greed, and homosexuality does not constitute historical progress, but is actually a cultural regression into ancient ways of being human that Christ came in order to replace with new life for individuals and cultures that genuinely reflect the character of God in Christ.

RULE

Paul prayed for peace and mercy to be part of the rule that Christians are to live by. This prayer hoped that the world would receive this new teaching, this new understanding of human history, this revelation of the ancient and then existing Temple establishment, with peace and mercy—toleration, kindness, understanding, sympathy. He prayed that the vision that God had given him would not be cause for any response other than peace and mercy. His hope was that, if he, who had been a high ranking Pharisee in the Second Temple establishment, could change his perspective about Jewish history in the light of Christ, then so could others.

And in order to help facilitate peace and mercy it was also a prayer that Christians who came to understand this new perspective would be filled with peace and mercy as they worked to advance Christ's kingdom. He understood the problem of establishing God's kingdom with war and violence, as the ancient Temple establishments had done. God's kingdom cannot be forced on people, it cannot be established through intimidation, violence, or war, nor by fiat, coercion, or control. This was the central lesson of the Old Testament that Paul's vision had shown him.

Yet, the momentum of ancient history had worked repeatedly to do just that! Not just the Jews, but every ancient culture advanced through warfare, violence, and intimidation. This was how the ancient cultures functioned. God separated Abraham in order to establish a new way, a new culture of forgiveness that would produce peace and mercy in Christ. But as the Jews grew increasingly successful by bringing other ancient peoples into their fold through military conquest, they found it increasingly necessary to employ the old ways in order to keep a measure of peace among unrepentant, sinful people.

Under David and Solomon they mastered the process by fusing the Temple and the palace, by wedding religion to the politics of domination and vengeance. This is what God had shown to Paul. This is what Jesus came to overcome, to fix, to replace. So, Jesus wedded religion to the politics of forgiveness and service in order to birth a new humanity, and new human culture in Christ.

This new way in Christ was not unordered. Rather, it was governed by a rule (κανών), a principle, a standard, a model, a norm. Because vengeance was required to satisfy an offense in the ancient religious culture, the new rule would work to eliminate offensive behaviors. The old way was to take vengeance on those who offended you, those who offended your honor. So, the new way in Christ was to forgive those who offended you, and to make every effort not to offend others. In order to simplify and standardize the complexity of knowing what would offend others, the rule established the idea of not offending God in Christ.

The plan was for people to adapt their behavior to the idea of not offending God—not simply the Old Testament God as understood by the ancient cultures, but the Old Testament God as exemplified by Jesus Christ. Jesus would be the new model for the new rule. He set the norms of behavior by living in accordance with the intention of God's ancient law. And He did this for two purposes: 1) to establish that conformity to the intention of God's law was possible, and 2) to put an end to the laws of Moses and the seventy by revealing their greater purpose.

However, the establishment of a new human culture threatened every existing culture because all cultures had inherited their fundamental structure from the sin of Adam and the ancient violence of Cain. The establishment of a new human culture threatened Second Temple Judaism and the Roman Empire, which were fused at the hip in Jerusalem. Both were threatened by Jesus, so they conspired together to put an end to the threat, thinking that they could contain and control those whom Jesus had touched. They were not aware of the reality of Christ's divinity, the clarity of Paul's vision, or of the great reservoir of spiritual potential that the Temple dam had created among their own people.

Paul worked to develop a rule that would provide a channel for the flow of the Spirit when the dam would finally break. He didn't know exactly when that would be, but he knew that it would be soon, not next week, but historically soon. And it was.

ISRAEL OF GOD

Paul also prayed for peace and mercy to be "upon the Israel of God" (v. 16), not on the God of Israel, but the *Israel of God*. This is the only place in the Bible that this phrase is used, so it has special meaning. There are two ways to understand who Paul was talking about here, and they both suggest the same thing.

The *Israel of God* could refer to those Israelites who actually loved God, "for not all who are descended from Israel belong to Israel" (Romans 9:6). Paul had mentioned that not all Israelites were faithful, and this term points to those who were. The Israel of God was composed of those Israelites who actually belonged to God.

But because Paul was advancing the gospel to the gentiles, the term also points forward to include faithful gentiles into God's fold. Paul's Israel of God was composed of all faithful Israelites and all faithful gentiles. In Christ both groups were fused into one. This is not simply replacement theology, where the Christian church is understood to have replaced Israel as the recipients of God's blessings. It does, however, suggest that the Mosaic covenant has been superseded by the New Covenant in Christ.

God's plan was not to replace all cultures with the culture of the Christian church, such that the world would be monocultural. God's creation reveals the necessity for biodiversity, which includes cultural diversity. Monolithic culture is neither desirable nor possible, at least not for long. God's intended change from vengeance to forgiveness does not necessitate or imply that the cultures in which Christianity takes a hold need all be alike. Different people can manifest Christ in different ways and still be in unity and union with Christ.

The drive for the unification of culture is a remnant of the ancient drive for cultural dominance, and plays no role where the necessity for cultural dominance does not exist. The old way was peace through cultural dominance, but Christ's new way is peace through forgiveness and mercy. Only in a culture motivated by forgiveness and mercy, rather than dominance and vengeance, can the freedom of diversity truly exist. Forgiveness and mercy are necessary where cultural diversity flourishes. A culture bathed in freedom allows diversity to flourish, but a culture driven by dominance cannot allow freedom to exist.

God was not replacing ancient Israel with the church as we have come to understand the church. He was not replacing one institution with another. He was not creating a new Temple establishment by the name of *church* on the model of the old Temple establishment. Rather, He was replacing one rule, one principle, one standard, one model, one norm with another. He was replacing the character of dominance and vengeance with the character of forgiveness and service. The spirit of forgiveness is not threatened by human diversity, unlike the spirit of domination, which is threatened by the spirit of human freedom.

However, there are limits to human freedom. One person's freedom must not violate the rights of another. My freedom does not allow me to steal your stuff. The origin of human freedom finds its roots in the emancipation of ancient Israel from slavery in Egypt, when Moses received the Ten Commandments from God. Those Commandments provide the rules for human flourishing. They provide maximum freedom without violating the rights of others. Those Commandments in their original presentation are eternal, or close enough.

Moses and the seventy worked with God's help to apply them to life in the wilderness. But we no longer live in the environment of that wilderness, nor in the environment of the Temple. Christ revealed the reality that He is the true Temple, and He refined the Ten Commandments into two. If we can truly abide by those two, we will satisfy the Ten. And this is the rule that establishes the Israel of God.

TROUBLE

"From now on let no one cause me trouble" (v. 17).

Calvin understood this verse in the sense of: "Let them cease to throw hindrances in the course of my preaching." Paul was not afraid to encounter various difficulties, but did not want to be contradicted anymore. Paul believed that he had sufficiently established his doctrine, and that it honored both the character of God in Christ and the veracity of the Old Testament. As Paul wrote to Timothy:

> "All Scripture is breathed out by God and profitable for teaching, for reproof, for correction, and for training in righteousness, that the man of God may be complete, equipped for every good work" (2 Timothy 3:16-17).

Paul was not discrediting the Old Testament, his doctrine was established on its veracity alone. He believed that the Old Testament was true, but he wasn't so foolish as to understand it woodenly. He believed that all of it was useful, helpful, beneficial, but only when it was understood correctly. As we all know, biblical ideas can be taken out of context, or understood wrongly, and result in much error. In fact, Paul understood the Temple establishment to have been guilty of such error for a very long time. But he also knew that without the light of Christ he would not have understood it as he did. It was only the light of Christ in the fullness of time that provided articulation to his message.

Paul took up (βαστάζω) the stigma (στίγμα) of Christ in his person (σῶμα). Of course he was scarred from his various beatings and troubles (2 Corinthians 11:25), but to think that he was talking about *that* at this point in his letter misses the larger point of his actively identifying with Christ in the stench of His crucifixion. He understood that there was a stigma, a mark of disgrace associated with Jesus Christ.

Crucifixion was usually used to punish political or religious agitators, pirates, slaves, or the underclass. In 519 B.C. Darius I, king of Persia—who authorized the building of the Second Temple, crucified three thousand political opponents in Babylon. In 88 B.C. Alexander Jannaeus, the Judaean king and high priest, crucified eight hundred Pharisaic opponents. Paul was well aware of what crucifixion meant and the stigma associated with it. But he also knew the power of God in Christ, and the truth of the message he taught. He knew that it was undeniable, that history would vindicate him, and that history desperately needed to understand his message.

He knew that the gospel he taught would cost him his life. He knew that there was a Jewish contract out on his life. Most of his missionary travels were as much fleeing from his Jewish persecutors and Roman authorities as they were opportunities for mission. These two interests coalesced as he traveled around the Mediterranean Sea when they finally captured him. But even that didn't stop him from preaching.

Jesus had graciously submitted to crucifixion. He had set his mind on it as something that He must endure for the life of the world. History was ripe for it. And He knew everything that Paul would later preach about. He hadn't met Paul yet, but He would. Shortly after His death, He met two disciples.

> "And beginning with Moses and all the Prophets, he interpreted to
> them in all the Scriptures the things concerning himself" (Luke
> 24:27).

He filled in *The Backstory* so that they could understand what He had done, and why He did it. He planted the seed that bloomed in Paul. It was a story of the grace of the God of Israel, who had sent His Son, the Lord Jesus Christ, to break open the flood gates and tear down the walls so that His story would flow again in the waters of life.

May the grace of Jesus Christ be with your spirit, brothers and sisters. Amen.

Postscript

If you have followed this argument to this point, you should be disturbed by its implications. I know that I am. Then again, if you have read the Bible and are not disturbed by it, you missed something important. Being disturbed by God is not intended to make us anxious or uneasy. Rather, it is to disturb us in the sense that "something in the room was disturbed," that is, *rearranged*. God's intention is our rearrangement in the light of Christ.

I have tried to be faithful to the spirit and intent of Paul's message to the Galatians from a twenty-first century perspective, to take what I know about the Bible, about Paul and the times in which he lived, and provide a realistic view of his perspective and the context of his understanding of Scripture and of Jesus Christ. In addition, I have tried to faithfully honor the character of God as revealed in Jesus Christ and the veracity of Scripture.

Many people today have trouble squaring the Old Testament, with its seemingly harsh laws and violence in the name of God, with the character of Jesus Christ. Consequently, many people abandon Christianity altogether or feel that they must either abandon the character of Christ or the veracity of Scripture. The effort to hold all of these things together has produced far more complexity than people like. Then again, our contemporary world has discovered that reality is far more complex than any of our ancestors could have possibly imagined. So, it should be no surprise that the Bible, a book that comports to be about reality, would be any less complex.

Nor should it be surprising that historic Christian doctrines must also submit to our awareness of the increasing complexity of reality. For instance the inerrancy of Scripture is a doctrine I love and ascribe to. However, I find the word *inerrancy* to be somewhat inadequate to the reality, and much prefer *veracity*, which is defined as the quality of being correct, true, or close to the true value. While every word of Scripture is true and can be trusted, it is incumbent to find the perspective from which it is true because that perspective will help us see things as God sees them.

Long ago I learned that when reading something in Scripture that is hard to believe—the miracles like turning water into wine, and whatnot—it is important not to simply dismiss the idea as being unrealistic. Rather, it is much more fruitful to trust its veracity, and to try to find the perspective from which such a thing or description of a thing *could* be true.

Modern science and technology are teaching us that much of what our ancestors believed about the world is simply not the case. God, if He is who He says He is, is not surprised by any of this. If God is really God, He knew all of what we are only recently learning about reality and about Scripture from the very beginning. And He also knew that we would discover it. Surely, He would have planned for such an eventuality.

I believe that He did, and that the Bible was written for just such a time, an end time, a time of change and transition. It is during such a time of transition, of endings and beginnings, that the value of the Bible increases greatly, not because it provides a prophetic window into the future, but because it provides continuity with the past so that we can see what God wants us to see about our future changes, what we need to retain, and how we need to adjust. The future will always be similar to and different from the past, and always far more similar than different. To expect something radically different in the immediate future is both ill-advised and silly. God is both a foundation of stability and a fulcrum for change. His purpose is not destruction, but rearrangement. And His time frame is immense, which is why we need patience and an historical perspective.

Whatever else you do, hold fast to the character of God in Christ and to the veracity of Scripture, and shine—not that little light of yours, but reflect the big light of Christ into everything. And illuminate the world for Christ.

Scripture Index

Alphabetical Index

www.ingramcontent.com/pod-product-compliance
Lightning Source LLC
LaVergne TN
LVHW051252080426
835509LV00020B/2936